Princes Shall Come out of Egypt, Texas, and Fort Worth

by
Reby Cary

DORRANCE PUBLISHING CO., INC.
PITTSBURGH, PENNSYLVANIA 15222

Permission acknowledgments to reprint and quote material are contained in the Notes following each Part.

ISBN # 0-8059-5862-2
Printed in the United States of America

First Printing

For information or to order additional books, please write:
Dorrance Publishing Co., Inc.
643 Smithfield Street
Pittsburgh, Pennsylvania 15222
U.S.A.
1-800-788-7654
Or visit our web site and on-line catalog at *www.dorrancepublishing.com*

Dedication

This book is dedicated to the affectionate memory of my parents, the late Reverend and Mrs. Smith Cary, who sacrificed unselfishly to provide for me opportunities of service. It is also dedicated to my wife and daughter, Nadine and Faith Annette, who today are able to share the fruits of a more enlightened American society.

DEDICATION OF MINORITIES CULTURAL CENTER, UNIVERSITY OF TEXAS - ARLINGTON

Reby Cary, Director of Minorities Affairs *(right)* and Chris Miller, Texas State Representative *(left)*

Contents

Thanks to...

Dr. Sandra Myres for her ever-ready advice and reassuring help in reading the manuscript.

Dr. Bob McDowell for his frank criticism and Betty Graham for her invaluable assistance in researching the material.

Norma Sue Lester for her patience and expertise in typing the initial manuscript, ands the yeoman's assistance of Elizabeth Hudson, Mary Anne Beatty, Cora Spencer, Gayle Hanson, and Toni Benford.

Credits and permission acknowledgments to reprint and quote material are contained in the Notes following each Part.

Introduction

The magnitude of the black problem today, and the subsequent social changes affected by the insistent demands of liberals and militants for first-class citizenship, mirrors the dilemma of a society whose racial dichotomy has perpetuated segregation and a caste system while trying to idealize the basic concepts of democracy.

The American experience in its various facets emerged from varied people, uprooted from many countries and amalgamated into a hetro-homogeneity which is distinctly American. Blacks left an indelible print on the institutions of this country and played a dominant role in most of the major issues in our political and cultural development. However, while other races have been absorbed into the "melting pot," the black man has been left outside the mainstream of American life as the invisible man, the forgotten "tenth." The long struggle of the black man to throw off the superimposed bondage of inferiority is part of the process of history. Yet the black man has been systematically dehumanized to the extent that it is commonplace for historians to treat him as having made no significant contributions to civilization. Subsequently, omissions and distortions have been part of American historiography. It is in this light that we must examine the forces and personalities who have rallied and persevered through centuries of bondage until they witnessed the day of "Jubilee" and the "Great Deliverance." The historiography of our day must be restructured in content and thought and become inclusive and valid enough to assert a corrective influence on many of the myths, distortions, and omissions glaringly evident in American history. Deliberate distortions by interpretation, omission, and application of pseudo-Christian concepts have been used to perpetuate and intensify racism in the United States. Authors have been the vehicles for minimizing and demeaning human dignity by ignoring significant achievements of a people who they assert had no history worth mentioning.

Today we are reevaluating the thoughtlessness and biases of historians of the past and are attempting to place the black man in his proper cultural and historical relationship to other people. An attempt is being made to publicize insistently and retell the story of the "invisible" men of American society who have made worthwhile contributions while being treated by historians as if they did not exist. We must not deny the historical luster of the real history of the United States nor these patriots who guided this country through the many stages of greatness, but at the same time we must illuminate the contributions and achievements of black men as cocontributors to the epic of American civilization. The interrelationship of blacks and whites as contributors to our culture must be highlighted and their togetherness portrayed as a perpetual and dynamic process.

Historians must not be misled by the rhetorical extremities of a small vocal group who misinterpret the nature of the Black Movement by distorting the goals to be achieved. The extreme left advocates complete separation from white society, while conservative segments of the black population propose total integration. This perplexing and divisionary condition emerges when blacks are divided as to the best strategy for obtaining equality. This dichotomy of goals is as paradoxical as the moral conflicts and values of a white society preaching Christianity and democracy on the one hand, and slavery, discrimination, and second-class citizenship on the other. Blacks in this new century must not be misled by a few irrationally exuberant leaders who demand monetary reparations for slavery for our forebears. Most of us were born in America and our struggle should be to remove all elements of visceral racism reflected in the segregation laws and move toward higher levels of independence and self-sufficiency.

America is witnessing a new birth of freedom. The inconsistencies of the Puritan heritage are being exposed and the hypocritical application of the Declaration of Independence is being reinterpreted to apply to the black man who was dehumanized by the compromise-acceptance of that document of human rights. The fulfillment of the American creed is nearer to fruition. We are witnessing a universal upheaval in which black men seek an identity in society through dismantling all vestiges of white supremacy. The growing acceptance of the black man as an integral part of our society, valued for his worth as an individual and not judged by the pigmentation of his skin, echoes the prophetic voice of Psalm 68, verse 31: "Princes shall come out of Egypt and Ethiopia would lift its hands to God."[1]

The emergence of new African nations and the surge of nationalism throughout the world has fired the restive spirit of blacks in rejuvenating concepts of their Afro-American heritage. The authors of *Black Rage* assert that "The psyche of black men has been distorted, but out of that deformity has risen a majesty."[2] Black men in Western countries, acquiring a new status of dignity and respect, metaphorically represent princes, while Egypt, a crossroads of civilization, is synonymous with the land of bondage. This prophecy was projected by David and is analogous to black hopes and aspirations in a world of human bondage in the twentieth century. Thutmose III, in Egyptianizing captive princes, kept the sons of defeated kings as hostages. These heirs became acclimated to Egyptian mores and folkways and soon developed loyalty to the pharaoh. David, while meditating and reflecting over the plight of the children of Israel held in bondage, longing for the day of deliverance, prophesied the return of these captives from captivity. The blacks, who have been systematically kept in captivity and denied equal participation in American society, look to the day when they will be accorded full citizenship.

Despite some negative racial attitudes reflected among the Hebrews when "Miriam and Aaron spoke against Moses for he had married an Ethiopian woman" (Numbers 12:1), the prophetic message "Princes shall come out of Egypt and Ethiopia shall lift her hands to God" still rings to fruition, loud and clear, as we see changes in American thought and in the political, social, and economic equality of the Negro and his acceptance as an individual in the democratic context.

Today new self-esteem encompasses the black man's princely dignity. The growing consciousness on the part of blacks throughout America to just be themselves, black but proud, finds manifestation in a new sense of identity. This affirmed dignity of humanity frees the black man from the mire of second-class citizenship and makes him equal to other ethnic groups. His acceptance as an individual will continue to be affected as the level of an enlightened morality, unflawed by prejudice, increases. This morality, yet to be engendered in white society, must cohabit and find nurture in black America. Only then will a new enlightenment cause Ethiopia to lift her hands to God.

PART 1:
A NATION BORN

African Background

The history of the African continent and Western civilization always seems to begin in Europe. Tentative conclusions persist that the predecessors of European civilization, Mesopotamia, Egypt, and perhaps India developed simultaneously in river valleys. Climatic changes that made it necessary for these inhabitants to subdue the torrential and residual effects of the flooding rivers resulted in the development of political and economic institutions. Such evidence is found in the great valley-state of Mesopotamia. It developed from fragmentations of many cities that came into existence because of nomadic trade in the Fertile Crescent. This trade produced a class of merchants and craftsmen who needed political organization for protection and a system of record-keeping in the transaction of business. The Sumerian codes and the famous Code of Hammurabi became the forerunners of our judicial systems. From this land between the Tigris and Euphrates rivers came the alphabet, astronomy, mathematics, metallurgy, and irrigation techniques.

But was the valley of the Tigris-Euphrates the cradle of civilization? Recently geologists and anthropologists have unearthed scientific evidence to give substance to previously doubtful philosophical and historical speculations that sub-Saharan Africa was the birthplace of early man and the cradle of European civilization. Africa has yielded the oldest human remains and artifacts yet discovered; the earliest anthropoid forms that could have begun the systematic invention of culture are indisputably associated with Africa. Africa seems to have been the home not merely of mankind, but also, and obviously, of human culture.[3] The transition of prehistoric man from the Eolithic to the Neolithic stages of development was characterized by his use of tools. Africa was also the place where early manlike creatures first became tool-making animals. This controversial projection is not intended to discount other probable theories of the site of the beginning of civilization, but to consider the historical perspective that Africa ranks with Southwest Asia, East Asia, and the New World as the scene of one of the major breakthroughs in the development of human culture.[5]

Robert Ardrey, author of *African Genesis* asserts, "The human genesis took place on that continent where nature today exhibits a minimum of innocence. Not in innocence, and not in Asia, was mankind born. The home of our fathers was that African highland reaching north from the cape of the Lakes of the Nile."[6] Experts estimate that as recently as 6000 B.C., the black man first appeared in the Sudanic grassland belt from the west coast to the headwater of the Nile.[7] Perhaps the most important hypothesis is that of Louis Leakey, the anthropologist who unearthed evidence and hypothesized that early man flourished in sub-Saharan Africa.

Historians formerly hypothesized that Western civilization began in the region of the Tigris-Euphrates, or a non-black Egyptian culture completely separate from sub-Saharan Africa. The noted historian Herodotus concluded that the Egyptians had no country at all except that which was formed by the Nile delta, further dethroning Egyptian claims as predecessors of civilization. They became the residue of African culture flowing down the Nile and leaving its varied cultural deposits. Thus Egypt became a crossroads of civilization where intermingling blacks left their imprints on several dynasties of Egyptians rule.

Egyptologists have recently closed the cultural gap of our knowledge of African civilization as far back as 2500 B.C. They have magnified and placed in historical perspective the reign of Pianky the Great, who ruled Egypt and Ethiopia before the culture of Greece blossomed and reached its heights. They have recaptured the prominence of the great pharaoh Aahmes I and his unexampled Queen Nefertari, who in 1580 B.C. established Egypt's eighteenth dynasty. Intellectual prominence has been given to one of the famous universities at Sankore in Timbuktu, where, says Immanuel Wallerstein, "the practice of medicine was much advanced and doctors performed some operations that were not known in Europe for another 250 years."[8] The ruins of Meroe reveal the smelting of bronze and iron as occupations long established in Africa.

The ancient kingdoms of Kush, Nubia, and Punt predate those of Mesopotamia. While Europe was still in the stone age and its inhabitants "swinging through the trees," highly developed kingdoms with organized social, political, and economic institutions functioned effectively in Africa.

The skeptic might still question Africa as the beginning of civilization when he attempts to explain the differences in the physical characteristics of the multifarious races throughout the world. The answer lies in the process of adaptation. As early man moved from the "Garden of Eden" in East Africa and migrated to Europe,[9] where climatic variations were at variance with his pigmentation, the texture and color his skin, influenced by environmental factors, had to change for the sake of survival. All mankind then is of the same racial stock, different only because of the genetic pigmentation of his skin.

Negroid anthropological characteristics have been discovered in the multiethnic groups in South America, Australia, and Eurasia. In *The Human Factor in Changing Africa*, Melville J. Herskovits explains, "Africa, when seen in perspective, was a full partner in the development of the Old World, participating in a continual process of cultural give-and-take that began long before European occupation."[10] The advanced civilization that Cortez and other Spanish explorers discovered had tinges of African culture as exemplified in the language and artifacts in the Western Hemisphere. Much of this culture was the result of the cultural attainment of earlier civilization in Africa. Many of the practices, rites, ceremonies, and words of the aborigines of the West Indian Archipelago came from Africa. Many supposedly Native American words are in reality of African origin; for example, *canoe*, and the appellation for the sweet potato, *yam*. Tobacco and its smoking were introduced into America by Africans long before Columbus crossed over to America from Guinea.[11]

These primitive migrants moved into the Western Hemisphere before the continental drift had occurred. Controversies still exist as to the possibility of drifting continents. An early explanation by Alfred Wegner hypothesized that by the end of the Paleozoic era the former union of landmass between Africa and South America had separated.[12] Recently the theory was confirmed by United States and Brazilian geologists, who made a computer study of shorelines on both sides of the Atlantic at a depth of 500 fathoms. The study revealed the continents would still match if they were set side by side.[13] Africa and South America, continents of the Southern Hemisphere (Gondwanaland), when reconstructed at 1,000-meter depth, fitted together almost perfectly with only one degree of error.[14] This scientific confirmation that the earth was once one continuous mass substantiates modern anthropological thought that man was originally black-skinned and originated in East Africa.

Why not a sub-Saharan beginning of Western culture? Would it be too much for a racist society to accept its origin as emanating from an ancient black continent or civilization? Unfortunately, most anthologies of African exploration are accounts of the European discovery of Africa conceived as a subject indigenous to the study of Europe or the New World. This attitude is strictly European and merely reflects European penetration and conquest. Yet this colonial stereotype is out of date. Sufficient evidence is now available to give credence to a sub-Saharan theory of the beginning of civilization, one that predated and provided the background for Western civilization.

Donald L. Wiedner, *A History of Africa South of the Sahara*, New York: Random House, 1962, p. 14.

THE ROLE OF THE NEGRO IN THE DISCOVERY AND EXPLORATION OF AMERICA

Throughout the fourth millennium African society continued to develop and interact with other cultures in Egypt. The diffusion of African ideas spread across the Mediterranean Sea, mixing with Greek and Roman culture. The periphery of Greco-Roman influence finally extended to the Atlantic coast in Western Europe. With the growth of new national states and the impact of mercantilism that fostered commercial rivalry among them during the fifteenth century, the stage was set for the discovery of America.

The discovery of America is an historical epoch which has captivated the sentiment of the whole world as the most dynamic and notable event to shape the destiny of our modern civilization. Black men accompanied many of the explorers and were initially with Columbus as he awoke the Western Hemisphere from its historical slumber.

Columbus' westward oceanic quest was not the beginning of his work but rather the culmination of efforts pursued through long years of disappointment. This mystical visionary was caught up in the restless quest for gold and the maddening race for power on the part of the sovereigns of Europe. The Spanish sovereigns, while not overly enthusiastic about the imaginary and unrealistic dream of a westward route to Cathay and Cinpango, made it possible for Columbus to fit out the *Santa Maria,* the *Pinta*, and the *Niña*. Whatever may be said of Columbus, the fact remains that he was persistent, persuasive in argument, and offered the monarchs of Europe the promise of glory, gold, and converts to Christianity.

As the "Enterprise of the Indies" got underway, the third ship of Columbus' fleet, the *Niña*, was commanded by Pedro Alonso (Peralonso) Niño. This heretofore obscure black personality gives further evidence that the United States is made up of many racial and ethnic groups, all of whom have contributed to the growth of our unique culture and civilization. Niño is typical of the many blacks who were remnants of the Moorish invaders of the Iberian Peninsula in A.D. 732 or the product of extensive miscegenation in Spain and Portugal which engulfed the population of the Iberian Peninsula.[15]

Pedro Alonso was a skillful sailor who remained faithful to Columbus. He sailed with him on subsequent voyages to the New World in 1493 and 1498. During the voyages in 1499-1500, Pedro Alonso was very successful in obtaining large quantities of pearls off the Venezuelan mainland, which were other incentives for adventure and exploration. His expedition got ninety-six pounds of pearls (at eight ounces to the pound), which they obtained at an average price of 2 1/2 dram.[16] Luis Guerra, the rich merchant of Seville who financed the expedition, had Pedro Alonso Niño incarcerated on charges of retaining a large number of pearls collected on the voyage. The black pilot was later released due to lack of evidence.

As other Spanish conquistadors and explorers took up the gauntlet of conquest to penetrate the land barrier which still barred the way to Cathay and Cipango, blacks accompanied them as guides and servants. The craving for gold and food compelled Vasco Nuñez de Balboa to shape a career for conquest that led to the discovery of the South Sea or Pacific Ocean. On September 25, 1513, Balboa, led by Nuflo de Olano, a black guide, and a company of soldiers including thirty black men, gazed on the Mar del Sur. These men helped carve a path through the Isthmus of Panama that became the gateway to potential treasures of the Far East.

We are prone to exaggerate the theory that the lust for gold was the primary motivating force behind the Spanish explorers. A good case to illustrate this contradiction is that of Hernando Cortez. After his conquest of Mexico, he was content to explore, and explore he did, all of the strange lands to the south of Mexico. Cortez not only explored and conquered, he also sought to develop and exploit the land and encouraged his followers to do the same.

One of his black followers made a far-reaching contribution and a dynamic impact on Western civilization. Juan Garrido introduced wheat into the Americas, as explained by German Arciniegas, author of *Latin America: A Cultural History*:

> He planted three grains of wheat he found in a sack of rice. He planted
> the three grains and two plants lived; one produced one hundred and
> eighty grains. Later they returned to plant the other grains and little by
> little there was an enormous amount of wheat.[17]

"Though wheat could not displace the cultivation of corn…its coming brought a new style of life to America, and it changed the landscape."[18] From this infinitesimal beginning Garrido paved the way for the United States, with its rich land, to become the "bread basket" of the world.

The epic conquest of Mexico challenged other Spaniards to match the exploits of Cortez. From Mexico, Spanish expansion radiated as a huge octopus. A staunch rival of Cortez was Panfilo de Narvaez, who sought to gain control of Mexico from Cortez. Narvaez failed in his diabolical bid for power and returned to Spain, where he received a grant from Charles V to explore the Western Hemisphere. In 1528 Narvaez led four hundred men, including a number of blacks, to Florida in search of fabulous wealth. They encountered disaster after disaster. After using their ingenuity and skill to build vessels to sail out of danger of the Native Americans, disease, and hunger, still the turbulent Antilles winds rose up in indomitable fury and repeatedly smashed their last rays of hope of returning to Mexico. Out of fourteen survivors, only four persons returned to Mexico: Alvar Nunez Cabeza de Vaca, Alonso del Castillo, Andres Dorantes, and Estevanico "el Negro," "the Black."

The experiences of Cabeza de Vaca after this catastrophe are an absorbing saga of survival in unsubdued Indian country by a man who had the sheer desire to live. He used every resource of human imagination to survive the sure death of an untamed wilderness. At one time the lack of food was so critical that, John Bartlett Brebner explains, "some of the whites resorted to cannibalism and dried the flesh of their dead companions to have food in reserve."[19]

The menace of hostile Indians was ever present along unexplored trails. Cabeza de Vaca was able to gain the confidence and admiration of the Native Americans by miraculously removing an arrow from the area above the heart of one of their warriors. This feat gained for the explorer the reputation of a "great medicine man." Always moving toward the southwest, he finally made it across this vast area under the pretext of healing sick tribes in the next village.

> With every day that passed, the countryside seemed more densely populated, and our shamans now progressed like masters instead of like slaves, causing great admiration among the natives in all the villages and on several occasions accompanied by a veritable multitude of Indians, like all holy men.[20]

All hope of seeing other Spaniards and Mexico City diminished with each passing day, until one day Castillo stared in amazement at a Spanish buckle that one of the Indians wore with his ornaments. This discovery brought renewed hope to the Spaniards that they were getting closer to Mexican civilization. The four survivors finally arrived in Mexico after the long and circuitous orbit across the plains of Texas. They gave many accounts of their travels and of the grandeur and wealth they heard about during their ordeal. These stories coincided with legendary myths of rich cities which Indians had previously told.

Estevanico el Negro, Moroccan by birth, was selected in 1539 by Viceroy Antonio de Mendoza to serve as guide to Fray Marcos de Niza in search of the fabled cities of Cibola. El Negro was to send back crosses as symbols of his progress and what he found ahead. He advanced into the land of the Zuni Indians in southwestern United States and in the process discovered Arizona and New Mexico. Estevanico sent gourds ahead of him by messengers as a symbol of authority and to command obedience from the numerous tribes of Indians. This technique had worked successfully in the western part of Texas when he was in company with Cabeza de Vaca.[21]

Hostile chiefs were unmoved by signs of the gourd and demanded Estevanico's departure from their land. The black explorer did not heed these warnings and subsequently the Indians killed him. They dismembered his body and distributed the pieces among the chiefs to satisfy them of his death.[22] Estevanico's contribution to America is that he was one of the first persons to explore the southwestern portion of the United States. Friar Marcos believed he had found the legendary Seven Cities of Cibola. With the death of Estevanico he returned to Mexico.

Other adventurous visionaries explored the eastern coast of North America. The early history of Virginia involved an ephemeral colonization by blacks. Endeavoring to go beyond the wind-swept Cape Hatteras the Spaniard Vasques de Allyon established a black settlement at Gualdape (San Miguel de Gualdape),[23] where the English in the next century founded Jamestown.[24] These blacks were so badly mistreated that they engaged in open rebellion and returned to Haiti from whence they had come. To expedite their return, Allyon, with the assistance of his black slaves, built the first ships constructed on the

United States' coast.[25]

Blacks also played important roles in French and English expeditions. Marquette and Joliet, French explorers, brought blacks with them as they explored Mississippi. These men of ebony were servants and not essentially slaves; they performed occupational chores, taking jobs such as laborers in lead and copper mines, farmers, blacksmiths, brewers, and carpenters.

One of the most prominent black explorers was Jean Baptiste du Sable, a fur trader and trapper. He was born in Haiti in 1745, the son of a successful businessman and a former Negro slave. Educated in Paris, du Sable migrated to New Orleans in 1765 as a representative of his father's expanding fur company. When the Spanish government took control of the French territory of Louisiana, du Sable moved to St. Louis where for two years he traded profitably with the Indians, exchanging goods for fur pelts. His business took him further north into Indian territory, where he settled among the Peoria and Potowatomy tribes. Traveling many times along the trails leading to the present sites of Chicago and Detroit, du Sable settled in 1772 at his trading post on the Chicago River near Lake Michigan. From this single cabin developed a growing trade center that today is the city of Chicago.

Black men also played prominent roles in the development of Louisiana. The French had black militia to protect the embryonic Company of the Indies that initiated the commercial development of the territory from 1718 to 1731. Too, these slaves were used to stave off Negro-Indian alliances and conspiracies; they helped save Louisiana from destruction by the Natchez and Chickasaw Indians, the colony's first formidable enemies.[26]

It is noteworthy that blacks were instrumental in diminishing the power of France in America and accelerating the opportunity for expanding the United States by the acquisition of the Louisiana Territory. Haiti, which had an economy based on slavery, was one of the most prosperous of French possessions in the Greater Antilles. The French Haitians were noted for extreme cruelty to slaves and their inhuman seasoning process designed to prevent uprisings and break the spirit of blacks for service in the Southern colonies. The obstinate and defiant blacks of this Caribbean island chose a native African, Macandal, who proclaimed himself the Black Messiah whose destiny was to drive the whites from the island. His plan of deliverance was to poison the water of LeCap. This scheme failed and Macandal was executed in 1758 for his conspiracy.

Many blacks and perhaps some whites were later to believe that Toussaint L'Ouverture was the reincarnation of Macandal.[27] Whether the legend was true or not, thirty-one years after the foiled insurrection of 1758, Toussaint L'Ouverture led a rebellion of a half-million black slaves against French rule in 1789. The principles of liberty, fraternity, and equality had also spread to the islands. When the French Revolution was over, new political rights were granted the mulattos, but the blacks were to be returned to slavery. Toussaint took up the gauntlet of leadership of the blacks against France. This prince of freedom was amazingly intelligent. He was self-taught and seemed to have natural military prowess. In *Citizen Toussaint*, Ralph Korngold describes Toussaint's abilities:

While still a slave Toussaint did considerable reading. That he was acquainted with Roman history is evident from his memorandum to Napoleon and several letters. He read Epictetus in a French translation and the influence of the noble Stoic upon his character is unmistakable.[28]

In 1798 Toussaint became commander of approximately 150,000 military personnel in Haiti and instituted needed reforms to bring about peace and harmony among the rival ethnic factions in the island. Tranquility was short-lived due to increasing jealousies among the islanders and Napoleon's attempt to use the conquest of Haiti as a springboard toward building an empire. France declared war on Haiti, and subsequently England and Spain intervened to protect the interests of French planters in Santo Domingo. French and Haitians mercilessly massacred each other in the years that followed and an epidemic of yellow fever reduced the number of General Leclerc's troops and almost depopulated the island.[29]

Toussaint's efforts against the French finally resulted in the defeat of the invaders, completely thwarted Napoleon's attempt to crush the rebellion, and ruined his dream of a new American empire. Napoleon realized the futility of governing colonies and slaves far from France and offered the entire Louisiana Territory in 1803 to the United States for $15,000,000.

This episode in world affairs marked a turning point for European powers in relationship to slavery. The Haitian revolution tempered the attitude of France toward the selling of human beings and their new philosophical concept extended to blacks, who also had a zeal for liberty, fraternity, and equality.

England searched its national conscience and became the main exponent of freeing the enslaved. A resurgence of Christianity throughout the English empire and the persistent denouncements of slavery by such men as John Wesley, Adam Smith, and Gilbert Wakefield brought up the execrable practice into moral focus. William Wilberforce and Lord Greenville engineered legislative sanctions in the House of Lords in 1807 against the slave trade. By 1811 slavery was legally abolished in all British dominions.

Spain, which had been more lenient than other powers in her treatment of slaves in her possession, abolished the system with comparative ease. A cultural enlightenment engulfed Spain with the drawing up of the "Rights of Man" in 1797, reaffirmed in 1811 in Spanish America.[30] It set the stage for the destruction of the system throughout Spain's empire.

Of the major powers, it remained for the United States to become the perpetuator of man's inhumanity to man and perfecter of the most inhuman system of slavery ever dreamed of by both civilized and uncivilized nations. The legacy of this slave heritage still lingers as a perpetual threat to racial harmony in American society.

The Colonial Period

Slavery in the United States developed as a manifestation of a capitalistic culture which grew out of a commercial revolution where property and materialism became a symbol of the Age of Reason. It justified the right to exploit the weaker and destroy the freedom of others. With the vast expanse of land and natural resources, men striving to conquer the virgin wilderness could acquire a vast amount of economic power if they could harness free labor in their crucibles of power. In 1645 Emanuel Downing, brother-in-law of Governor John Winthrop of Massachusetts, asserted that the "Massachusetts colony will never thrive until we get a stock of slaves sufficient to do all our business."[31]

The racial characteristics of slaves were unimportant at first to the colonists. But in a society made up primarily of yeomen, there was still a distinct preference for white English servants, who fitted readily into the life about them.[32] White servitude was the forerunner and finally became the blueprint for black servitude in the United States. The economic demands for free labor found a ready market in the poor and dispossessed lower class of whites in European society.

When attempts at enslaving Native Americans proved futile, the colonists acquired white laborers from Europe where severe vagrancy and poor laws were used to fill the pool of laborers. The Tower of London was emptied of political and religious dissenters to fill the quota of indentured servants in the New World. In lieu of prison sentences, convicts and vagrants signed contracts of varying lengths from seven to fourteen years of forced labor. There were some redemptioners who sold themselves to pay for their fare aboard ships coming to the New World.

When a pirate Dutch man-of-war plundered a Spanish slave ship and traded nineteen blacks for rations in 1619, the government of Jamestown became overseer of these indentured servants. The system of servitude was indelibly imprinted on colonial America and the white population lingering under the threat of perpetual slavery. Even though they were looked upon as inferior beings, the blacks retained their status until white agricultural entrepreneurs found it uneconomical to replace their servants. Too, because of the pigmentation of their skins, blacks found it difficult to lose their physical identity in a white society. But the loss of their names was the most demeaning thing done to the personality of the blacks. When in 1662 a Virginia law used the word "slaves" to designate an already existing class, slavery became recognized in law, as for some years it had been in practice.[33] Thus, through gradual implementation of laws, the indentured black servant became a slave in perpetuity.

Despite the growing practices that treated blacks as inferior and conditioned them to perpetual servitude as inferiors, the creative genius of the African was not totally subjugated. Out of the depths of slavery blacks made a number of important contributions to colonial development.

A slave named Cesar was liberated and given an annual grant of one hundred pounds sterling by special act of the South Carolina General Assembly for developing a cure for rattlesnake poisoning. The legislature also ordered a Charleston newspaper to publish the prescription for public use. Copies of the newspaper were much in demand when the cure was published on February 25, 1751. Also publicized widely outside South Carolina, the cure for poisoning was published in 1799 in a journal called *Domestic Medicine*. Cesar described in full the symptoms accompanying snakebite and outlined in detail the preparation and administration of his antidote, which was a mixture of roots, rum, and lye.[34]

Blacks were still uprooted against their will. Many were princes and rulers of kingdoms who came in chains to moisten this virgin land with their blood and sweat. They came from Ibo, Senegal, and all the western Sudan. From the Gold Coast came Atmun, prince of the Atmunshi, a victim of one of the many African tribal wars and greed of white slavers. Atmun spent two gruesome months in the notorious "Middle Passage" on the *White Falcon* before arriving in Boston, Massachusetts, on the first Sunday in July 1725. He was purchased for thirty pounds of sterling by Caleb Copeland, who gave the uprooted prince the name of Amos.

Caleb Copeland and his wife, Celia, were Christians who abhorred slavery. They needed domestic help to cord, spin, and operate the loom on which they made cloth to be sold at the market. Amos was brought up with the Copeland children, which is how he learned to read, write, and count. His friends used to call him Mr. Fortunatus because he had had good fortune in being well treated.[35] After Caleb was killed by the British during the French and Indian War, Amos was sold in 1740 to Ichabod Richardson, a tanner of Woburn, Massachusetts, for sixty-two pounds of sterling. On May 9, 1769, Amos, who was by then sixty years of age, was given his freedom by Mrs. Richardson.

Amos continued the business of his deceased master and in four years had a lucrative trade as a free man. To share his newly gained freedom with another, Amos purchased a wife, who died in October 1775. In order to fill the void in his life caused by the loss of his sister to the same slavers who brought him to America, Amos decided to purchase another slave. He watched intently for a female who had a lame leg. This affliction allowed him to transfer his love for his sister to Lydia, whom he purchased in 1778. She died a short time after.

In 1787 Amos moved to Jaffrey, where he became the leading tanner in that part of New Hampshire. By 1789 he had saved enough money to buy twenty-five acres of land and build himself a New England salt-box house near Tyler Brook, where it still stands today. Amos continued to use his affluence to buy blacks out of slavery[36] and to provide schools for the children of the neighborhood. He also owned six shares in the Jaffrey Library Society, of which he was a founder.[37] The inscription on Amos Fortune's tombstone is a living monument to the life of this freed slave who contributed greatly to New England colonial life. It reads:

> Sacred to the memory of Amos Fortune
> Who was born free in Africa.
> A slave in America, he purchased liberty,
> Professed Christianity,

Lived reputably, died hopefully—
November 17, 1801. AE + 91[38]

A prince had come out of "Egypt" and Ethiopia lifted its hands to God for deliverance.

Historiographically, blacks have experienced a new sense of dignity and respect, not because of their color but because of their outstanding contributions. The panorama of individuals who have made a cultural impact on America by their contributions has continued from the colonial period until today. Born as a free person in the small village of Ellicott's Mill, Maryland, Benjamin Banneker was to become a life-long student of many subjects and a scholar in his own right. Banneker's grandmother, Molly Walsh, was one of the white Americans who bought slaves and then married one of them. She had been a victim of the cruel practice in England of legalized indentureship whereby she was convicted by the court in Wessex, England, and shipped to the Colony of Maryland in 1683.

When her seven years on indentured servitude were up she bought two slaves and married the one named Bannaka, who was a native of Africa. Their eldest daughter begat Benjamin Banneker. Like many prominent blacks before and after him, Banneker was mostly self-educated. His lack of formal education proved no insurmountable obstacle as his thirst for knowledge provided him the motivation necessary to pursue his studies and effectively apply his many talents.

Using borrowed tools, Banneker constructed what is believed to be the first clock made in America. A wooden model of acceptable accuracy, it not only told the time but also chimed the hour. As a surveyor and astronomer Banneker was recommended to George Washington by Thomas Jefferson to carry out the plans for the design of Washington, D.C., as previously developed by Major L'Enfant. After completing his work on the capital in 1791, he returned home and in the following year published an almanac that has since been favorably compared to that of Benjamin Franklin. Prior to the final printing of the almanac, Banneker sent a copy of the manuscript to Thomas Jefferson, who, overwhelmed by its contents, then dispatched it to the Academy of Sciences in Paris as documentary evidence of the author's brilliance.

Of unique study habits, Banneker would oftimes study the heavens late into the night, not going to rest until dawn. When he was not sleeping, he would work on mathematical computations and correspond with other mathematicians in pursuit of difficult solutions. Tables filled with books and papers marked the interior of his home. In later life, still a confirmed bachelor, he devoted all his remaining time and energy to scientific work.

With minor exceptions, black slaves were not permitted to obtain patents to register their inventions. Since they could not enter into contracts, they had to rely on whites to obtain patent registration. In doing so they risked the loss of any rights to benefit from their efforts. The breakthrough for blacks' acquiring patents developed during the Civil War. An irony of history is that this lifting of the patent barrier to many of the "dispossessed" was probably instigated by the Confederate president, Jefferson Davis. In a futile endeavor to solicit some foreign powers to aid the South in the war against the North, Davis proposed to the government of the South that

Early provision should be made to secure to the subjects of foreign nations the full enjoyment of their property in valuable inventions, and to extend to our own citizens protection, not only for their own inventions, but for such as may have been assigned to them or may hereafter be assigned by persons not alien enemies.[39]

Nevertheless, prior to the Civil War, some blacks did develop inventions that stimulated the economic growth of industry in the United States and the world. Free men of color were not so restricted. According to Patent Office records, free-born Henry Blair of Maryland was the first black to be granted a patent.[40] In 1834 and 1836 Blair received patents for two similar corn harvesters.[41]

A plaque in honor of Norbert Rillieux hangs in the Louisiana State Museum in recognition of his outstanding contributions to American society. Born in New Orleans, Rillieux was sent by his father to France for his education. After his return, Rillieux became chief engineer of the Louisiana Sugar Refining Company. Because the old "Jamaica train" method of refining sugar was slow and expensive, Rillieux in 1846 developed a vacuum evaporating pan that revolutionized the refining of raw sugar. The new method reduced the production cost of granulated sugar, which lost its dark color but retained its sweetness. The engineer's invention established the scientific principles that are basic to all modern industrial evaporation.

The son of a black woman and Dutch engineer, Jan Matzeliger was born in Dutch Guiana in 1852 and in the 1870s came to the United States. He worked as a shoemaker's apprentice and later moved to Lynn, Massachusetts, where he pursued his occupation. After ten years of repeated failures, Jan Matzeliger finally perfected a shoe-lasting machine that could attach the uppers of shoes to the soles. This had previously been a slow, tedious task done by hand. Where skilled workers had been able to produce between forty and fifty pairs of shoes per day, Matzeliger's new invention made possible mass production of four hundred shoes per day. This shoe-lasting machine could hold a shoe on its last, grip and pull the leather around the heel, insert the nails, and then eject the completed shoe.

In 1883 Jan obtained a patent on his machine and the shoe industry was completely revolutionized. The patent was bought by the United States Shoe Manufacturing Company, which grew to control 98 percent of the shoe machinery trade. Income from shoe manufacturing in New England increased three and one-half times, and Matzeliger's invention was adopted in factories around the world. In spite of the tremendous success of his invention, Matzeliger died a poor man at the age of thirty-six.

The North offered opportunities for blacks that were nonexistent in the South. Born in Columbus, Ohio, Granville T. Woods worked for a time in a machine shop, then took a job as railroad fireman and engineer in Missouri, all the while studying electrical and mechanical engineering at night. After two years of employment on a British steamship, in 1880 he became an engineer on the Danville and Southern Railroad. During these varied work experiences Woods was formulating ideas for improving transportation and communication devices.

Woods later established a factory in Cincinnati which manufactured telephone, telegraph and electrical equipment. His first invention, a steam boiler furnace, was introduced in 1884. Later inventions included an amusement apparatus, automatic air brakes, an incubator, and a system for sending telegrams for trains in transit. Woods was granted over fifteen patents for electrical railway devices and sold various inventions to the American Engineering Company, Westinghouse Air Brake Company, American Bell Telephone Company, and General Electric Company.

Another black inventor was Elijah McCoy, who was born in Canada and later moved to Detroit, Michigan. Between 1872 and 1920 he was granted fifty-seven patents, all dealing with ways to lubricate machinery. His principal invention was a result of his job as lubricator of locomotive engines. To save time and increase productivity, McCoy designed a lubricating cup that made it possible to apply oil to various parts without stopping the engine. He also patented a steam dome for locomotives in 1885 and later organized the Elijah McCoy Manufacturing Company in Detroit.

A noteworthy black contributor to the field of electronics was Lewis Howard Latimer. Born in Chelsea, Massachusetts, in 1848, he became imbued at an early age with the spirit of liberty and devoted part of his youth to selling the *Liberator*, the abolitionist newspaper of William L. Garrison. During the Civil War, Latimer served aboard the *Massasoit*, a Union naval vessel. After Appomatox, Latimer worked for a solicitor in a patent office, where he gained invaluable technical knowledge. In 1876 he coupled his creative genius with that of Alexander Graham Bell by executing the drawings and assisting in preparation of the applications for a patent on the telephone.[42]

One of Latimer's most outstanding accomplishments was his discovery of a suitable filament for the incandescent bulb, which today lights up the world. In this endeavor he worked very closely with the noted inventor Hiram S. Maxim. In 1884 he became chief draftsman for both the General Electric and Westinghouse companies[43] and in 1890 published a book to give the public an explanation of the art of electric lighting by incandescence.[44] Latimer held numerous patents, including one for a carbon-manufacturing process (issued in 1882), another for a cooling and disinfecting apparatus (1886), and one for a "locking rack" for hats, coats, and umbrellas (1896).

It is surmised that Latimer found the climate right for him to acquire patents and participate in making worthwhile contributions to American science and technology. As a member of the original team of the Famous Edison Pioneers in 1919, many of the installations of electric lights in New York, Philadelphia, Montreal, and London were installed under the supervision of this black inventor. Because Latimer was one of the persons responsible for the schematic drawings and specifications, very often he was one of the star witnesses in many of the patent suits in which Edison Enterprises were involved.

Blacks in the American Revolution

In spite of slavery, there were many blacks who had a zeal for freedom and fought side by side with the colonials who were throwing off the shackles of oppression from Great Britain. One early freedom fighter was Crispus Attucks, a dockworker who was well known around Boston. In the months following the dispatch of British troops to Boston, street fights and tavern brawls between soldiers and colonists were common. Tension increased in the spring of 1770, after a disagreement between some ropemakers and three soldiers grew into a fight. Three days later, on March 5, 1770, armed soldiers emerged from a barracks to face a group of townspeople, with the giant-like Attucks standing in the center. Fearless and commanding, Attucks urged the people to hold their ground. Insults led to blows, and soldiers began using bayonets against the furious crowd. Attucks urged the colonists not to be afraid, saying the soldiers dared not fire. A stick sailing through the air struck a soldier, Private Hugh Montgomery, who fell back and then fired his musket, killing Attucks. After the volley of shots several others also lay dead. Thus Attucks became the first casualty of the American Revolution.

During the Revolutionary War, the British promised freedom to male slaves who enlisted in their army. This strategic plan was promulgated by Lord Dunmore. On November 7, 1775, the royal governor of Virginia, while aboard the ship *Norfolk*, took official action in his proclamation, where he stated:

> I do hereby declare all indented servants, Negroes, or others, free that are able and willing to bear arms, they joining His Majesty's Troops, as soon as may be, for the more speedingly reducing the Colony to a proper sense of their duty to His Majesty's crown and dignity.[45]

Frightened by Negro response to the British promise and military reverses, General Washington reversed an earlier decision and allowed free Negroes to enlist in the Colonial army.

On June 17, 1775, under the command of Major John Pitcarin, British forces stormed Breed's (Bunker) Hill. Among the black American defenders were Prince Hall, originally a native of Barbados in the West Indies, and Peter Salem, who fired the shot that mortally wounded Major Pitcarin and changed Bunker Hill from a defeat to a moral victory.

Prince Whipple also served in the Revolution to gain his freedom. He was a bodyguard to General William Whipple of New Hampshire, an aide to George Washington. When Washington crossed the Delaware River on Christmas night, 1776, to provide reinforcement against the British, Prince Whipple was with him in the boat. Another black patriot, Oliver Cromwell, enlisted in the Second New Jersey Regiment, and accompanied Washington as he crossed the Delaware River.

A remarkable black spy during the American Revolution was James Armistead, who later took the name of James Lafayette in honor of the French hero of the War of Independence. Armistead carried out many dangerous missions in 1781 to acquire information concerning English troops. The Virginia legislature granted him his freedom in 1786.

Other blacks who served as spies during the Revolutionary War were Saul Matthews, of the Commonwealth of Virginia, who served under Baron Von Steuben; and Jack Sission, a commando who succeeded in capturing a British officer as a hostage for Major General Charles Lee, who was a prisoner of the British.

A New Government
and the Quest for Equality

Despite their services and contributions which helped the Americans win in the struggle for independence, blacks were not included in the egalitarian concept in the Declaration of Independence that "all men were created equal." J. Franklin Jameson writes,

> ...for at this time the contrast between American freedom and American slavery comes out, for the first time, with startling distinctness. It has often been asked: How could men who were engaged in a great and inspiring struggle for liberty fail to perceive the inconsistency between their professions and endeavors in that contest and their actions with respect to their doctrines respecting the rights of man to the Black men who were held among them in bondage far more reprehensible than that to which they indignantly proclaimed themselves to have been subjected by the King of Great Britain.[46]

There is no doubt that Jefferson turned his back on his own morality and political views, based on the "rights of man." Perhaps the exaggerated charges blaming the slave trade on George III were too obvious.

> He [George III] has waged cruel war against human nature itself, violating its most sacred rights of life and liberty in the persons of a distant people who never offended him—captivating and carrying them into slavery in another hemisphere, or to incur miserable death in their transportation thither. This piratical warfare, the opprobrium of infidel powers, is the warfare of the Christian King of Great Britain. Determined to keep open a market where Men Should be brought and sold, he has prostituted his negative [royal veto] for suppressing every legislative attempt to prohibit or to restrain this execrable commerce. And that this assemblage of horrors might want no fact of distinguished dye [might lack no flagrant crime], he is now exciting those very people to rise in arms among us, and to purchase that liberty of which he has deprived them by murdering the people upon whom he also obtruded them: thus paying off former crimes committed against the liberties of one people with crimes which he urges them to commit against the lives of another.[47]

Even if his political philosophy had included blacks, Jefferson knew that Southerners and Northerners made wealthy by the slave trade would not support black freedom. So the section of the Declaration condemning slavery was deleted as a compromise in order to continue human depravity. The subsequent adoption of the Declaration of Independence by the Constitutional Convention in Philadelphia reflects the victory of the reactionaries who were attempting to check the trend toward social upheaval and give sanction to the protection of human (slave) property.

Categorical pronouncements that blacks were property, had no rights, and were not included within the egalitarian concepts of the founding fathers were affirmed in the famous Dred Scott Case (1857) and later in the Slaughterhouse Cases, which affirmed "that a man of African descent, whether a slave or not, could not be a citizen of the United States."[48] The Declaration lighted the flame of liberty for white America but snuffed out the candle of freedom for black America. The American Revolution was brought to fruition at Yorktown. To some extent it democratized American society and slightly elevated black slaves, who were the most debased people in the New World. Their status improved because of new social changes effected by the political upheaval of the American Revolution.

The presumptive evidence of another real revolution was omnipresent. The economic fiber of colonial life had been weakened by the war, and the subsequent discontent spilled over into the social strata as reflected in Shays' Rebellion of 1786. White and black farmers, artisans, and laborers who had lost their land due to delinquent taxed and mortgage foreclosures revolted. They were led by Daniel Shays, a former officer of the American Revolution, who sought a redress of grievances from the legislature at Springfield and the wealthy creditor class in Massachusetts. This spontaneous rebellion demanded not only land reforms but freedom for slaves in adherence to the principles of freedom and equality which the American revolutionaries had articulated as a cause of their rebellion against England.

Of the two thousand evergreen twig-wearing insurgents, Moses Sash was one of the black agrarians from Worthington who marched along with Shays as his assistant in this post-revolutionary protest.[49] He was one of the dissidents who was to lead the detachment of men to seize muskets, powder, and other weapons from the United States arsenal at Springfield. Governor James Bowdoin of Massachusetts sent General Benjamin Lincoln with five thousand army regulars and successfully put down the rebellion. Shays sought political asylum in Vermont. For his part in the rebellion Sash was indicted twice for this act of securing warlike supplies.[50] Blacks paid the price and fought for freedom from oppression just as other colonials. When John Hancock was elected governor of Massachusetts, he pardoned Shays and Sash in 1788. This rebellion justified the need for a strong central government, resulted in the movement to revise the Articles of Confederation, and the subsequent adoption of the Constitution.

When the founding fathers met in Philadelphia to consider revision of the Articles of Confederation, they came to the conclusion that the articles were inadequate for the floundering republic as constituted in 1787. The Constitutional Convention was a series of compromises. The large states sought to dominate the convention and suggested that population should be the basis for representation. The South, scheming to gain control of the new government, proposed counting slaves in the census enumeration. Slaves were temporarily considered people; the North, seeing the disadvantages to its political future, rejected the proposal. Finally a compromise was adopted whereby five slaves would be equivalent to three whites.[51] Thus, constitutional fractionalization demeaned the identity of black people in the United States.

Another compromise in the convention further demeaned the legal status of blacks by giving constitutional sanctions to the continuance of slavery. New England merchants pressed their representatives for the deletion of the two-thirds requirement in the Constitution that was necessary to pass navigation acts. They proposed that a simple majority of Congress be empowered to pass this type of legislation. Both South Carolina and Georgia engaged in log-rolling tactics to support the New England proposal in return for permitting the slave trade to continue until 1808.

What came out of the Constitutional Convention had to be the miracle of all ages. Forrest McDonald attests to the assumption that the American Revolution and the American people—of all the world's peoples the most materialistic and most vulgar and least disciplined—should have produced a governmental system adequate to check the very forces they unleashed; this was the miracle of the age, and of the succeeding age, and of all the ages to come.[52] Both white and black leaders expressed their dissatisfaction with the Convention, which was designed to solidify and crystallize basic political ideologies of liberty, justice, and equality, yet had extended these concepts to only white men, excluding women and blacks, in the New World. George Mason, an affluent Virginia planter, was especially critical of the compromise that extended African slave trade twenty more years. Franklin decried the feasibility and economics of slaveholding in order to compete with cheap wages of factory workers in Great Britain. He calculated the total cost of maintaining slaves after their original cost was too high, but he justified American slavery because the slaves could be held in perpetuity while "hired men are continually leaving their masters."[53]

Richard Allen led a "kneel-in" in 1787 at the conclusion of the Constitutional Convention to focus attention on the evils of slavery. He and Absolom Jones had earlier organized the Free African Society in Philadelphia. The embarrassment and dehumanizing aspect of being pulled from their knees while praying in the St. George Methodist Church of Philadelphia led them to form the organization. The Free African Society passed several resolutions urging the abolition of slavery and opposing proposals by the American Colonization Society of sending free blacks back to Africa.

The majority of blacks did not support the various movements to send blacks back to Africa but felt that the solution had to be in America. A staunch black foe of the back-to-Africa movement was James Forten. He was a former powder boy who served with Stephen Decatur on the *Royal Louis* privateer during the Revolutionary War. The Somerset case of 1771 had nullified slave laws in England and Forten sailed to England to enjoy the fruits of freedom. While living on the Isle of Liberty, Granville Sharp's electrifying oratory against slavery inspired Forten to lead a life dedicated to the abolition of slavery. Shortly after, Forten returned to Philadelphia, where he became an apprentice to sailmaker Robert Bridges, who died in 1798 and left the business venture to the free black man.

This black entrepreneur invented a device which aided in the control of sails and netted him more than one hundred thousand dollars in profits. He became a very rich and patriotic citizen. During the War of 1812 Forten recruited 2,500 blacks to help defend Philadelphia against the British. He fought with the same fervor against the American Colonization Society and its plan to send blacks back to Africa. This prominent citizen of Philadelphia felt that blacks should enjoy the blessings of the America they helped create with their toil, sweat, and tears, rather than follow the circuitous route to perpetual bondage in Africa.[54]

James Forten was the guiding spirit behind William Lloyd Garrison and contributed considerable support to the *Liberator* and abolition societies. The black philanthropist used his wealth for various causes, including women's rights, temperance, peace, and first-class citizenship for blacks. His dreams were realized in his children, Ray Allen Billington writes, "when Abraham Lincoln's Emancipation Proclamation completed the reform to which he devoted his life."[55]

Although many blacks opposed recolonization in Africa, some thought avoidance was a good technique for mitigating the racial problem. Paul Cuffee was a free black who taught himself to read and write. He was born in New Bedford, Massachusetts, and spent most of his early life on the sea. Because of his ingenuity and business skill he built a fleet of ships, plying the seas to ports the world over.

When his own children were denied the right to attend school, Cuffee used his accumulated wealth to build a schoolhouse and hire a teacher. Thus the black children of New Bedford had the opportunity to gain a formal education. Cuffee, with other Quakers, became concerned over the continuing enslavement of blacks in the United States. In 1811 he visited Sierra Leone, a British colony on the west coast of Africa, and founded the Friendly Society of Sierra Leone to encourage American blacks to emigrate there. In 1815, at a personal expense of three or four thousand dollars, Cuffee transported forty free blacks to Sierra Leone. His failing health prevented the completion of further expeditions.

Encouragement for blacks to immigrate to Africa also came from many whites. Free slaves were a continuous menace to the docility of the enslaved. Their very presence and unrelenting instigations to revolt or escape were a physical threat and potential economic loss to slave owners. So in 1817 Justice Bushrod Washington, Henry Clay, and John Randolph put into reality Thomas Jefferson's idea of gradual manumission and exportation of slaves by organizing the American Colonization Society. Its purpose was to remove as many free blacks as possible from the United States and send them to West Africa, where most of their ancestors had originally been enslaved. This would provide greater security to the institution of slavery[56] and too, by having a colony on the West Coast of Africa,

> ...this could also provide an answer to the embarrassing question of what to do with the Ibos, Dahomeans, Congolese, and other Africans taken away from slaving vessels intercepted by the United States Navy following the ban on importation of slaves after 1808 and the agreement of 1879 to help suppress the slave trade on the high seas.[57]

Even though the basic motive was a selfish one, the movement was a manifestation of the national sentiment for the betterment of humanity. Too, the American Colonization Society temporarily became a safety valve that allowed the cauldron of sectional hatred to simmer a little longer in postponing the Civil War. Pressure from the abolitionists was diverted into a more cooperative endeavor to mitigate the misery of blacks in this country.

In 1818 the Society sent Samuel J. Mills and E. Burgess to Sierra Leone to make a study of the black settlement there. They later made a favorable feasibility report for the inauguration of the humanitarian undertaking south of Leone.[58] Political patronage and pressure was exacted by influential Southerners, who persuaded Congress to appropriate $100,000 in initial grant to purchase the desired land from African chiefs and provide the means necessary for settlement and development. In 1821 the site was chosen and the new "cradle of liberty" was named Liberia. Its capital was appropriately designated Monrovia as a tribute to President Monroe.

After successfully putting down several tribal wars which threatened the peaceful existence of Liberia and the renewal of the slave trade, and settling sporadic boundary disputes and interferences from Great Britain, on July 26, 1847, the Liberians drew up a Declaration of Independence. Its preamble's literary quality is similar to that immortal document drawn up by Thomas Jefferson in 1776.

THE REPUBLIC OF LIBERIA
Declaration of Independence
In Convention
Town of Monrovia; June and July 1847.

> We, the representatives of the people of the Commonwealth of Liberia, in Convention assembled, invested with authority for forming a new Government, relying upon the aid and protection of the Great Arbiter of human events, do hereby, in the name and on behalf of the people of this Commonwealth, publish and declare the said Commonwealth a FREE, SOVEREIGH and INDEPENDENT STATE, by the name and style of the REPUBLIC OF LIBERIA.[59]

On the same day the Declaration was proclaimed, a constitution, based on the political ideology of the United States, was adopted by the Liberian constituent assembly. The state was constituted as the Free and Independent Republic of Liberia, and Joseph Jenkins Roberts became its first president. The colonizing enterprise envisaged by its founders never attracted the number of blacks it was intended to lure to this haven of freedom, however. By 1830 there were only 1,420 blacks in the colony. The following table is a summary of the dismal percentage of blacks who migrated to Liberia in the first forty-five years of its existence.

Table 1. Status of Liberian immigrants, 1822-1876[60]
Born free 4,541
Purchased their freedom 344

Emancipated to go to Liberia 5,957
Emancipated for other reasons 753
Arrived from Barbados, 1865 346
Unknown 68
Settled in Maryland County, 1831-1862, Origins not indicated 1,227
Recaptured Africans sent by the United States Navy 5,722
Total 18,958

Many of the free blacks in the United States during this period were generations removed from their ancestors who had been enslaved, and most of the younger generation had developed Western cultural fixations and a deep attachment for America in spite of being forced to live in a hostile society. They were determined not to leave the land of their birth. Those blacks who went to Liberia did so with a higher sense of liberty than the Founding Fathers of America did when they left the despotism and tyranny of Europe. Princes were coming out of "Egypt" and Liberia was the home of the exiles returning from captivity. The national motto inscribed on the seal of Liberia says, "THE LOVE OF LIBERTY BROUGHT US HERE." These pioneers were launching a new government where men would be immune from injustices and oppression based on the pigmentation of their skin. The number of blacks who might have sought a new life in Africa was reduced by the advent of the Civil War and the subsequent emancipation of the slaves.[61]

The Liberians had to nurture the development of the new republic without much assistance from the United States. Throughout its infancy, and even today, the United States has maintained the position that it would make Liberia a sovereign partner and a not a protectorate. The contrast between this interested partnership and the sometime ruthless exploitation that has marred much of the development of Africa by the European colonial powers is striking.[62] Nevertheless, the successful development of African countries controlled by blacks as a solution to their racial problems remains a misty dream awaiting the "Day of Jubilee."

THE VOYAGE, PROTEST, AND FLIGHT TO FREEDOM

The failure of the Founding Fathers to eliminate slavery and extend the constitutional guarantees to all Americans gave further encouragement to the importation of Africans. This trade corrupted African tribal life and frustrated the development of native civilizations in Africa.[63] Removed completely from their native culture, "princes" were brought from their kingdoms inside the low-lying African deltas to the slave depots on the western coast for shipment to the New World. Most times they were victims of the increasing number of tribal wars and the greed of Europeans who traded Dutch and Portuguese commodities for human cargo.

Liverpool merchants became so rich from the slave trade that they invested heavily in mills, factories, mines, canals, and railways. In New England that process was repeated, and black cargo provided much of the capital that was needed for the industrial revolution.[64] The invention of the cotton gin by Eli Whitney and the resultant demand for cotton accelerated the need for slaves and an increase in the traffic of human cargo.

Southern plantation owners sensed the key to economic survival in cotton and black merchandise. This new economic concept of success in America, unhampered by religious and moral restraints, made blacks the spring and doormat of American capitalism. Thus man became property to be pawned, bought, and sold for profit. In order to increase their profits, ship captains joined the progenitors of inhumanity. They packed the quarters below deck to capacity; slaves were shackled together in cramped spaces that made it difficult to stand or move during the entire voyage. The stench and odor below deck was unbearable. Observers indicated that in certain states of the weather they could detect the odor of a slaver further away than they could see her on a clear night. The odor was often unmistakable at a distance of five miles downwind.[65] But the lure of profits from those blacks who would survive the ordeal of the voyage nullified the unpleasant odor. The slavers devised means of making the voyage more profitable by arriving in the New World with a reasonable number of slaves. As Daniel P. Mannix, in *Black Cargoes*, explains, "The usual procedure was to batten both men and women below hatches and leave them there until the ship dropped anchor. Then, under armed guards, the hatches were opened and the living allowed to go ashore to their new masters. The dead were thrown into the bay."[66]

Only estimates and conjectures can be made as to the loss in lives exacted by the slave trade. Conservative estimates indicate "that about one third of the Negroes died on the way to the coast and at the embarkation stations, and that another third died crossing the ocean and in the seasoning, so that only one third finally survived to become the laborers and colonizers of the New World."[67]

Because they were warriors, many of the slaves' hostile spirits surged against the chains in violent protest during the ordeals of the "Middle Passage." Mutinies were frequent. In 1839 the slave Joseph Cinque led a mutiny on the slave ship *Amistad*. Kidnapped and shipped to Cuba, Cinque, the royal blood of a Mendi chief coursing through his veins, recruited fifty other slaves, mutinied, killed Captain Ferrer of the *Amistad*, and sailed the ship to Long Island. While Cinque awaited trial in New Haven, abolitionists rallied to his cause and formed an Amistad Committee. On March 9, 1841, the articulate John Quincy Adams, Congressman from Massachusetts, addressed the Supreme Court as counsel for the defendants. The court freed the Africans. Charles Sumner became the chief counsel for another group of 130 black mutineers who took over the slave ship *Creole* in 1841 and killed the captain. The British held the ship at the port of Nassau and eventually freed the blacks.

When mutiny failed, suicide became the means of escape. Prince Olaudah Equiana (Gustavius Vassa) tells in his narrative, written in England in 1789, of two of his fellow countrymen who, "preferring death to such a life of misery, somehow made it through the netting and jumped into the sea; immediately another quite dejected fellow, who on account of his illness was suffered to be out of irons, also followed their example."[68]

Resistance to slavery was quite often subtle but always omnipresent. The oppressed attempted to find their way to freedom without shedding the blood of their oppressors. Even when the ships had discharged their human cargo and the slaves had been carted away to the plantations, protests were expressed in the religious fervor of the spirituals. The slaves' hope for a better world in the life to come eased their miserable conditions and enabled them to find an element of freedom from the shackles of involuntary servitude. These blacks embraced Christianity and eulogized that the experiences of the Hebrews in their deliverance from Pharaoh were analogous to conditions in America. They expressed their feeling in melodies that exemplified the jubilant liberty of a soul which no chains could hold in submission or oppression. The book *Seventy Negro Spirituals* explains,

> Hymns more genuine than those have never been sung since the psalmists of Israel relieved their burdened hearts and expressed their exaltation. Nor will they die, because they sprang like these from hearts on fire with a sense of the reality of spiritual truths.[69]

The universality of the verse "Sometimes I feel like a motherless child, a long ways from home" remains today as a symbol of the lonely and longing spirit of these human beings who were uprooted and carried into captivity in a strange and hostile land. But their hopes of freedom were constantly renewed by a song of deliverance that they appropriated for their own use from the Hebrews:

Go Down, Moses, Way down in Egypt land,
Tell ol' Pharaoh, To let my people go.
When Israel was in Egypt land, let my people go,
Oppressed so hard they could not stand,
Let my people go...

But freedom did not come. The louder the blacks cried, the harder the callous overseers whipped these helpless creatures. This inhumanity to man produced harmonic utterances among blacks that reflected an unwavering faith that one day they would be free. Their patience and forbearance was harmonized in a moving spiritual:

Soon I will be done with the troubles of this world
Troubles of this world
Goin' home to live with God.

So blacks remained the most ardent worshippers in the Christian churches of their oppressors. For a while the slaves worshipped in the same sanctuaries with whites, until they were ostracized from regular worship. The slaves accepted their separation with the customary exhortation which they expressed in song: "O, Mary, don't you weep, don't you moan…Pharaoh's army got drowned…." Whites who held them in bondage were looked upon as Pharaoh. The whites became suspicious and alarmed and restricted slaves' assembling together unless there was a white person present. It was thought that this regulation would lessen the likelihood of conspiracies. So the slaves resigned themselves to the new restrictions and sought secret meetings where they could worship and plan for liberation. The slaves would exhort each other to

Steal away, steal away, steal away to Jesus,
Steal away, steal away home,
I ain't got long to stay here.
My Lord, He calls me, He calls me by the thunder,
The trumpet sounds within-a my soul,
I ain't got long to stay here.

The dual nature of the spirituals was often overlooked by the overseers, who were spellbound by the antiphonal music of the slaves as they lifted their voices in harmony. While the songs might have been ones of hope and longing, they were used as signals for escaping to freedom by way of the Underground Railroad. The repetitious phrases of "Get on board, little children…there's room for many-a more" or "I'm bound for the Promised Land" provided an opportunity for those who wanted freedom to be ready to leave in the darkening shadows of evening. Then if they were successful in making it across the Delaware River and thence into Canada, they would join in the chorus of "Free at Last":

Free at last, free at last,
I thank God I'm free at last.

However, to some who dreamed of freedom this was an illusion; they never made it to Canada. The disappointments, imaginative hope, and fervor of the enslaved contributed to American culture through the spirituals. Negro spirituals are one of the outstanding cultural contributions of the black man to America. He is, according to James Work, "the creator of the only things artistic that have yet sprung from American soil and been universally acknowledged as distinctive American products."[70]

When mutiny, suicide, and religion failed to extricate the African from his plight in the Middle Passage and subsequent slavery, he often resorted to revolt. In the southern United States in the nineteenth century, a body of laws known as the Black Codes was established to regulate blacks. Slaves were considered property, not persons; they could not own property, strike a white person (even in self-defense), possess firearms, buy or sell goods, assemble with other blacks unless a white person was present, or be taught to read or write. Offenders of these laws were punished by shipping, branding, imprisonment, or death. These harsh laws made enslavement more and more unbearable, and an increasing number of revolts occurred.

One of the earliest revolutionaries was Gabriel P. Prosser. Like many leaders of American black slave revolts, Prosser was deeply religious and an avid reader of the Bible. Prosser claimed he was the slaves' divinely chosen leader. During the spring and summer of 1800, Prosser made elaborate plans for his uprising. Taking careful notes of strategic points in Richmond, Virginia, he formulated his plot. His two thousand to fifty thousand participants would form three columns: one column would seize the arsenal, another would take the powder house, and the main column would enter Richmond simultaneously from two sides, cutting down every white person except Quakers, Methodists, and Frenchmen. Prosser hoped to then attack other cities and eventually become the King of Virginia. The time chosen was midnight, August 20.

Unknown to Prosser, Tom and Pharaoh, slaves of Mosby Sheppard, informed their master of the plot. Sheppard, in turn, notified the governor, who immediately and secretly called in over six hundred militiamen. Before Prosser and his followers (estimates of their numbers range from two to five thousand) could march into Richmond from their meeting place, a violent thunderstorm descended on the area, washing out bridges and making roads impassable. Thus Prosser was forced to postpone his invasion. Meantime, after word of the betrayal reached him, Prosser attempted to escape to Norfolk but was captured there on September 25. Refusing to give authorities any information, the twenty-three-year-old Prosser was hanged on October 7. On the same day, fifteen of Prosser's accomplices also died.

Several years after Prosser's death, Denmark Vesey, a native of Hispañola, led another revolt. Vesey, the property of a Charleston trader, purchased his freedom with money he won in a lottery. Working in Charleston as a carpenter, he accumulated money and property and gained the respect of blacks and whites. But Vesey could not erase the memories of his twenty years as servant to a slave trader. He harbored a deep, unquenchable hatred for slavery and slaveholders. For four or five years Vesey talked to slaves, spreading dissatisfaction and revolt. Ridiculing, threatening, taunting, Vesey gained influence over blacks around Charleston. According to some sources, many slaves feared Vesey more than they feared their masters.

Vesey then switched from agitator to organizer. He chose Peter Poyas, who had amazing administrative ability, as his first assistant. He also enlisted the talents of Gullah Jack, an African-born sorcerer, and Bland Phillip, who could reportedly see ghosts, to influence timid slaves. Vesey and his associates recruited an estimated nine thousand slaves and finalized their plans. On July 16, 1822, the slave army was to strike Charleston, capturing arsenals, naval equipment, and ammunition, and killing all white persons. Then disaster struck. A house servant betrayed Vesey's painstaking efforts. Authorities, notified of the conspiracy, labored for two weeks to uncover details of the plot and names of the leaders. During this time the bold Vesey continued to hold secret meetings. Soon another slave, entrusted with details of the plot, gave the authorities important information which led to the arrest and subsequent execution of Vesey and thirty-four other blacks.

The most famous slave revolt, perpetrated by Nat Turner, had tremendous impact upon the people of the South. Described as a religious fanatic and mystic, a dreamer and terrorist, Turner immersed himself in religion and came to believe that God had chosen him to lead the Negroes out of bondage. Turner ran away when he was placed under an overseer he did not like. Nevertheless, he returned within thirty days because he was convinced that he was to do the will of God.[71] Believing that he had received a sign from God, Turner gathered his six "disciples" on the banks of Cabin Pond in Southampton County, Virginia, on the evening of August 21, 1831. Here he outlined plans to kill every white man, woman, and child. Armed with a hatchet and broadax, the insurrectionists proceeded house by house. Striking first at his master's house and continuing on through the night, gathering followers at every stop, Turner carried on his massacre until there were some sixty white dead.

Throughout the two months Turner was at large, much of the South remained in a state of apprehension and hysteria. Historian Lerone Bennett quotes an eyewitness as saying, "Fear was seen in every face; women pale and terror-stricken, children crying for protection, men fearful and full of foreboding, but determined to be ready for the worst."[72] As news of the insurrection spread, three thousand soldiers and militiamen from warships and forts thronged Southampton. During the massacre that followed, the enraged white burned, tortured, and murdered a number of innocent blacks. After his capture, Turner, nicknamed "The Prophet," was taken in chains to the nearby town of Jerusalem. Although he pleaded not guilty at his trial, a jury sentenced Nat Turner to death. He and sixteen of his followers were hanged; twelve others were convicted and sent out of the state.

Other slaves chose escape rather than revolt. To escape from "Egypt," the land of bondage, and get to the Promised Land was a tactical operation that was a perilous undertaking by those along the Underground Railroad and makes one of the most exciting chapters of American history. An organizer of the underground "Freedom Road" and the man who earned the title of "spokesman" for his race was born Frederick Augustus Washington Bailey in Tuckahoe, Maryland. Like many other slave children, he was separated from his mother at an early age. Frederick lived with his grandmother until at the age of seven years, he was sent to reside with "Aunt Kay," an ill-tempered slave woman who often starved him and the other children. His master's daughter, to whom he had been temporarily loaned, taught him to read. Lessons ended abruptly when her husband angrily interfered. Frederick later acquired a copy of the *Columbian Orator* and was moved by speeches supporting liberty and freedom.

He learned to hate slavery early in life after being brutally flogged, whipped, and kicked. At the age of twenty-one Frederick disguised himself as a sailor and escaped to New York, where he married a free black girl he had earlier courted in Baltimore. He then took the name of Frederick Douglass.

Prevailed upon by abolitionists to tell his story of life under slavery, the eloquent Douglass rapidly became one of the best-known orators in the United States. In 1845 he went to England and Ireland for nineteen months, where his antislavery lectures gained the sympathy of rich and poor alike. In 1852 Douglass delivered the following outstanding oration:

WHAT IS YOUR FOURTH OF JULY TO ME?
1852

Fellow Citizens: Pardon me, and allow me to ask, why am I called upon to speak here today? What have I, or those I represent, to do with your national independence? Are the great principles of political freedom and of natural justice, embodied in that Declaration of Independence, extended to us?

What to the American slave is your Fourth of July? I answer, a day that reveals to him more than all other days of the year, the gross injustice and cruelty to which he is the constant victim. To him your celebration is a sham; your boasted liberty an unholy license; your national greatness, swelling vanity; your sounds of rejoicing are empty and heartless; your denunciation of tyrants, brass-fronted impudence; your shouts of liberty and equality, hollow mockery; your prayers and hymns, your sermons and thanksgivings, with all your religious parade and solemnity, are to him mere bombast, fraud, deception, impiety, and hypocrisy—a thin veil to cover up crimes which would disgrace a nation of the earth guilty of practices more shocking and bloody than are the people of these United States at this very hour.

Go where you may, search where you will, roam through all the monarchies and despotisms of the Old World, travel through South America, search out every abuse and when you have found the last, lay your facts by the side of the everyday practices of this nation, and you will say with me that, for revolting barbarity and shameless hypocrisy, America reigns without rival....[73]

For seventeen years, beginning in 1847, Douglass published a widely read antislavery paper entitled the *North Star* (later changed to *Frederick Douglass' Paper*), so named because slaves on their way to freedom in Canada traveled at night following the North Star. The *North Star* was the voice of the trumpet and the guiding light of the Underground Railroad.

Douglass, active in the Republican Party, advised President Lincoln on the possible role of the black in the Civil War. He was elected president of the Freedman's Bank and Trust Company in 1874, and later was appointed to various offices, including marshal and recorder of deeds for the District of Columbia, charge d'affaires to Santo Domingo, and minister-resident and consul general to Haiti.

Another organizer of the Underground Railroad, Harriet Tubman, was born on a slave-breeding plantation in Maryland. She had two brothers who escaped in 1849, but the brothers later returned, fearing recapture. Traveling at night and guided by the North Star, Harriet eventually reached Philadelphia and freedom. She returned to Maryland for her husband two years later, but he had married another woman. This disappointment increased her determination to liberate more slaves. Over a period of years she rescued her parents and five brothers and sisters.

Harriet became a legend in antislavery circles by returning to the South nineteen times and bringing out more than three hundred slaves. Rewards for her capture mounted to $40,000, but still she continued her dangerous journeys. Her tactics as conductor on the Underground Railroad, a secret system of guiding fugitive slaves to the free states and Canada, were effective; she threatened to shoot any slave who wished to turn back. Fanatically religious, Harriet trusted in God and prayed often. During the Civil War she was a spy for Union troops along the seacoast, and in the South acted as Union scout, making courageous raids inside the enemy lines. As a nurse for blacks, she tended and comforted hundreds of black men.

Yet another woman was prominent in antislavery work. A child slave named Isabella was brought to New York from Africa and later, when New York abolished slavery in 1827, Isabella became a prominent exponent of the antislavery movement. She took a new name, Sojourner Truth, because she felt she had been commissioned by God to "tell the truth" as she traveled across the United States. Whenever Sojourner Truth spoke, she wore a banner proclaiming the words inscribed on the Liberty Bell: "Proclaim liberty throughout the land unto all the inhabitants thereof." Sojourner kept the evils of slavery constantly before the nation. When the slaves were discouraged, she assured them that God was not dead and in Him rested the hope of their people.

In 1852 she attended the National Woman's Suffrage Convention in Akron, Ohio, and through her eloquence helped make substantial gains for the right of women to vote. The Civil War brought Sojourner Truth to Washington, D.C., where she spent her time as a Union spy. She also helped care for the wounded and provided comfort for thousands of black refugees. In the fall of 1864 she was received by President Lincoln and presented him a Bible as a token of appreciation of the blacks in Baltimore. She emphasized to Lincoln the necessity of arming free northern blacks to help preserve the Union.

Slaves kept running away from the South and the nation was gradually coming to the belief that a conflict was inevitable. One of the significant steps toward this confrontation was the judicial decision of the Supreme Court in the case of *Dred Scott v. Sanford* in 1857. Scott sued Sanford, his master, for freedom after the slave had gone from Missouri to the free states of Illinois and Wisconsin and lived there for five years. He maintained that residence in free territory automatically made him free.

The lower courts ruled against the allegations of Dred Scott and he appealed to the Supreme Court. Justice Tawney announced the 5-4 majority opinion of the court, which maintained that Dred Scott could not bring legal suit in a federal court because he was not a citizen. Tawney theorized that "the enslaved African race were not intended to be included and formed no part of the people who framed and adopted this Declaration [Independence]...and by common consent, had been excluded from civilized governments and the family of nations, and doomed to slavery."[74]

A second reason for denying Dred Scott a favorable decision on his appeal was based on the assumption that Scott was property and going into free territory would not make him otherwise. More important was the *obiter dictum* influenced by President Buchanan, which announced that Congress had no right to prohibit slavery in the territories and that the Missouri Compromise had been null and void since its enactment in 1820. This decision stripped the black man of any chance he had to become a recognized human being and relegated blacks to nonfamily organization. Blacks became dehumanized abstractions. The decision nationalized slavery and marred the *sacred* history of republican government.

The slaves now became the focal point of a struggle in which black men would be the national scapegoats. Disregard the economic clash between the entrepreneurs in the East and the Plantation Bourbons of the South; reject the issue of states' rights, or egocentric sectionalism, and we are left with slavery as the vehicle by which the sectional struggle began.

The Negro Soldier in the Civil War

During the first year of the Civil War, only white soldiers were permitted to engage in combat. Both the North and South feared that white men might refuse to fight beside black troops. Too, as in the American Revolution and the War of 1812, whites were reluctant about training blacks to fight and giving them arms because they might revolt at the end of the war. The North was afraid that border states might join the Confederacy if blacks were given arms. Blacks performed a variety of supportive tasks, however, which released more whites for direct fighting. Affluent Confederates took their slaves to war to wash clothes, polish swords, run errands, cook food, and cut hair, but when fighting grew fierce most servants were sent home. Slaves toiled in mines and arsenals, repaired railroads and bridges, acted as mechanics, hospital attendants, ambulance drivers, cooks, and waiters. They served aboard naval ships of both sides.

A former slave born in Reaufort, South Carolina, Robert Smalls is believed to have taught himself to read and write; he was compelled to work without pay on a Confederate transport, the *Planter*, which was used as a special dispatch boat of General Ripley, the Confederate post commander at Charleston. One May night in 1862, the white officers of the *Planter* were sleeping ashore in the Charleston homes, leaving only the black crew aboard the ship. Seizing the opportunity, Smalls smuggled his wife and children and several other close relatives aboard. The *Planter* then proceeded down the bay, giving its usual salutes and signals as it passed forts Johnson and Sumpter. Heading directly toward vessels of the Union Navy blockading Charleston, Smalls surrendered the ship to Union possession. Smalls' daring escape brought him into national prominence.

From the beginning of the war, blacks were anxious to enlist in the Union Army, and in some cities formed drill units. Frederick Douglass and other abolitionists tried to get the government to enlist blacks. Repeated reverses made the Union Army plead for assistance from the transplanted blacks of Africa. Finally, after the Battle of Antietam, Lincoln appealed to black volunteers for help. In August 1862, Union general Ben Butler, without Lincoln's approval, issued a call for colored volunteers in New Orleans. Thus the First Regiment, Louisiana Native Guards, composed of free men, many of them French-speaking, was the first Negro unit actually mustered into the Union Army. Three months later the First South Carolina Volunteers and the First Kansas Colored Regiment were given official standing.

General enlistment of blacks was possible only after January 1863, when Lincoln issued his Emancipation Proclamation,[75] freeing the slaves and accepting blacks into paid military service. However, they received only about half the salary of white soldiers, and in protest, some black regiments served without pay. Later the inequality was corrected.

The Confederacy was outraged by the Northern acceptance of blacks into the Union Army and said it would return captured blacks to bondage. In an ugly incident, rebel forces led by an ex-slave trader, Major General Nathan Bedford Forest, massacred black troops at Fort Pillow, Tennessee. A congressional investigating committee later said the Confederates murdered three hundred men, women, and children after the fort surrendered. Black soldiers began entering battle with the cry, "Remember Fort Pillow."

They proved their valor and bravery in battle after battle: at Forts Wagner, Hudson, and Milliken's Bend in 1863, and at Forts Olustee and Petersburg in 1864. Approximately two hundred thousand Negroes participated in the Civil War, sixteen of them receiving Congressional Medals of Honor for gallantry in action. More than thirty-eight thousand Negroes were killed in conflict. The following statement appeared in *Chicago Tribune* on August 1, 1863:

> Whenever a Negro has been tried, the courage, steadfastness, and endurance of the African race have been triumphantly vindicated. The Negro will fight for his liberty, for his place among men, for his right to develop himself in whatever direction he chooses; he will prove himself a hero, and if need be, a martyr.[76]

The Negro in the West

At the time the frontier was providing a natural laboratory for the seeds of democracy, it was simultaneously creating the incentive for the expansion of slavery. It was to the southwest that Southerners looked after the Ordinance of 1787 prohibited slavery in the northwestern territories. The Ostend Manifesto was also a manifestation of the attitude of the expansionist who made belligerent demands to Spain that if she did not give the United States Cuba, the U.S. would take it by force. President Pierce and his Secretary of State repudiated the document and refused to be dictated to by the sentiments of slaveholders who wanted fertile land to raise crops and exploit black labor.

The expansionists looked toward Texas for the fulfillment of their dreams for a government dominated by landed aristocracy supported by a slavocracy. The Louisiana Purchase had accelerated western emigration of blacks from the United States into Texas. This movement westward was a spontaneous and individualized phenomenon motivated by the same reasons as much of the white movement. The children of bondage now moved into the wilderness to get away from Pharaoh and the shackles of slavery. Moses Austin set the stage for moving into Texas by securing permission from the Mexican government in January 1821 to establish a colony in the advancing frontier of the southwest. He died shortly after receiving a charter of settlement, and his son, Stephen F. Austin, made his dream a reality by settling in the area between the Brazos and Colorado rivers.

As with other pioneers, black men were part of this westward movement. A Negro was among the original three hundred families that Austin carried with him into Texas. Hendricks Arnold, whose father was a member of Austin's cavalcade, was one of the first Negro freedmen in Texas. His fame as a scout and hunter parallels that of his companions, Erasmus (Deaf) Smith and Henry Wax Karnes. Later, during the Texas Revolution, Colonel Benjamin Milan refused to march without Arnold as his guide. Arnold also distinguished himself at the Battle of San Jacinto.

Three other Negroes were among the pioneering families Austin accepted as colonists and granted land. Lewis B. Jones, a farmer, came in 1826 from Mississippi; Greenbury Logan, a blacksmith, came in 1831 from Missouri; and Samuel Hardin, given title to half a league of land in Waller County, moved into Texas in March of 1822.[77] Plans for colonization of Negroes were envisioned by nonwhites. In April 1834, Nicholas Drouett, a mulatto and a retired Mexican army officer, came to Texas seeking the privilege of introducing five hundred Negro families from New Orleans. The project failed due to racism, which barred the black man from acquiring black land in a white society.[78]

Hundreds of slaves were brought to Texas, but the Mexican government insisted on the Texans adhering to their laws which prohibited slavery. The Mexicans' political philosophy of freedom for the individual had been crystallized in their revolution and subsequent independence. This creed was expressed in the Colonization Law of 1824, proclaimed by the republican congress under Santa Ana, "prohibiting forever the commerce and traffic in slaves and declaring all slaves introduced in Mexico in violation of the law, free by the mere act of treading Mexican soil."[79] Anglo settlers managed to circumvent the laws of Mexico through scheming, protests, and finally support from the United States, whereby Texas threw off the yoke of Mexican rule by revolution. The black man's contribution to Texan independence is noteworthy because it indicates his ultimate desire for liberty. To some it seems ironic that men would fight for rights they themselves are denied; yet black men sacrificed their lives for the apparent impossible dream. When the Texas Revolution broke out, black men were still willing to shed their blood for liberty in spite of being bound by the laws of slavery. However, some enlisted in the Mexican army to insure their continued freedom.[80]

Samuel McCullough, Jr., legally a free man, was wounded near Matagorda Bay in October 1835 and became the first to fight and give his blood for the independence of Texas against Mexico. As a result of his wounds, McCullough was an invalid for life.[81] After the war, McCullough, Jr. desired to acquire land to support his family but found that "the laws of the Country, for Independence for which he had fought and bled, still suffers, he is deprived of citizenship by reason of an unfortunate admixture of African blood."[82] President Houston gave formal recognition to the veteran's heroic gallantry and later granted him permanent residence, but rejected his plea for land and citizenship.

A historic landmark in Texas is the Alamo, in which Santa Ana, the Mexican commander, annihilated Colonel William B. Travis and his contingent of 187 men who valiantly defended the fortress. After the dramatic siege and heroic defense of the Alamo that ended on March 6, 1836, the tragedy of the slaughter was witnessed by five survivors, one of whom was "Joe," Travis's slave.[83] This twenty-three-year-old black had been a constant companion to Travis and was a full-fledged member of the American citadel.[84] During the attack on the fort by the Mexican army, Joe fought alongside Travis until his master was mortally wounded. The black defender of the Alamo went into hiding until he was discovered by the Mexicans, who were looking for blacks in the Alamo. Santa Ana's soldiers hurriedly brought Joe before the victorious Mexican general, who conveyed to the former slave that his life was not in jeopardy. However, Joe did not trust the Mexicans and he left with another survivor, Mrs. Dickinson, who was on her way to Gonzales. No known records indicate the surname of the black survivors of the Alamo, but the name "Joe" must be recorded in the annals of Texas history as one of the heroic defenders of the Alamo. Thirteen days later three hundred Americans, under the leadership of Colonel James Fannin, were massacred at Goliad. Blacks were also with these defenders.

As the fighting intensified between the Texans and Mexicans, blacks answered the call for volunteers in every instance. When Stephen F. Austin became commander-in-chief, Greenbury Logan, a free black, marched with him in his attack on Bexar. Later, when Texans were rallying under the battle cry of "Remember the Alamo" at the Battle of San Jacinto, April 21, 1836, another black man, "Dick the Drummer," distinguished himself in the battle whereby Texas won its independence. According to one observer, "this gray-headed descendant of Ham carried consternation into the ranks of Santa Ana's myrmidons."[85]

By 1840 blacks in Texas experienced a drastic legal setback to their enjoying the fruits of their participation in the Texas Revolution. Texans' yielding to the pressure of the "peculiar institution" passed the Definitive Act of February 5, 1840,[86] which made it mandatory that all free blacks who were in Texas would have to get out within two years or be placed back in slavery. This act led to the annexation of Texas, clouded the black man's future as a free man in Texas, and made his sojourn in the "wilderness" untenable. In no frontier state could he vote or hold office; many state constitutions forbade blacks from even entering their boundaries. The flower of democracy that flourished in Western soil was lily-white.[87]

While black men were prohibited and discouraged from settling in many places in the West, there were whites and blacks who encouraged all-black communities as a solution to the race problem. The origin of the majority of these towns and settlements in the North was due to antebellum masters in the South who freed their slaves, purchased land in the North, and settled them there.[88]

Between 1889 and 1910 some twenty-six black towns were established in the Oklahoma Territory. W. H. Boley was one white man who believed in the self-determination of blacks and assisted Thomas M. Haynes, a Negro, in organizing a town that is still all black and has a population of 557. The township of Boley developed its own schools, hospital, hotels, theaters, and utilities, and prospered economically. At the zenith of its development in 1912 economic repression by whites stymied further growth in the cotton economy of Boley.

When the political solidarity and potential challenge of Boley's all black community was realized, whites negated the political power by gerrymandering so it would lose its effectiveness. Later the Oklahoma legislature passed the "grandfather clause," which practically eliminated Boley's electorate. This "Aesopian formula"[89] for systematic disenfranchisement of the newly emancipated blacks established a literacy test for voters but exempted those persons whose forebearers were eligible to vote prior to January 1, 1866. This excluded most blacks from the privilege of voting and carried out its basic intent "to make white domination secure."[90] In 1915 the Supreme Court declared the "grandfather clause" unconstitutional because it violated the Fifteenth Amendment.[91]

Northern politicians had constantly fought for the exclusion of slavery from the territories in order to maintain the political balance between slave and free states, yet settlers in the far Northwest territory resisted free blacks' settling in that area more than other parts of the United States. The absences of a sizable number of blacks today in that section is attributed to earlier laws and attitudes which persisted over the questions of slavery.

The term "free black" is a classical misnomer, and in its strictest connotation denotes a vague political and theoretical generalization. As the history of America has been recorded, blacks have systematically and consistently been denied rights and privileges other Americans have taken for granted in their democratic society. Numerous blacks fled from the oppressive tyranny of southern slavery to the territories, seeking an opportunity to enjoy the freedom which frontier life afforded. They soon found that they were not included in the democratic formula of American life and that their fancied freedom was a delusion. If American ideology developed as a result of the frontier, then the nature of the frontier was one of color that excluded blacks from its environs.

With rare exceptions, most territorial legislatures prohibited free blacks from settling within their boundaries. One of the most effective ways of judging the status of free blacks in the westward expansion of the United States is to examine territorial legislation that forbade or discouraged their movement westward. The majority of territorial legislatures established north of the Ohio River, after the Ordinance of 1787, attempted to adhere to the nonslavery restrictions. Most went beyond prohibiting slavery by also excluding free blacks. In 1802, Ohio, while prohibiting slavery, passed an act requiring blacks and mulatto persons to have in their possession a certificate of freedom if they wished to remain in that state.[92] This discriminatory exclusion of blacks was an indication of racial prejudices against ethnic groups seeking refuge in western lands, and, John D. Barnhart writes, "a determination was expressed to establish a white man's civilization" in the West.[93]

In 1807 the Ohio legislature imposed restraints to reduce the number of blacks entering its domain. It enacted a law that prohibited blacks from settling in that state unless they could acquire a bond of $500 "to assure his good behavior and to guarantee that he would not become a public charge."[94] From 1827 to 1830, the number of black laborers in Ohio increased and authorities rigidly enforced the law to compel blacks to leave Ohio, sometimes using physical coercion. In Cincinnati in 1830, "a mob attacked the homes of Blacks, killed a number of them, and forced twelve hundred others to leave for Canada West, where they established the settlement known as Wilberforce."[95]

Even when they permitted blacks to remain in a state, legislative authorities denied them the right to vote, and, in most instances, refrained from counting them in the census for the apportionment of representatives. In an act which extended the right of suffrage in the Indiana territory, the general assembly received the power to apportion the representatives of the several counties according to the number of free white male inhabitants above the age of twenty-one.[96] Neither free blacks nor three-fifths of the slaves were counted in the enumeration. On March 3, 1811, in a bill extending the right of suffrage in Indiana, voting was still limited to free white male inhabitants;[97] this continued in subsequent legislation in 1828 and 1829. This racial disenfranchisement was a contrivance repeatedly used by Americans to deny blacks the right to live as other citizens in a democratic society and leave them powerless.

Blacks followed the southern currents of settlers, from 1802 to the next decade, over the Blue Ridge Mountains to Tennessee in large numbers. The geography of Tennessee created a clashing dichotomy of attitudes in relationship to slavery and free blacks. Eastern Tennessee inherited the liberal attitude of its neighbor, North Carolina, where there was little need for slave labor because of the mountainous terrain, which was not conducive to farming. In a few communities in the eastern part of North Carolina, the Carolinians' extraordinary liberality bore fruit because they put into practice a social arrangement that reduced racial tension. Instead of ostracizing large numbers of slaves on plantations, they integrated their slaves with small landowners. This arrangement placed blacks in closer contact with whites and created a condition where there was better mutual understanding and toleration.[98]

Free blacks in North Carolina also fared better than their counterparts in other slaveholding states. Prior to 1835, they could exercise their privileges of suffrage if they also held real estate, which was prohibited in many other states, and in some instances even became slaveowners themselves.[99] This enviable position aroused the ire of other blacks and the avarice of those mercenary men who dealt in human cargo and jeopardized the safety of free blacks in Tennessee. Frequently, notices in newspapers reported the kidnapping of free mulatto children, who were carried to Missouri and other states and sold as slaves.[100] There was no legal protection for free blacks from such periodic slave sorties.

Nevertheless, blacks fared better in North Carolina, and eastern Tennessee simulated this benevolent attitude. But in western Tennessee, the rolling countryside beckoned to slave labor and became a deterrent to free blacks. The provocative insurrection perpetrated by Nat Turner in Southampton County, Virginia, in 1831, caused Tennessee and several states to pass laws that prohibited free blacks from entering their territory. From Tennessee some free blacks moved into Arkansas, where they also found the climate hostile to people of color. When the French controlled what became the Arkansas Territory, they adopted Black Codes in 1724 to perpetuate and control slaves. In 1819 Congress formally created the Arkansas Territory, with no legal restrictions on slavery. This part of the West became a natural haven for slaveholders. As they moved into the territory, settlers adopted laws similar to those of their neighbors to the east.

In 1836 Arkansas became a state, and two years later the legislature of Arkansas passed the following law prohibiting further emigration of free Negroes to Arkansas:

> No free Negro or mulatto shall hereafter be permitted to emigrate or settle in this state unless he shall produce to the clerk of the county court of the county in which he wishes to settle, within twenty days after his arrival therein, a certificate of his freedom, and enter into bond to the State of Arkansas for the use of any county that may be damnified by such Negro or mulatto, with good and sufficient security in any sum not less than five hundred dollars, before the clerk of the county court, conditioned for the good behavior of such Negro or mulatto and to pay for the support of such Negro or mulatto in case he shall any time thereafter be unable to support himself and become chargeable to any county of this state.[101]

This provision severely restricted blacks from moving into Arkansas.

Geographic features of the Oregon Territory made slavery impractical, but in organizing the territory in 1847, provisions of the Wilmot Proviso, prohibiting slavery in newly acquired territory, were rejected. Racial overtones were very much evident because the Oregon legislature subsequently passed laws barring free blacks from entering or remaining in that territory. In an act in regard to slavery and free Negroes and mulattos, it provided "that when any free Negro or Mulatto shall have come to Oregon he or she, as the case may be, if of the age of eighteen or upwards, shall remove from and leave the country within the term of two years."[102] Whatever credit Frederick Jackson Turner might have given the West as the cradle of democratic concepts, the resistance to blacks raises questions as to the credibility of his concept.

Yet despite such prohibitions, blacks did move west and made major contributions to the development of the region. The adventurous life of James P. Beckworth provides much evidence concerning the role played by Negroes in westward expansion. An experienced frontiersman and Indian fighter, Beckworth traveled the length of the continent from Virginia, his birthplace, to the Rocky Mountains. During 1824-25 Beckworth journeyed to the Rocky Mountains as member and guide of a fur-trading expedition under the employ of General William Ashley's Fur Company. During this period he discovered a mountain pass which today bears his name. (The pass is located in northern California at the junction of U.S. Alternate 40 and State Highway 395.) The nearby small community of Beckworth is also named for him.[103]

Beckworth ranged the West as hunter, trapper, and Indian fighter, living at times with the Blackfoot tribe and the Crow Indians. The friendly relationship of the Native Americans to Beckworth was one of the exceptions rather than the rule. The remotely allied ethnic groups were the victims of deliberate agitation from whites moving westward. Widespread fear that the two exploited races would recognize a commonality in their servile conditions and unite to drive out the enslavers caused frontiersmen to use the old imperialistic technique of "divide and rule."[104] To meet the nightmare of an Indian-black combination, whites deliberately maintained social distance between Indians and blacks and created antagonism between them.[105]

Nevertheless, Beckworth claimed to be a Crow chief. In 1854 he dictated his memoirs, published two years later by Harper & Brothers. He followed the gold rush stampede to Colorado in 1859 and fought in the Cheyenne wars of 1864. He died there years later while on a government peace mission to the Crow Nation.

While the Civil War was raging, Native Americans in the West took advantage of the federal troops' preoccupation in the South and conducted a number of sorties to reclaim large segments of land previously taken by white settlers. To resist this threatening offensive by the Indians, Congress passed legislation in July 1866, reorganizing the army to include black soldiers who had fought valiantly in the War Between the States. The act stipulated that white officers would be in command of the black regiments, and a policy developed where these ebony soldiers would be assigned to duty in the West. This would provide a safety valve for the racial tension that inevitably developed whenever blacks were armed and given authority. By 1867 a full-scale Indian war was taking place. It took black men of the Ninth Cavalry, stationed at Brownsville, Texas, and the Tenth Cavalry in central Kansas to help quell the Indian uprising. These "Buffalo Soldiers" assisted in paving the way for peaceful settlement of the Central Plains, West Texas, and along the meandering Rio Grande.[106]

The saga of the West would be incomplete without the black cowboy being put in his proper perspective. Thousands of blacks have ridden the western plains unnoticed by the colorful fiction writers and historians who developed static concepts of white cowboys. Black riders could ride over the ridges and trails of the western frontiers; they could cross the "Great Divide"; but they could not ride over the color lines of the recorders of history.

In *The Cowboy*, Philip Ashton Rollins explains that "While men of the Range were mainly English or Irish descent...the Southwest added to its quota of such bloods numerous men of Mexican extraction, and a more than occasional Negro..."[107] Most of these black cowboys who faced the setting sun came from the Lone Star State. They all began their trade as slaves when their masters moved to Texas and acquired cattle.[108] Valuable skills in riding, roping, and handling cattle were learned from the Native Americans and Mexicans. The cowboy's hope for survival lay in his equestrian skill and his quickness with a gun. In some areas of the West there were two kinds of people: the quick and the dead. Occasionally, when blacks are recognized as cowboys, they are stereotyped as being house servants and cooks. Most black cooks on the range were ex-cowboys of all nationalities, who were unable to do hard riding because of injury or age. After the Civil War the black cowboy "moved out across the Plains to play a significant role in the development of the cattle industry and became a part of the Spirit of the West— a spirit which demanded a conscience but cared little for color."[109]

The earliest concentration of black cowboys was in east Texas, and it is here that the story of these actors on the Western stage of American civilization begins. In what are now Orange and Jefferson counties, Aaron Ashworth, a free black who had come to Texas in 1833, by 1859 owned 2,570 head of cattle, a herd larger than that of anyone else in his county.[110] His affluence enabled him to purchase slaves and hire tutors for his children. Ashworth became one of the most influential ranchers in all of east Texas. He was a staunch supporter and generous contributor of funds and property in support of the Texans' struggle for independence. As a result of his outstanding service, he was recognized as a prominent citizen, so much so that when the Definitive Act of 1840 was passed by the Texas Legislature, requiring all blacks to leave Texas, Ashworth's neighbors interceded. A special act by the Texas Congress permitted Ashworth to remain in Texas and retain ownership of his land.[111]

A classic Western narrative of the black cowboy is that of Nat Love, who was later given names such as Red River Dick and Deadwood Dick. He was born in Davidson County, Tennessee, in 1854, the son of slave parents. After fifteen years on the plantation, Nat Love emigrated westward to a Kansas cattle town in 1869. Gaining recognition because of his prowess in roping and riding, Deadwood Dick (Nat) hired out to work in all the big roundups throughout west Texas, Arizona, and South Dakota.

His escapades brought him into contact with famous dignitaries of the West, such as Billy the Kid and Bat Masterson. In his autobiography, Deadwood Dick asserted that he had been all man: daredevil, wild, reckless, free, and afraid of nothing. He had often been exposed to the crudeness of the West. Suffering from a snake bite he encountered on the range,

> ...he rode into the chuck wagon sucking his thumb, his hand and arm badly swollen. One of the cowboys immediately drew a knife and gashed—almost hashed—the thumb around the fang marks. He then opened a pistol cartridge, poured powder over the wound, and lighted it with a match.[112]

It was not unusual for a Negro cowboy to serve as a peace officer.[113] One episode concerns a Negro in the role of a peace officer losing his life in an attempt to bring in the notorious outlaw John Wesley Harden.[114] And on the other end of the rope was the case of Texas' Cherokee Bill, a black, "who murdered for profit, seduced for fun, and was hanged a month before his twentieth birthday. He told the crowd gathered around the gallows: 'I came here to die—not to make a speech.'"

Black cowboys left an indelible heritage which only the colorblind and those who are guilty of unsound and incomplete historical scholarship will continue to ignore. To tell the true story of the West, historians must rescue from oblivion the black cowboy's role in westward expansion.

Princes Emerge from Egypt

The Civil War resulted in the legal freedom for blacks as portended in Lincoln's Emancipation Proclamation and the subsequent passage of the thirteenth, fourteenth, and fifteenth amendments, which were designed to give equality to the newly freed slaves. Many blacks and northern liberals had common aspirations that attitudes in the South would be for the better and the freedmen would be free in the true sense of the word. The Civil Rights Act of 1866 was enacted to aid in carrying out this dream. Sections one and two of the Act provided

> An Act to protect all Persons in the United States in their Civil Rights, and Furnish the Means of their Vindication.

> Be it enacted, that all Persons in the United States and not subject to any foreign power, excluding Indians not taxed, are hereby declared to be citizens of the United States; and such citizens, of every race and color, without regard to any previous condition of slavery or involuntary servitude, except as a punishment for crime whereof the party shall have been duly convicted, shall have the same right, in every State and Territory in the United States, to make and enforce contracts, to sue, be parties, and give evidence, to inherit, purchase, lease, sell, hold, and convey real and personal property, and to full and equal benefit of all laws and proceedings for the security of person and property, as is enjoyed by white citizens, and shall be subject to like punishment, pains, and penalties, and to none other, any law, statute, ordinance, regulation, or custom, to the contrary notwithstanding.[115]

President Andrew Johnson vetoed the act, but Congress passed it over the chief executive's veto. As the Reconstruction president, Johnson cooperated with the South in maintaining the status quo and ignored the Black Codes, political coercion, and violence that were perpetrated on helpless blacks. Vagrancy and apprenticeship laws were used to return blacks to slavery and circumscribe their freedom. Other laws required blacks to sign labor contracts that gave the employer the authority to treat them as chattel. All other civil liberties were systematically denied blacks by men who were sworn to uphold the law. All this was done under the guise of preventing irreparable harm to southern society and thwarting the progress of Reconstruction.

Contrary to popular belief that Reconstruction was a time of calamity and regression for the South and that all blacks who participated in Southern governments were uncivilized and immoral, several states had black men who made outstanding contributions to American political life. Doors of opportunity for black political participation were provided by a large number of whites who were consistent proponents of freedom and equality. Persistent efforts by United States Senator Charles Sumner resulted in black lawyers having the opportunity to argue cases before the Supreme Court. He had to overcome prejudicial adjudications of the high tribunal, articulated by Justice Tawney, that blacks were property and had no rights white men were bound to respect.

On February 1, 1865, Charles Sumner presented John S. Rock, a black, to the court. The new chief justice, Salmon P. Chase, gave his assent and Rock became the first man of color to be certified to argue cases before the Supreme Court of the United States. Rock was an eloquent orator and had studied dentistry and medicine prior to his becoming a Massachusetts judge and a barrister of the Supreme Court.

Another black political leader of the Reconstruction period was Hiram Rhodes Revels, born a free man in Fayetteville, North Carolina. As a young man Revels entered the Quaker Seminary in Union County, Indiana, and graduated about 1847 from Knox College in Galesburg, Illinois. He traveled throughout Missouri, Indiana, Illinois, and Ohio, preaching and lecturing. Pastor of a Methodist church in Baltimore when the Civil War began, he helped organize the first colored regiment in Maryland. In 1863 and 1864 Revels taught former slaves in Missouri, then moved to Vicksburg, Mississippi, where he worked with the Freedmen's Bureau, an agency of the U.S. government established to aid and protect newly freed slaves.

After the war, Revels resided in Natchez, Mississippi, and entered politics as a state senator in 1869. In 1870 he was elected to fill Jefferson Davis' seat in the United States Senate. The election of Revels as the first black senator created much surprise and comment, but signified the changed status of the black from slave to free man.

Blanche Kelso Bruce was born a slave in Farmville, Virginia, and received a rudimentary education from his master's son. During the war he escaped to Hannibal, Missouri, where he worked as a printer and teacher. In 1868 he settled in Bolivar County, Mississippi, as a planter. He entered politics as conductor of elections for Tallahatchie County and later held several other offices.

In 1874 Bruce was elected to the United States Senate. Serving from 1875 to 1881, Senator Bruce sought to improve the conditions of Negroes. His wide range of interests as a lawmaker is reflected in his activities as member of committees on manufactures, education and labor, pensions, and improvement of the Mississippi River and its tributaries. He also served as chairman of the committee investigating the defunct Freedmen's Bank.

In 1881, at the close of Bruce's Senate term, President Garfield appointed him register of the Treasury. President Harrison later selected him as the District of Columbia's recorder of deeds, and President McKinley appointed him register of the Treasury again in 1897.

Evaluations as to the success or failure of Reconstruction are still in conflict. An affirmative or negative response depends on the evaluator's point of view. If it was a failure, then America's claim to democracy was a failure. Blacks were caught up in the same basic struggle for economic dominance that had been the main cause of the Civil War. Both major parties used blacks in their political strategy to maintain control over the government. The white backwoodsmen and newly arrived immigrants, who were just as illiterate as the newly freed slaves, were manipulated in the struggle for political power.

Periodically, economic depressions have been the catalytic agents to temporarily solidify dissident racial groups in America. In 1890 a severe catastrophic recession, accompanied by a rise in unemployment and devaluation of the currency, mushroomed in the United States. Submarginal blacks and whites discovered a commonality of interest which enabled them to disregard for a short while their racial prejudices. They sought to alleviate their plight by merging the colored Farmers' Alliance, which claimed a membership of 700,000, with conservative sections of the Populist Party and focusing their efforts against those they blamed for their miserable economic conditions. Actually, the Southern Populists directed their rebellion against the newer ruling class, the industrialists and businessmen of the new South, instead of the old planters.[116] In *The Burden of Southern History*, C. Vann Woodward asserts that "Never since the Civil War had the ruling economic group been defied so openly by so many people."[117]

The Harrison administration had continued the political practices of former presidents and the government, catering mainly to the needs of big business. State and federal troops were used daily to repress the demands and needs of the laboring and agrarian classes. Blacks were systematically denied equal opportunities and physically repressed by the many political subdivisions of government. When the poor whites settled at the bottom of the economic cauldron with the former slaves, they came to the stark reality that they too were victims of exploitation and economic pressures of the business elite. Thus they aligned themselves with blacks into a political party, seeking ways of improving their helpless lot.

To effect this political coalition, Tom Watson of Georgia, a criminal lawyer whose father was a veteran of the Confederacy, led the drive to solicit and organize black votes for the new third party, the Populists (People's Party). He appealed to blacks and whites alike by telling them they were kept apart so that they could be "fleeced" separately. The organizer employed the strategy of political tokenism by supporting and seconding the nomination of a black to be on the State Executive Committee of the People's Party in 1894.

Blacks thronged to the ranks of the party in large numbers. A black minister of the gospel, H. S. Doyle, became one of Watson's most courageous and articulate supporters. Watson aroused the ire of many whites when he assembled some two thousand armed farmers to protect Doyle from violence and possibly a lynching. Watson's sincerity was demonstrated in the episode when he affirmed "that we are determined in this free country that the humblest white or black man that wants to talk our doctrine shall do it, and the man doesn't live who shall touch a hair of his head, without fighting every man in the People's Party."[118]

In North Carolina four blacks were elected to Congress, and in 1892 and 1894 the Populists attained unprecedented success and domination of state governments in Nebraska, South Dakota, Alabama, Virginia, Minnesota, and South Carolina. Flushed by their success in the November of 1890, the Farmers' Alliance laid plans to bring the urban wage-earners into the movement.[119] This plan was thwarted when both major parties recognized the danger of the growing coalition to their existence, and became apprehensive that this was a prelude to the domino capitulation of other states. Consequently, blacks had to be eliminated from their strategic position as the "balancer of power" in both parties. Whites immediately banished their equalitarian ideas and recognized blacks as a political threat to white supremacy in both the North and South. This attitude put a new dimension on the ephemeral-harmonious race relations between the races. As voters Blacks were both hated and cajoled, intimidated and courted but could never be ignored as long as they voted.[120] Members of the Farmers' Alliance went back to the Democratic Party during the election of 1892 and joined in legal and extra-legal strategies to disfranchise blacks. Literacy tests, the poll tax, the "grandfather clause," whipping, and lynching became common techniques endorsed and administered by those who were "the keepers of the gate."

After 1896 even Tom Watson, the former organizer of black voters, joined the ranks of the racists who became resentful and disappointed that the blacks whose cooperation they had expected had instead become tools of the Bourbons.[121] This segment of the Democratic Party used racism and token legislators to create a one-party system in the South that would not give Republicans a chance to utilize black votes. Regardless of the many criticisms of the Populists, C. Woodward Vann says, "in the efforts made for racial justice and political rights they went further toward extending the Negro political fellowship, recognition and equality than any native white political movement has ever gone before or since in the South."[122]

Black legislators indulged in log-rolling for improvements in their states, just as any white legislator. They were able to obtain funds for developing rivers and harbors and supporting public school systems. These black politicians responded to the lobbyists who wanted protective tariffs for their products and succumbed to pressures for railroad subsidies like any other legislator. The corruption that was so evident during this period of political and economic readjustment was not at the instigation of black legislators but of white congressmen and manipulators of government as well. Nevertheless, black voices were heard above the din of party manipulations.

Every once in a while, prophets' voices were heard sounding the trumpet of deliverance. Some voices were soft and pleading; others were loud and threatening. One of the soft-spoken strategists was Booker T. Washington. The death of Frederick Douglass in 1895, the year of Booker T. Washington's Atlanta Compromise, symbolized the shift from the militant strategy of agitation for equal rights to the conservative philosophy of racial segregation in return for jobs. In his famous speech at the Atlanta Exposition in 1895, Washington extolled the idea that "the wisest among my race understand that the agitation of questions of social equality is the extremist folly, and that the progress in the enjoyment of all the privileges that will come to us must be the result of severe and constant struggle rather than of artificial forcing."[123] Washington's speech skyrocketed him to fame and a position of leadership, though his critics lambasted him for his "Uncle Tomism." He proposed gradualism and submission to the will of white society and believed that blacks should desist from seeking immediate political power and civil rights.

Washington understood the failure of Reconstruction and the basic ingredients of the American economic system. His conceptual framework for freedom included the idea that, for the black man to be free, he had to first of all free himself economically through self-improvement. He believed that blacks should pursue more industrial training and minimize higher education in the liberal arts. Since proficiency in academic subjects might have given lie to the Southern belief that Negroes were intellectually inferior to whites, such subjects were avoided.[124] Whites readily accepted this accommodative philosophy and made Washington a black leader. Having raised him to power, it was in white America's interest to keep him there.[125]

Despite his conservatism and capitulation to white interests, Washington did help to improve the black's economic condition through the establishment of the National Negro Business League, which played a significant part in the development and organizational scheme of Negro economic improvement institutions throughout the United States. As Washington traveled the country and studied the economic conditions of the black people, he sensed a deep need for a clear-cut analysis of their status and possible solutions for the alleviation or mitigation of their varied problems. Along this line of thinking he deemed it expedient to call together the leading Negro men then engaged in successful business pursuits and to discuss pertinent problems that, by achieving feasible solutions, would enhance the growth and development of their individual businesses.

Booker T. Washington describes the formation of the National Negro Business League as follows:

> In the summer of 1900, with the assistance of such prominent coloured men as Mr. T. Fortune, who has always upheld my hand in every effort, I organized the National Negro Business League, which held its first meeting in Boston, and brought together for the first time a large number of the coloured men who are engaged in various lines of trade or business in different parts of the United States. Thirty states were represented at our first meeting. Out of this national meeting grew state and local business leagues.[126]

The purpose of the Business League from the outset was the promotion of industrial and commercial achievement, whereby the influence of the race could be increased and enabled to maintain a position of influence in the American economy and eventually obtain economic freedom. Ralph Bunche later said,

> However, in terms of its influence on economic betterment of the Negro, the National Negro Business League has been inconsequential as a factor in shaping the psychology and thinking of Negroes. Nevertheless, it has been vastly important…it has pursued the narrowest type of racial chauvinism, for it has organized, not business, but Negro business and has employed the racial situation as its main stock in trade in bidding for the support of Negro patronage.[127]

Washington's ideas for self-improvement were basically sound. But blacks could not make inroads into the economic stream of American society for the policy of gradualism proved futile. When blacks who were trained in special skills applied for employment, they were rebuffed by white racists in laboring groups in the North and South. Washington's philosophy of race improvement took seed at Tuskegee Institute in

Alabama, which Washington headed from 1881 to 1915.

The greatest contrast in the leadership of the black movement is found between Booker T. Washington and W. E. B. DuBois. DuBois, the voice of black protests during the 1920s, was one of the most dynamic and compelling leaders the black man has known. His life was dedicated to the herculean task of freeing the oppressed captives in America and Africa. Scholarly preparation for such a mammoth undertaking had been initiated while he was nineteen years old and an undergraduate student at Fisk University. He later studied at Harvard under the masters of American universities—James in psychology, Albert Bushell Hart in history, Shaler in geology, Santayana in philosophy. By training, DuBois was a philosopher-historian and firmly convinced that it would take the leadership of black intellectuals and professionals to lift the black man out of the mire of racial prejudice and retardation.

He set out to reject the accommodation and conciliation proposed by Booker T. Washington in his Atlanta Compromise. Instead, DuBois' Declaration of Principles demanded equality in all facets of life. Washington preferred economic advances and the relinquishing of immediate political rights. He was content to "cast down your bucket where you are." DuBois wanted political power first. His aims were the attainment of all civil rights, including suffrage, economic opportunity, and the abolition of all legal discrimination. He believed that "black men could not make effective progress in economic lines if they are deprived of political rights, made a servile caste and allowed only the most meager chance for developing their exceptional men."[128]

To begin the task, DuBois assembled a coordinated group at Niagara, Canada, in 1905, which was the beginning of the National Association for the Advancement of Colored People. At its first national meeting at Harpers Ferry in 1906, the group voiced reaffirmation of the aims of blacks in the United States. DuBois succinctly stated that "we will not be satisfied to take one jot or tittle less than our full manhood rights...and until we get these rights we will never cease to protest and assail the ears of America."[129] Nevertheless, after launching the NAACP into the thick of the Civil Rights movement, DuBois became frustrated as prominent whites took over leadership and blacks were subordinated in the organization.

The influence of his grandmother, who was of the Bantu tribe in Africa, left DuBois with an indelible belief that black Americans had never completely severed their ties with Africa. His work in the Races Congress of 1911 in Europe gave him fame as the patron saint of Pan-Africans and "the evangel of African Freedom." He was painfully aware of his dilemma in the United States as an American and a black. The dual quality in the black mind and soul is a recurring theme in his black awareness:

> One ever feels his two-ness an American, a Negro; two souls, two thoughts, two unreconciled strivings; two warring ideals in one dark body, whose dogged strength alone keeps it from being torn asunder.[130]

DuBois' philosophical training and his Christian views of brotherhood caused him to embrace socialism as the one great hope of black America. His disenchantment with the failure of intellectuals to bring about changes in the helplessness of blacks forced him further toward the brink of socialism as a panacea for black America. In 1928, DuBois began to identify blacks as being in the vanguard of the proletariat, he wrote, "in the hearts of black laborers alone lie those ideals of democracy in politics and industry which may in time make the workers of the world effective dictators of civilization."[131]

In 1933 and 1934 DuBois reasoned that the solution to the black man's problem was segregation of the black economy and cooperation with whites in the mainstream of American society. NAACP integrationists, led by Walter White, removed the mantle of leadership from DuBois by accusing him of adhering to the accommodation philosophy of Booker T. Washington.

If Booker T. Washington was too accommodating for DuBois, Marcus Garvey was too radical in his approach to alleviating the problems of blacks in America. Both shared a commonality in principle in solving the black man's problem that differed only in geographical location. Washington believed in self-help through education in the South. Perhaps the arrogant egotism with which Garvey emerged on the American scene created a sense of resentment and jealousy on the part of other black leaders at the apparent success of this rising militant.

Garvey appealed to blacks by preaching the doctrine of racial separation from white society, and, as DuBois had projected, renewing the ties with African civilization. Garvey was among the first to create a "new vision," based on a revolution of the African cultural heritage, as a source of inspiration to the blacks in America and in the world. This expounder of black nationalism was a princely remnant of the Maroons, who were African descendants residing on the island of Jamaica. Garvey's parents had hoped for a son who would lead black people out of bondage just as Moses had led the children of Israel. Marcus Mosiah Garvey was to be acclaimed the "Black Moses." He abandoned black intellectuals and directed his appeal to the masses who were poor and uneducated.

The results of Garvey's emotional appeal were the marvel of the nineteenth century. His philosophy hammered black pride into the anvil of racial solidarity by using unique techniques of motivation, resplendent uniforms, and weird titles to enhance blacks' concept of dignity and respect as a people. He attempted to modify the stigma of blackness as the equivalent of evil and inferiority and extolled the idea that there was virtue in being black. This prophet of militancy hypothesized "that racial prejudice was so much a part of the civilization of the white man that it was futile to appeal to his sense of justice and his high-sounding democratic principles,"[132] a philosophy that attracted many converts. In 1920 he claimed four million dues-paying members of the Universal Negro Improvement Association, a number which increased to six million by 1923.[133]

Washington believed in self-help through education in the South. Garvey editorialized self-help but advocated removing blacks to Africa. In August 1920 the flamboyant Garvey arrived in Liberty Hall in New York City to draft a "Declaration of the Rights of the Negro Peoples of the World," at which time he was elected provisional President of Africa. "Visionaries as we are in the Universal Negro Improvement Association," he said, "we are fighting for the founding of a Negro nation in Africa so that there will be no clash between black and white…"[134]

To carry out his pilgrimage to Africa, Garvey organized the Black Star Steamship Line, which met financial disaster due to his lack of entrepreneurial skill and economic pressure applied from unknown sources. This program to colonize Africa met opposition from the European powers who already dominated the continent.

To further hush the voice of this chauvinistic black, Garvey was accused by the U.S. government of fraud and using the mail to swindle the public. His wife claimed that he netted some "ten million dollars in three years from 1919 to 1921."[135] In 1921 he was convicted and assessed a five-year sentence in the federal penitentiary. Garvey never visited Africa and died in London in 1940, but his vision of a Black Africa was never dimmed.

Many black leaders opposed Garvey's philosophy of racial separation. This separation seemed unnecessary due to the temporary solidarity which was exemplified by American engagement in a war on the behalf of Cubans in the West Indies. The Spanish-American War was attractive enough to the South to induce them to unite with the North in an imperialistic cause. Reluctantly both sections succumbed to the plea of black men to participate in a war surreptitiously designed to protect black men in Cuba and the "little brown brothers" in the Philippines. Several black fighting units participated in the war against Spain. Hardened buffalo soldiers, veterans of Indian fighting and searing suns and stinging sands of the southwestern Badlands, made up the Ninth and Tenth Cavalries. The Twenty-fourth and Twenty-fifth Infantry were made up of black soldiers summoned from garrison duty in the eastern states. These Negro regulars went into action at El Caney, Las Guasimas, and San Juan. There is no doubt that in the battle of San Juan the Negro cavalry turned a defeat into victory and saved the honor and the hides of Teddy Roosevelt's Rough Riders.[136]

The gratitude of white society seemed to mark the beginning of a new attitude and a new day for the millions of blacks. Black laborers were sought to help develop the territorial fruits of the Spanish-American War. The Hays-Buanau-Varilla treaty of 1903 ushered the United States into the accomplishment of one of the most spectacular military and cultural feats of all times, the construction of the Panama Canal. As Gustave Anguizola explains in his article "Negroes in the Building of the Panama Canal," "Toiling under the most unfavorable conditions, Negroes left in that ditch their share of sweat, tears and blood, a permanent contribution toward the shaping of the United States as a super power...80 percent of the hard work was performed by them."[137]

McKinley and his successor, Theodore Roosevelt, both assumed a new posture in race relations. They appointed blacks to federal positions heretofore denied them because of the pigmentation of their skins. A mirage of princes coming out of Egypt was dimly seen as a new day for blacks seeming to break forth from the dark past. The hopes and aspirations of the enslaved "tenth" who had waited patiently for acceptance into the mainstream of American society appeared nearer to reality. So bright was the future that in 1900 the literary genius of James Weldon Johnson blossomed forth with aesthetic sensitivity, and, with the musical skills of his brother, J. Rosamond Johnson, composed the stirring Negro National Anthem.

"Lift Every Voice and Sing"

Lift every voice and sing

Till earth and heaven ring,
Ring with the harmonies of liberty;
Let our rejoicing rise
High as the listening skies,
Let it resound loud as the rolling sea.
Sing a song full of the faith that the dark past has taught us,
Sing a song full of the hope that the present has brought us,
Facing the rising sun of our new day begun
Let us march on till victory is won.

Stony the road we trod,
Bitter the chastening rod,
Felt in the days when hope unborn had died;
Yet with a steady beat,
Have not our weary feet
Come to the place for which our fathers sighed?
We have come over a way that with tears has been watered,
We have come, treading our path through the blood of the slaughtered,
Out of the gloomy past,
Till now we stand at last
Where the white gleam of our bright star is cast.

God of our weary years,
God of our silent tears,
Thou who has brought us thus far on the way;
Thou who has by Thy might
Led us into the light,
Keep us forever in the path, we pray.
Lest our feet stray from the places, our God, where we met Thee,
Lest, our hearts drunk with the wine of the world, we forget Thee;
Shadowed beneath Thy hand,
May we forever stand.
True to our God,
True to our native land.[138]

The bubble of hope burst as quickly as the mirage became a reality. Subtle but ever-present racial tensions struck suddenly to retard black progress. "Pharaoh" changed his mind about blacks leaving bondage in Egypt. The Brownsville affray in Texas alienated the black community from Roosevelt and was the prelude of things to come, where white supremacy would remain the basic tenet for America. The constant racism that overshadows the American nation came to the forefront in August 1906 when Theodore Roosevelt flexed his domestic "Big Stick" and, without civil or military trial, summarily court-martialed three companies of black soldiers who comprised the Twenty-fifth Infantry at Fort Brown (Brownsville, Texas).

The animosity of white citizens had been rekindled on August 1, 1906 when the black infantrymen arrived in Brownsville from duty at Niobrara, Nebraska. The local citizenry resented the armed black soldiers and set out to demonstrate their opposition, hostility, and displeasure. An inspector of customs, a Mr. Tate, struck a soldier on his head with a revolver when the black trooper didn't get out of his way quickly enough; two more soldiers were knocked in a ditch for no apparent reason at all; and, to add to the tension, on August 12 a white girl claimed she had been intimidated by Black soldiers.[139] The following night the polarized community completed the perpetuated conspiracy to get the black soldiers removed from Brownsville.

Even though Major Charles Penrose, commander of the fort, had restricted all but two of his 160 men to their quarters and all had answered the roll calls, authorities reported that from nine to twenty soldiers had slipped out of the fort about midnight and attacked the town. An unsubstantiated report also stated that

> They went through the town, shooting whomsoever they saw moving and firing into houses wherever they saw lights. They fired upon and hit in the arm the lieutenant of police...fired also at two policemen, killed one bartender man in a saloon and wounded another, and came very near to killing several women and children.[140]

No one actually saw the black soldiers return to camp,[141] but white witnesses and circumstantial evidence convinced army investigators that some of the blacks must have participated.[142] Relying on reports by Texas Ranger Captain Bill McDonald and Major August P. Blocksom, Roosevelt ordered a summary court martial of all the black soldiers, regardless of their involvement. Guilt by association was the arbitrary rule of law invoked by Roosevelt. These men were denied due process of law and were never tried before a military tribunal or a civil court of law.

To offset the political impact his handling of the situation at Brownsville would have had on the congressional election on November 6, Roosevelt signed the "discharge without honor" order on November 5 and held it until the day after the election. The northern black vote was crucial to many Republican congressmen who would have to face the ire of the black electorate for another Republican president who turned his back on blacks in the United States.

Outrage continued unabated at the court-martial and the incident was kept vociferously in focus by senators Tillman and Foraker. They introduced a resolution in 1908 demanding an investigation of the episode and persisted so ably that in 1909 the President accepted a compromise measure setting up a special military court to hear those denying any implication in the incident.[143] Foraker offered impressive facts in support of the theory that the shooting had been the work of residents of Brownsville, who then placed the blame on the Twenty-fifth Infantry.[144] Of the eighty-four soldiers who testified before the tribunal, fourteen were finally declared eligible for reinstatement in the army.

This episode clearly demonstrated that the black man had not gained enough political status to guarantee him equal justice where whites were involved. James Weldon Johnson's bubbles of hope kept bursting. He watched blacks in Florida become more pessimistic as they experienced a social revolution that transformed them into a quagmire of racism. Lynching of blacks took place at the smallest and most inconclusive provocation. In *They Came in Chains*, Saunders Redding writes that "In the first decade of the century, nearly a thousand of them were lynched in public spectacles that outmatched the Roman Circus for savagery and obscenity,"[145] and James Weldon Johnson joined with W. E. B. DuBois to protest injustices heaped on blacks in America. He was a man of tough temperament who opened the black renaissance in literature. In his *Autobiography of an Ex-Coloured Man* (1912), Johnson redefined and gave new meaning to America's connotation of the "Negro" as a race. In 1916 Johnson became field secretary of the NAACP and an avid exponent of the cultural attainment of blacks in the United States, vehemently rejecting the Christ-like Negro image previously expounded by W. E. B. DuBois.

An agnostic by proclamation, Johnson's literary works, especially his poetry, contradicted his denial of a religious faith. Even though he claimed no ties with the spiritual fervor of blacks, in *God's Trombone* (1927) he exemplified deep sensitivity to Negro spirituals, which he maintained were the true measure of America's creativity and greatness.

Where voices of protests cried out, denouncing injustices, there was less tendency for legalized retaliation and Klan-like organizations to impose coercive tactics to enforce silence. There were many blacks who took advantage of the more liberal climate of protests. One such man was Asa Phillip Randolph, who was educated in a Florida high school, moved to New York City, and became an outspoken leader for Negro workingmen by organizing them within the framework of the American Federation of Labor.

Technological unemployment brought on by the rapid mechanical changes in railroad caused black employees to descend to the bottom of this country's economic ladder. While working as a waiter on the Fall River Line in New York, Randolph tried to organize his fellow workers as a protest to their poor living and working conditions on the boat. He was subsequently fired. This episode opened new avenues to A. Phillip Randolph in trying to find answers to the economic and racial problems of blacks in the United States. He teamed with Chandler Owen to publish the *Messenger*, which was to many people a radical journal of black militancy. After a riot occurred in East St. Louis in 1917, in which forty lives were lost, Randolph and his partner published an article entitled "Pro-Germanism Among Negroes." It severely criticized the foreign policy of the United States and suggested an illicit alliance of Germans and blacks. Randolph and Chandler, incarcerated by the Justice Department, were both given a probated sentence of two and a half years.

In the fall of 1925 Randolph was asked to speak at a meeting of the Pullman Porter's Athletic Association. There he outlined a campaign to organize a union. Although he had never been a porter on a railroad, he was persuaded to be the organizer and president of the union, which was not recognized by any constituted authority. The *Messenger* automatically became the official organ of the newly formed Brotherhood of Sleeping Car Porters. By 1928 Randolph had organized about half of the maids and porters and felt it was time to strike for better wages and a shorter work week. The strike failed because other unions would not honor the porters' union. But through perseverance and the assistance of members of the American Federation of Labor, the Brotherhood became an important part of the American labor movement.

In 1941, when the nation was about to become involved in another global war, A. Phillip Randolph again spoke out against American involvement, but his pacifist position was altered by the nature of the fascists' and Nazi aggression. He surmised that this war was different from World War I, even though the black man was again fighting in a war for principles which he was denied the privilege of enjoying. The fascist powers had to be defeated in order to preserve the theoretic principles of democracy, he asserted. In his essay "Why Should We March?", Randolph expounded:

> Though I have found no Negroes who want to see the United Nations lose this war, I have found many who, before the war ends, want to see the stuffing knocked out of white supremacy and of empire over subject peoples. American Negroes, involved as we are in the general issues of the conflict, are confronted not with a choice but with the challenge both to win democracy for ourselves at home and to help win the war for democracy the world over.[146]

A. Phillip Randolph used the Brotherhood of Sleeping Car Porters as the springboard for combating discrimination. Blacks were summarily discriminated against in the armed forces and employment by companies given government contracts to produce material for the war effort. Randolph maintained the point of view that "if race prejudice is to be eliminated from the trade unions movement, it is going to be eliminated by the workers themselves, and not at polite conferences."[147] A march on Washington was scheduled for July 1941, with about 50,000 people participating. There was speculation that a race riot would erupt. Franklin D. Roosevelt conferred with Randolph and shortly afterwards issued Executive Order No. 8803, establishing the President's Committee on Fair Employment Practice. Randolph had clearly demonstrated the power of racial solidarity in bringing America face to face with its moral conscious and defense of its political ideology.

A. Randolph proved himself over and over to be one of the greatest leaders in American History. He was adviser to presidents Roosevelt, Truman, Eisenhower, Kennedy, and Johnson. In August 1963 more than 200,000 Negroes and whites from many parts of the United States marched in Washington, D.C., in a gigantic demonstration for jobs and freedom. To many this impressive spectacular, organized by Randolph, was the climax of a long career of fighting to get into the mainstream of American society. But to the gallant leader this was not the climax to the black man's struggle, but a new beginning.

Black power advocates did not find much support from Asa Phillip Randolph. He thought the slogan "Black Power" was a step backward and just as repugnant as the term "white racism." His life-long dedication was to the integration of "existing AFL-CIO unions, free from bias and discrimination."[148] He was integrated into the hierarchy of the AFL-CIO by being elected a vice-president of the organization and a policy-making executive council member.

Malcolm X

A drastic change in the black movement was ushered in with the resurgence and rise in popularity of Islam. The movement was able to catch the imagination of a large number of blacks who looked at the futility of legal attempts to integrate. The proponents of the Muslim sect advocated the meeting of violence with violence, using the same methods whites had used to intimidate and demean blacks ever since slavery. "The nation of Islam," James Hope Franklin writes, "bitter in its denunciation of American racism, was a voice of disgust and despair. It was as much a political and social movement as it was a religious organization."[149]

According to Harvey Wish's *The Negro Since Emancipation*, the Muslims further "repudiated American society, rejected Christianity as a hypocritical religion..., denounced integrationists as Uncle Toms, and charged that the National Association for the Advancement of Colored People was a tool of the Zionists and encouraged anti-Semitism by picturing the Jew as an exploiter of cheap Negro labor."[150] Institutionalized racism had created separate institutions that now became goals for Muslims. White Christianity became the focal point of Malcolm X's attack:

> Christianity is the white man's religion. The Holy Bible in the white man's hands and his interpretations of it have been the greatest single ideological weapon for enslaving millions of non-white human beings.[151]

In the mystical rhetoric of traditional theology, slaves of the pre-Civil War days and modern black militants questioned the doctrine of Christian faith. They could not see a Christ created in the image of their oppressor. Their Christ was viewed as a non-white.

Out of the Black Muslim movement emerged a lieutenant and defector, Malcolm X, who became one of the most dynamic and revolutionary leaders in the Black Nationalist movement. His father had been an organizer for Marcus Garvey's Universal Negro Improvement Association in Nebraska. The elder Garvey was lynched by the Ku Klux Klan in Nebraska and Malcolm became a juvenile delinquent after a number of crimes which led him to prison. While in prison he was converted to Islam. Malcolm's rhetoric and philosophy were almost carbon copies of those upon which Marcus Garvey had expounded years earlier.

Malcolm came into conflict with the leader of the Muslims, Elijah Muhammed, and after much dissension and disagreement he severed their relationship. Determined to make a frontal assault on white racism in America, Malcolm X founded the Organization of Afro-American Unity. He tried to establish African ties with the black man in the United States in order to restore the dignity that had been destroyed by white society. Malcolm was a natural adversary of American society. His anti-white tirades, his clarion call for separation and bluntness invoked hatred in the hearts of most Caucasians. To blacks he was a man with a mission who had emerged from the depth of human depravity and cloaked himself with a Black Puritanism symbolic of his Muslim faith.

As a strict adherent to Islam, Malcolm X insisted on a strict moral code. "The white man wants Black men to stay immoral, unclean, and ignorant," he said. "As long as we stay in these conditions we will keep on begging him and he will control us. We never can win freedom and justice and equality until we are doing something for ourselves! We have to keep in mind at all times that we are not fighting for integration, nor are we fighting for the right to live as free humans in this society. In fact, we are actually fighting for rights that are even greater than civil rights and that is human rights."[152]

Malcolm X completely rejected his idea of the separation of blacks and whites after he made a pilgrimage to Mecca in 1964. He claimed to have received fresh insight into racism throughout the world. His experience with white Muslims and dignitaries convinced him that there were sympathetic and sincere whites who could not be classed as racists and consequently shunned. However, Malcolm X was never allowed to test the effectiveness of his new philosophy because, while speaking to a group in New York City, he was shot by a black assassin. Ossie Davis, giving the eulogy at Malcolm X's funeral, said that:

> ...secure in the knowledge that what we place in the ground is no more now a man—but a seed—which, after the winter of our discontent will come forth again to meet us, and we will know him for what he was and is—A Prince—our own Black shining Prince![153]

A prince had come out of Egypt and his young black followers were united and lifting their hands to God. Malcolm X left a legacy of dignity. A harmonious reaction is evident in young blacks as they proclaim a new birth of freedom and equality for people of color all over the world.

At the time Malcolm X was murdered, the militant prototype, Elridge Cleaver, was serving a term in Folsom Prison in California for the possession of marijuana. He had been an ardent disciple of the slain leader and had also severed his relationship with the followers of Muhammed. Cleaver had many things in common with Malcolm X. It seems that prison was the common denominator and shaper of a black nationalists philosophy for both, for, like Malcolm X, Cleaver experienced a religious change.

Cleaver's devotion to Malcolm X was such a close one that he constantly expressed gratitude to his prophet for altering his radical view points concerning all whites and "liberating him from a doctrine of hate and racial supremacy."[154] The alteration of his attitude toward whites was attributed to his new-found moral enlightenment, which he received from Malcolm X. He noticed and praised the revolution going on within the young whites who were rebelling against the mores and folkways of their forebears and parents. Cleaver hypothesized that "there is in America today a generation of white youth that is truly worthy of a Black man's respect...if I myself and other former Muslims can change, if young whites can change, then there is hope for America."[155]

During the period of discontent which followed the assassination of Martin Luther King, Jr., Cleaver, while attempting to maintain tranquility among black ghetto dwellers, was arrested for possession of firearms. His continual harassment by California law enforcement officers is a tragedy of the dual nature of justice applied to blacks who challenge "the system."

Taking advantage of his literary prowess, Cleaver became the voice of *Ramparts*, and it was this journalistic affiliation that opened many doors to him for public appearances and speeches. Before his parole was revoked, a big controversy between students and faculty at the University of California at Berkeley erupted over Cleaver's right to speak on the campus and to be hired as an instructor. Governor Ronald Reagan used political pressure on the Board of Regents to deny academic credit to students who matriculated in the course of sociology that Cleaver was to teach.

In 1968 Cleaver ran for President of the United States on the Peace and Freedom Party's platform. He received 30,000 votes. On November 22, 1968, the parolee made his last speech in San Francisco, in which he asserted his intentions of never returning to prison. State governmental agencies continued to use repressive measures to still the voice of Cleaver, and after the California Appeals Court denied him a writ of habeas corpus, he left the United States to escape legal entanglements and seek political asylum in Algiers.

Martin Luther King, Jr.

An unflinching faith in God and a firm belief that the dormant moral conscience of America would be awakened to alter the black man's unequal position in a democratic society was the fundamental credo of Martin Luther King, Jr. As violence mushroomed with destructive fury throughout the United States, King sought an effective way of changing America's attitude toward blacks by utilizing the nonviolent philosophy of Mohandas Gandhi. This immortal prophet and leader of India had used his political shrewdness and tenacious faith in translating his belief into effective action in awakening oppressed people in India, Africa, and the United States to a sense of their dignity and freedom. So Martin Luther King, Jr. became a disciple of the revered Gandhi in every respect. With messianic humility he preached "turning the other cheek" when the rabid hounds of racial hostility assailed helpless blacks in an open and permissive climate of violence. King had a firm conviction that man had the capacity to do right and that white society, confronted by moral indignation, would help turn the blacks' disillusionment and bitterness into hope and faith.

A third-generation Baptist minister, Martin Luther King, Jr. was born in Atlanta, Georgia. He attended Morehouse College and the Crozer Theological Seminary, where he earned the Pearl Plafkner Prize for scholarship. His Ph.D. was granted in 1955 by Boston University, and his D.D. degrees were awarded by both the University of Chicago Theological Seminary and the Boston Theological Seminary.

Practicing his theory of nonviolent positive resistance, Dr. King led blacks in a bus boycott in Montgomery, Alabama. The thirteen-month boycott followed the arrest on December 5, 1955 of Mrs. Rosa Parks, a seamstress who refused to yield her seat to a white man. Blacks now challenged the legality of man-made laws and brought to the forefront the higher law of morality. They employed a strategy of power and protest[156] through a large mass of people withdrawing their economic power and engaging in civil disobedience to effect desirable changes in the community. This boycott ended segregation on city buses, and for his leadership of the boycott, King won the Springarm Medal in 1957. It was in this year in Atlanta, Georgia, that King organized the Southern

Christian Leadership Conference, a nonviolent action group that staged massive demonstrations. He continued to advocate the use of direct nonviolent action, legal redress, ballots, and economic boycotts to improve the status of black people in the U.S. King led various sit-in demonstrations against segregation in Georgia and Alabama and was arrested, beaten, and slandered time and time again for his opposition to state segregation laws.

As we draw upon the memorabilia of our minds, this writer and wife, Nadine, cherish the opportunity we had to hear Martin L. King when he appeared at the Majestic Theater in Fort Worth, Texas, on October 22, 1959. For once, blacks were permitted use of the entire theater; the Palace, Ideal, Isis, Worth, Hollywood, and other theaters limited blacks to special doors and seats in the balcony. Dr. King was invited to this city by Ms. Vada P. Felder, wife of the Reverend O. P. Felder who followed the Reverend W. S. Brent as pastor of the St. James Baptist Church in 1950. Ms. Felder was a social and religious leader and a scholar of the first class. She was one of the first blacks to graduate from Texas Christian University's Brite School of Divinity in 1954. Ms. Felder made an excellent hostess for Dr. King and several other dignitaries who later visited Fort Worth.

Many of the leading black ministers disassociated themselves from the public meeting because they were intimidated by the racial threats against Dr. King and didn't want to alienate some of the whites who classified him as a troublemaker. Nevertheless, Dr. King challenged the group to take up the new challenge of liberty and freedom and he continued his crusade in America.

In 1963 King's antisegregation demonstrations in Birmingham, Alabama, culminated in the brutal beatings and mass arrest of both black and white people by the Alabama police. Public outrage at the brutality helped gain stronger support for federal civil rights legislation. Support for earlier civil rights legislation had been nil. The Civil Rights Act of 1866 and 1875 had been passed to guard the rights of the recently emancipated slaves and protect them against discrimination. The Act of 1866 had been vetoed by President Andrew Johnson and the Supreme Court ruled in 1883 in the Civil Rights Cases that the acts were unconstitutional. Both acts were almost identical to more recent legislation providing for equal protection, employment, housing, and desegregated education.

In 1896 the Supreme Court in *Plessy v. Ferguson* established its "separate but equal" doctrine, which it later repudiated in 1954 in the historic ruling in *Brown v. Board of Education*. Consequently, in 1957 Congress passed the first civil rights laws since Reconstruction.

In August of 1963 King helped to organize a march of 200,000 persons on Washington, D.C., to emphasize desire for expanded civil rights legislation. It was at this march that he gave his famous oratorical masterpiece, "I Have a Dream," on the steps of the Lincoln Memorial. Part of the speech follows.

> Now is the time to make real the promises of democracy.
> Now is the time to rise from the dark and desolate valley of segregation
> to the sunlit path of racial justice. Now is the time to lift our nation from
> the quicksands of racial injustice to the solid rock of brotherhood. Now
> is the time to make justice a reality for all of God's children....

There will be neither rest nor tranquility in America until the Negro is granted his citizenship rights. The whirlwinds of revolt will continue to shake the foundations of our nation until the bright day of justice emerges.

But there is something that I must say to my people who stand on the warm threshold which leads into the palace of justice. In the process of gaining our rightful place we must not be guilty of wrongful deeds.... Again and again we must rise to the majestic heights of meeting physical force with soul force.

The marvelous new militancy which has engulfed the Negro community must not lead us to a distrust of all white people, for many of our white brothers, as evidenced by their presence here today, have come to realize that their destiny is tied up with our destiny....

There are those who are asking the devotees of civil rights, "When will you be satisfied?" We can never be satisfied as long as the Negro is the victim of the unspeakable horrors of police brutality.... We can never be satisfied as long as a Negro in Mississippi cannot vote and a Negro in New York believes he has nothing for which to vote. No, no, we are not satisfied and we will not be satisfied until justice rolls down like waters and righteousness like a mighty stream.

I am not unmindful that some of you have come here out of great trials and tribulations. Some of you have come fresh from narrow jail cells.... Continue to work with the faith that unearned suffering is redemptive. Go back to Mississippi, go back to Alabama, go back to South Carolina, go back to Georgia, go back to Louisiana, go back to the slums and ghettos of our northern cities, knowing that somehow this situation can and will be changed. Let us not wallow in the valley of despair. I say to you today, my friends, so even though we face the difficulties of today and tomorrow, I still have a dream. It is a dream deeply rooted in the American dream.

I have a dream that one day this nation will rise up and live out the true meaning of its creed: "We hold these truths to be self-evident that all men are created equal."

I have a dream that one day on the red hills of Georgia the sons of former slaves and the sons of former slaveowners will be able to sit down together at the table of brotherhood.

I have a dream that one day even the state of Mississippi, a state sweltering with the heat of injustice, sweltering with the heat of oppression, will be transformed into an oasis of freedom and justice.

I have a dream that my four little children will one day live in a nation where they will not be judged by the color of their skin but by the content of their character....

This is our hope. This is the faith that I will go back to the South with. With this faith we will be able to hew out of the mountain of despair a stone of hope.[157]

Martin Luther King, Jr. was awarded the Nobel Prize for Peace in 1964. Among the books King wrote concerning his civil rights activities are *Why We Can't Wait, Strength and Love, Stride Toward Freedom,* and *Where Do We Go from Here: Chaos or Community?*

In Memphis, Tennessee, on April 4, 1968, Dr. King was assassinated. King was in Memphis to aid in the strike of 1,300 predominantly black garbage workers. The assassination set off a wave of black rioting and looting in 125 cities across the nation. President Lyndon Johnson proclaimed April 7 a day of mourning for Dr. King. A white man, James Earl Ray, was convicted of King's murder and in March 1969 was sentenced to ninety-nine years in prison.

The Reverend Ralph Abernathy became the titular head of the Southern Christian Leadership Conference and was not able to generate and maintain the enthusiasm King did as its leader. Perhaps the spark died with Dr. King. Certainly Dr. Abernathy was not able to sustain the organization he helped Dr. King create.

The last person to talk to Dr. King was the Reverend Jesse Jackson, a close confidante of the slain civil rights leader, who refuses to admit that the mantle of King has fallen to him. Reverend Jackson appears to be more sensitive to the needs of blacks than other SCLC leaders. His attire and mannerisms identify with militants, and yet he does not condemn any other persons because of their philosophies and techniques in the Civil Rights Movement. Jackson believes that America is schizophrenic in its concept and application of the basic tenets of democracy.[158]

To offset the reality of racism, Jackson operates under the premise that economic coercion and economic power are successful techniques for mitigating problems blacks face in capitalistic America. He promoted the largest Black Expo Trade Fair in history. This mammoth undertaking was a program of "Operation Breadbasket," the economic counterpart of the Southern Christian Leadership Conference. This fair, with more than 200 exhibits, was designed to develop cultural pride in black achievements and open markets to black corporations for goods they produce. It attracted more than 900,000 persons to Chicago's International Amphitheater in November 1969. The current phase of "Operation Breadbasket" is essentially a good one, designed to mitigate the economic woes of blacks.

Too often in the past, blacks looked over Jordan into the Promised Land and gained renewed hope to replace their poor experiences of the wilderness. They marched with steady feet in a great migration with the expectation that when they reached the urban cities in the North, their plight would be better. Unfortunately, this mass movement compounded their problems. Black migrants found themselves systematically shunted from white society. They were retained in the burgeoning stockade—ghettoes of the United States metropolis where their social, economic, and political problems were multiplied. The cancerous growth of white racism continued to harden the impregnable attitude of a society which was determined to maintain its own exclusive and special brand of democracy. Blacks in cities were placed in a quandary as to which way they were going to be forced to go to achieve a semblance of decency and equality.

Booker T. Washington took the initiative in 1911 to give direction to alleviating the plight of those in the ghettoes by organizing the National Urban League. Today, under the leadership of Whitney Young, this organization has grown in importance because its programs have been structured to help overcome discrimination in jobs, housing, and employment. Young scoffed at tokenism and sought a major role for blacks in effecting changes in the mainstream of American life. He championed his beliefs during the administration of the last four presidents and insisted that a decade of special affirmative effort was needed to close the cultural gap created from decades of slavery and deprivation.

Young continued the early policy of the Urban League of seeking cooperation from employers and avoiding involvement in the rank and file of trade unionism. His association and influence with the power elite in government and industry was the basis of the severest type of criticism from his critics. But Young had to maintain the goodwill of his benefactors and had not developed the flexibility of his counterparts in effecting changes with those who were not in agreement. Consequently, when Martin Luther King, Jr. turned his attack on the "hawks" in the Vietnam War, Young had to alter his stance and not follow the new directions of the Civil Rights Movement, the course of which King was attempting to charter, if he was to maintain the good graces of his benefactors.

Until his death, Whitney Young remained in the front ranks of the black revolution and had a penetrating insight into the democratic formula of racial equality. He proposed in his "Marshall Plan" that America must make a compensatory and special effort that would include the cooperative endeavors of private, public, and voluntary organizations. It would attempt to overcome serious disabilities resulting from historic handicaps, more positively to develop human potential of black citizens and provide to blacks with the best education available. Blacks would be hired at all levels of employment and named to all public and private boards and commissions in order to participate in decision-making. Positive action would be taken to eliminate racial ghettoes and develop strong leadership among Blacks.[159] Such concerted efforts would move the nation nearer to the day when all of its citizens would be able to enjoy the fruits of the American dream of equality and justice for all.

Blacks in Modern Politics

The vociferousness of militant voices has been softened by the suave and outspoken leader Julian Bond. According to *Time* magazine, news media analysts categorize Bond as "a militant activist, but not a revolutionary, ...representing those Blacks seeking to influence the nation through the existing governmental system."[160] Bond possesses the varied qualities necessary to become a dynamic leader like the late Dr. Martin Luther King, Jr. Bond studied philosophy under King while enrolled as a student at Morehouse College and was inspired by King's ideals and philosophy. Yet Bond's nonviolent philosophy is tempered by his admiration of such notable militants as Malcolm X, Stokeley Carmichael, and Rap Brown. His association with the middle and lower classes of blacks makes him more responsive to their needs. Bond's earlier membership and affiliation as communications director of SNCC in Atlanta sharpened his zeal for black unity through organizations.

The organizational technique of SNCC, which changed ideas into action, was especially appealing to Julian Bond. Members of this organization recognized the princely leadership qualities in Bond and persuaded him to run for the 11th legislative district in the state of Georgia. His political philosophy was that "politics does not represent salvation for black people...but black people can, through the political process, get some of the things we need."[161]

In 1965 Bond won a seat in the Georgia legislature, but the speaker of that body refused to swear him in. According to his political opponents, their refusal came because Bond had supported a resolution by SNCC that protested American involvement in Vietnam. It took a ruling by the Supreme Court to compel the Georgia legislature to seat him.

At the Democratic Convention in Chicago in 1968, Bond was nominated as a vice-presidential candidate, but he had to decline because he did not meet the constitutional requirement of age. But this gesture was a prelude of things to come and of the leadership role Bond would assume in helping blacks fit into the democratic formula of this country. He asserted that "we must strive for the day when the nation that fights wars to make the world safe for democracy can assure its citizens that democracy is safe for them."[162] In 2001 Julian Bond became chairman of the board of the NAACP. At this point in history it is not clear whether his "Democratic" criticism and opposition to current president George W. Bush is in the best interest of that organization and black America.

The most spectacular achievements of Negroes have been through the persistent, conservative leadership of the National Association for the Advancement of Colored People (NAACP). To many it may appear that the tactics of this organization are too slow in effecting changes through legal processes, and this has been a source of irritation to the more aggressive and militant blacks since the late 1950s. Major criticisms have been hurled at the organization's techniques in implementing the decision of the Supreme Court in the *Brown v. Board of Education* desegregation case in 1954.

The NAACP has been criticized for following middle class and black elite standards. Roy Wilkins, the executive director of the NAACP, attempted to hold the helm of the conservative civil rights organization through turbulent times of dissent while militants were advocating radical methods of bringing about revolutionary changes. Nevertheless, Wilkins continues to believe that the legal processes of constitutional change will bring blacks into the mainstream of American society, and he adheres to the NAACP's basic philosophy that "its work in the civil liberties sphere is important enough not to be lightheartedly jeopardized by radical adventures in other directions."[163]

Roy Wilkins fought off the young activists who were trying to make the NAACP more militant and instead has moved toward a more positive concept of Black Power and separatism. He answered the dichotomy of the movement by asserting that "The separatism called for by a highly vocal minority of Negro-Americans will harm the multiracial, pluralistic society America is seeking to perfect."[164] Many of Wilkins' critics have forgotten or know nothing of the outstanding pioneering and legal aid achievements of the NAACP.

The diffusion of leadership and more individualistic expressions of blacks are symptoms of the changing awareness and resultant involvement of this minority group in the fulfillment of the American dream. No one person speaks for the black race, but the commonality of black demands is beginning to be known through the ballot boxes. Blacks are using their political power to assist in electing their peers to office. The election of blacks in recent mayoral races throughout the United States is growing evidence of the political maturity of this previously impotent and disfranchised group, which has gained success in developing political coalitions with white liberal factions. There is demographic interest in selecting persons who understand and can identify with the diversified elements of urban problems.

One of the most important events in the past decade was the election in November 1967 of Carl Stokes to the office of mayor of Cleveland, Ohio, against a strong white opponent, Seth Taft. This multinationality-oriented city, plagued with a multiplicity of urban problems, could sympathize with Mordecai's query in the Old Testament to Esther in a similar setting: "And who knoweth whether thou art come to the kingdom for such a time as this?" (Esther 4:14) This metropolis was typical of the other major cities in the United States. It had been beset with administrations that continually ignored the plight of the poor in relation to employment, housing, and other social problems effected and compounded by mass movement of the more affluent to suburbia.

Carl Stokes had a wide range of experiences which prepared him to effectively deal with the problems of Cleveland, a city in danger of greater racial polarization. He was the son of a poor laundry worker who died in 1950. This untimely demise of his father left his mother a widow and Carl and his brother, Jon, fatherless. Carl's ambition was to be a prizefighter, but he dropped out of school when he was fifteen years of age to work for the Thompson Products Company, inspecting valves. World War II gave him an opportunity to fight for his country and serve with the army of occupation in Germany, 1945-46.

When Carl Stokes was discharged from the army, he matriculated at West Virginia State College for two years and for one year at the University of Washington. Later he graduated from Cleveland-Marshall Law School, which provided him with the necessary educational credentials to serve as an investigator for the State Liquor Control Board and as the Assistant City Prosecutor. In 1962 he became the first black democrat elected to the Ohio General Assembly.

In 1965 Stokes placed his name in nomination for mayor as an independent. Kenneth Weinberg writes, in *Black Victory*,

But what hurts most of all, and what probably cost him the election, was a whispering campaign calculated to exploit the fears and prejudice of apprehensive whites who had nervously observed tensions increasing between blacks and whites, not only in Cleveland but throughout the country.[165]

Ralph Lockner won the election and Carl Stokes immediately began another campaign to defeat the incumbent in the next election. The campaign picked up momentum in July 1966, when riots in the Hough area disrupted Cleveland and Stokes decided it would be in his favor to run on the Democratic ticket to help save Cleveland from destruction. His job was to convince the 300,000 suspicious blacks that he would not sell out to the white power elite, and to persuade white supporters that he would work for the good of the total community. Stokes' ultimate challenge was to develop a community consciousness, a monumental task silhouetted against insurmountable odds. The faucet of federal funds had been cut off due to mismanaged projects; the demoralizing condition of the slums continued its octopus-grip on the poor; and a rising crime rate and inadequate schools alienated the haves from the have-nots.

With an unquenchable faith in the morality of American society, Stokes embarked on a well-planned political campaign with the idea foremost in his mind that "a massive attack must be made on the economic problems of Black America, and Negroes must be convinced that through political activity they can become full partners in American society."[166] Too, the guiding light for this political realist was his firm belief that the city of Cleveland was desperately reaching for a high level of enlightened morality that would elect him because he was the answer to Cleveland's problems, not because he was black. His faith in democracy was restored when he won the Democratic nomination and the support of his party.

The veteran politico and flag-bearer of the Democratic Party took on the challenge of Seth Taft, his Republican adversary, by putting his energetic efforts behind the slogan, "Cleveland Now!"[167] He seemed to have rejuvenated the whole community. Stokes used the news media and solicited and received participation by all factions of the city. This great-grandson of a slave received 129,829 votes; his opponent, 127,328. A prince had come out of Egypt and America was apparently experiencing a new renaissance in human dignity. The fourth-largest city in the United States, where whites outnumbered blacks two to one, had lifted itself out of the quagmire of racism and elected itself a black mayor who was not just a black mayor, but an exemplar of the new renaissance in American thought.

The campaign promises of Carl Stokes were partially carried to fruition during his first year as mayor. He built houses, provided jobs, and constructed service centers in the various communities. His basic belief was that

> If black people are really going to become a part of America, they're going to have to become real parties in the American society. And that means more than simply having good jobs. They'll have to be profit-sharers, profit-makers. They'll have to be producers and employers. This is a capitalist country, so the black man has got to be a capitalist. That's when he'll realize his role as an equal—when he's part of

America's profit-making system.[168]

In Newark, New Jersey; Gary, Indiana; and Washington, D.C., blacks have also been elected to important municipal offices.

At all levels of legislature, an increasing number are now active in the legislative process. Thurgood Marshall was one of the first blacks to practice law before the Supreme Court of the United States, and he became the first black Supreme Court Justice. In his birthplace of Baltimore, he won distinction in *Murry v. Pearson*, a decision that gave blacks the right to attend the University of Maryland Law School.

In 1945, as chief counsel for the NAACP, Marshall initiated the current Civil Rights Movement by his success in *Brown v. Topeka Board of Education*, which revoked the "separate but equal" doctrine formerly sanctioned in *Plessy v. Ferguson*. This barrister was the dynamo of cases that have become contemporary social and legal history. As a lawyer he won twenty-nine of the thirty-two cases he brought before the U.S. Supreme Court.

The sensitivity of President John F. Kennedy to the absence of blacks from high offices led to the 1962 appointment of Marshall to the Second Circuit Court of Appeals. In 1965 he became the first black to serve as Solicitor General and in 1967 was appointed as Associate Justice of the U.S. Supreme Court, where he served with dignity and distinction until his retirement in 1991.

The legal barriers against blacks in America have been eliminated. De facto segregation is slowly being gnawed away by a more enlightened morality and a new generation of young people who have slowed the transmittal of stereotyped racial myths. The recent aberration of Southern governors from promoting fratricidal strife is symptomatic of a new enlightenment. Changing attitudes articulated in the 1971 gubernatorial inaugurations of governors John C. West of South Carolina, who pledged support to a government that was totally colorblind, and Jimmy Carter of Georgia, who pronounced that the time for discrimination was over, are an ebbless movement of this century. As Prince Hall wrote many years ago, once again "The scene is changed…thus Ethiopia begins to stretch forth her hand from a sink of slavery to freedom and equality."[169] Blacks remain in the vanguard of political and social change in the United States and are determined to become an integral part of American society.

The appointment of Colin Powell by President George W. Bush as his Secretary of State made Powell the first African-American to hold this high an office of governmental administration. This may be a major step toward blacks being included as an integral part of American society. Blacks are proud, yet skeptical of being "the first" African-American to do something, but one has to recognize that being Secretary of State is not a token position. Very few citizens opposed his selection. Previously, Colin Powell was a prime candidate for the 2000 presidential election. This articulate military genius had served under several presidents: as a budget-fellow in the Nixon administration in 1972; National Security Adviser for Ronald Reagan; Chairman of the Joint Chiefs of Staff under George Bush, overseeing Operation Desert Storm in 1991. He was also the recipient of the Springarm Medal from former NAACP executive director, Benjamin Hooks, and he was part of an historic peace mission to Haiti with President Carter and Sam Nunn.

However, this writer and many other blacks didn't want him to run for president. Many were not convinced that the Republican majority would whole-heartedly support him, and he could not win running with the Democratic Party or as an Independent. Evidently his wife, Alma, wouldn't consent either. So the second President Bush, recognizing the statute and quality of leadership in this military genius, appointed Colin Powell as Secretary of State. In *Time* magazine, John Stacks explained that "The Powell success story is reassuring to those Americans who want to believe that although racism persists, the system is not so corrupted by it to prevent talented minorities from succeeding."[170] His influence is in keeping with strong American traditions of passing opportunities on to succeeding generations: his son, Michael K. Powell, is chairman of the Federal Communications Commission.

The real challenge for young blacks in America is to mimic the ability of Colin Powell to overcome the pitfalls of his youth and racism in America. Powell was born April 5, 1937, in New York City, where his parents had emigrated from Jamaica. When Powell was four, his parents moved to the South Bronx, where he attended Public School 39 and Morris High School.

Upon graduating from high school in February 1954, Colin Powell enrolled as an engineering major at the City College of New York; he didn't do well in his major so he changed to geology. In 1954 he joined the Reserve Officers Training Corps and graduated as an outstanding recruit for the United States Army. The rest is history. Powell could be on the threshold of attaining the presidency of this dynamic and changing America. However, the opprobrious and villainous September 11, 2001 attack on New York City and the Pentagon in Washington, D.C., is a test to the ability of a black man to be an aggressive and competent Secretary of State and retain the confidence of the American people. Colin Powell's experience in the Persian Gulf and other military theaters help forge his leadership expertise and style. This national catastrophe has further helped to dispel doubts about his grasp of the complexity and nuance of international relations. The progressive, general, and gradual acceptance of black America into the melting pot is a modern-day epiphany of David's prophetic revelation that "Princes would come out of Egypt, and Ethiopia would lift her hands to God."

There is currently an historical resurgence of the advancement of black women in America. Simultaneously, with the appointment of Colin Powell as Secretary of State, President George W. Bush selected Condoleezza Rice as the National Security Advisor. She had previously served with the former President George Bush as director of Soviet and Eastern European Affairs in 1990. She, too, had grown up in the segregated Bastille of Birmingham, Alabama, with its Ku Klux Klan, Alabama Women's League For White Supremacy, police dogs, and water hoses directed toward blacks. Condoleezza Rice proved that regardless of her experience with racial hatred and hostility, she could overcome. This highly acclaimed educator realized that having intellectual skills was good, but it required putting them to use for the good of yourself and society. She was chosen in 1993 as the first black provost at Stanford University in California, and she is now in charge of the White House's largest policy staff.

President George Bush has demonstrated that he is not putting blacks in token positions for political purposes; he exceeded the achievements of other presidents by also appointing Rod Paige to a top cabinet post as the seventh Secretary of Education. Rod Paige's educational prowess preceded him; he had made dynamic changes as Superintendent of the Houston Independent School District beginning in 1994. This former football coach served on the HISD Board of Education from 1989 to 1994 and was well acquainted with many problems of the Houston School District. He understood the importance of working with the business communities in evaluating and improving the academic and vocational qualities needed for success. Rod Paige created the PEER examination, evaluation, and redesign program and expanded the concept of charter schools by initiating performance contracts patterned after those in various private schools. Student achievement in math and writing skills soared to national prominence. He included teacher incentive-pay, which rewards teachers for outstanding academic performance. On December 18, 2001, the U.S. Congress helped Rod Paige to reach his goals by passing President Bush's $26.5 billion education bill requiring schools to adopt plans to close the achievement gaps between low-income and middle-class students and between white and minority students.

Rod Paige was born in Monticello, Mississippi. He earned his bachelor's degree from Jackson State University in Mississippi and a master's degree and doctorate from Indiana University. For ten years Dr. Paige was employed as Dean of the College of Education at Texas Southern University. In 2001 he was named the National Superintendent of the Year by the American Association of School Administrators. President George W. Bush wanted a proven educational leader, and he knew that Paige, who had changed the lives of so many students in Texas, would carry his expertise to the national level. Often dressed in his lizard, snake, ostrich, and alligator cowboy boots, Rod Paige is another prince who has come out of Texas.

The inevitable cultural changes which follow an enlightened society that has simultaneously been tempered with an enlightened morality will enhance the humanistic traditions of our American society. The descendants of those black princes who were brought into the land of bondage by "pharaoh" and experienced their traumatic wilderness travail are Americanized in their ideals. American concepts of dignity, respect, equality, and individualism are now a part of their heritage.

The continued struggle to transcend the barriers of color is the spiritual odyssey of the black movement in this century. Any concerted effort to turn back the clock of progress will be met with stiff resistance. Blacks will not tolerate prolonged denial of human and civil rights. The prophecy is one of determination: Princes *will* come out of Egypt.

America is experiencing a new birth of freedom. Cracks in the melting pot are being plugged so that the "dredge" which formerly sank to the bottom will permit black men to be absorbed in the mainstream of society. As an editorial in the *Fort Worth Star-Telegram* once stated,

> All effective action is fueled by hope. If there is a chance that we can replace brutality with reason, inequity with justice, ignorance with enlightenment, we must try. And our chances are better if we have not convinced ourselves that the cause is hopeless.[171]

NOTES, PART I

1. Psalm 68:31.
2. William G. Grier and Price Cobb, *Black Rage* (New York: Basic Books, Inc., 1968), p. 38.
3. Paul Bohanna, *Africa and Africans* (New York: Doubleday & Company, Inc., 1964), pp. 48, 58.
4. Victor C. Ferkiss, *Africa's Search for Identity* (New York: The World Publishing Company, 1967), p. 21.
5. Ibid., p. 23.
6. Robert Ardrey, *African Genesis* (New York: Atheneum, 1963), pp. 283, 289.
7. Ferkiss, p. 22. See also Basil Davidson, *The Lost Cities of Africa* (Boston: Little, Brown & Co., 1959), p. 7.
8. Immanuel Wallerstein, *Africa: The Politics of Independence* (New York: Random House, 1961), p. 18.
9. Sonia Cole, *The Prehistory of East Africa* (London: Macmillan Publishing Co., Inc., 1954), p. 24.
10. Melville J. Herskovits, *The Human Factor in Changing Africa* (New York: Vintage Books, 1962), p. 3.
11. Monroe H. Work, *Negro Yearbook, 1937-1938* (Tuskegee: Negro Year Book Publishing Company, 1937), p. 293.
12. *Origins of Continents* in the Britannica Encyclopedia, Vol. 6, p. 339.
13. "The Continental Drift," in *Time* (August 18, 1967), p. 36.
14. Patrick Hurley, "The Confirmation of Continental Drift," in *Scientific American* (August 1968), pp. 61, 64.
15. R. P. Jackson, "Elizabethan Seamen and the African Slave Trade," in *The Journal of Negro History* (January 1924), p. 2.
16. Charles Gibson, *Spain in America* (New York: Harper & Row, Publishers, 1966), pp. 12-13. See also John Bartlett Brebner, *The Explorers of North America, 1492-1806* (New York: The World Publishing Company, 1966), p. 13.
17. Francisco Lopez de Gomara, *Historia General De Las Indios* (Madrid: Espassa-Calpe, S.A., 1954), p. 431.
18. German Arciniegas, *Latin America: A Cultural History* (New York: Alfred A. Knopf, 1967), p. 45.
19. John Bartlett Brebner, *The Explorers of North America, 1492-1806* (New York: World Publishing Company, 1966), p. 59.
20. Dario Fernandez Florez, *The Spanish Heritage in the United States* (Madrid: Publicaciones Espanolas, 1965), p. 59.
21. Woodbury Lowery, *The Spanish Settlements within the Present Limits of the United States, 1513-1561* (New York: Russell & Russell, 1959 [1901]), p. 278.
22. Ibid., p. 280.

23. Shea, in Justin Winsor's *Narrative and Critical History of America*, II (Reprint edition by AMS Press, Inc.), p. 241.

24. Lowery, p. 451.

25. August Meier and Elliot Rudwick, *The Making of Black America*, Vol. 1 (New York: Atheneum, 1969), p. 28.

26. Robert C. McConnell, *Negro Troops of Antebellum Louisiana: A History of the Battalion of Free Men of Color* (Baton Rouge: Louisiana State University Press, 1968), p. 14.

27. John Hope Franklin, *From Slavery to Freedom: A History of Negro Americans* (New York: Vintage Books, 1969), p. 68.

28. Ralph Korngold, *Citizen Toussaint* (Boston: Little, Brown & Co., 1945), p. 57.

29. Henry Wendt, *The Red, White and Black Continent: Latin America—Land of Reformers and Rebels* (New York: Doubleday & Company, Inc., 1966), p. 87.

30. Ibid., p. 261.

31. Lorenzo J. Greene, *The Negro in Colonial New England* (New York: Atheneum, 1968), p. 60.

32. Oscar Handlin, *The History of the United States*, Vol. 1 (New York: Holt, Rinehart and Winston, 1967), p. 95.

33. Work, p. 296.

34. Herbert M. Morias, *The History of the Negro in Medicine*, 1967, pp. 12-13. Reprinted by permission of the Association for the Study of Life and History, Washington, D.C.

35. Elizabeth Yates, *Amos Fortune: Free Man*, p. 48, copyright 1950 by Elizabeth Yates. Published by E. P. Dutton & Co., Inc., and reprinted with their permission.

36. Henry W. Bragdon and Samuel P. McCutchen, *History of a Free People* (New York: Macmillan Publishing Co., Inc., 1956), p. 17.

37. Helen Worden, "To the Glory of Amos Fortune," *Collier's* Vol. 125 (January 7, 1950), p. 72.

38. Ibid., p. 39.

39. James D. Richardson, *A Compilation of the Messages and Papers of the Confederacy* (Nashville: United States Publishing Company, 1905), p. 78.

40. Langston Hughes and Milton Meltzer, *A Pictorial History of the Negro in America* (New York: Crown Publishers, 1956), p. 227.

41. Booker T. Washington, *The Story of the Negro* (New York: Doubleday & Company, Inc., 1940), p. 77. By permission of Mrs. Portio Pitman.

42. William Loren Katz, *Eyewitness: The Negro in America* (New York: Dell Publishing Co., 1969), pp. 300-301.

43. Henry A. Ploski and Roscoe C. Brown, Jr., *The Negro Almanac* (New York: Bellwether Publishing Company, 1967), p. 637.

44. L. H. Latimer, *Incandescent Electric Lighting: A Practical Description of the Edison System* (New York: D. Van Nostrand, 1890), p. 9.

45. Benjamin Quarles, *Lord Dunmore as Liberator* in The Bobbs Merrill Reprint Series in Black Studies, p. 494. (Reprinted from *William and Mary Quarterly*, Vol. XV, No. 4, October 1958.)

46. J. Franklin Jameson, *The American Revolution Considered as a Social Movement*, in A short quote from *The Status of Persons*, p. 21. Copyright 1926 by Princeton University Press: Princeton Paperback, 1967.

47. J. H. Hazelton, *The Declaration of Independence* (New York: Da Capo Press, Plenum Publishing Company, 1906), p. 144.

48. 12 Wall. 36, 21 L.E.D. 394 (1873).

49. Bryan Fulks, *Black Struggle: A History of the Negro in America* (New York: Dell Publishing Company, 1969), p. 42.

50. Katz, p. 49.

51. United States Constitution, Article I, Section 2.

52. Forrest McDonald, *E Pluribus Unum* (Cambridge: Houghton-Mifflin Company, 1965), p. 236.

53. Jared Sparks, *The Works of Benjamin Franklin, 1840*, II pp. 313-315.

54. Louis R. Mehlinger, "The Attitude of the Free Negro toward African Colonization," *Journal of Negro History*, Volume I (June 1916), pp. 276-301.

55. Ray Allen Billington, "James Forten: Forgotten Abolitionist," in *Negro History Bulletin*, Association for the Study of Negro Life and History, Vol. XIII (November 1949), p. 45.

56. John Hope Franklin, *From Slavery to Freedom: A History of Negro Americans* (New York: Alfred A. Knopf, 1969), p. 240.

57. Reprinted from J. Gus Liebenow, *Liberia: The Evolution of Privilege*, p. 2. Copyright 1969 by Cornell University. Used by permission of Cornell University Press. See also Early Lee Fox, *The American Colonization Society, 1817-1840* (Baltimore: The John Hopkins Press, 1919), p. 226.

58. R. C. F. Maugham, *The Republic of Liberia* (New York: Charles Scribner's Sons, 1920), p. 34.

59. Ibid., pp. 60-63.

60. Adapted from Merran Fraenkel, *Tribe and Class in Monrovia* (London: Oxford University Press, 1964). Reprinted from Liebenow, p. 8.

61. Edwin S. Redkey, *Black Exodus: Black Nationalist and Back-to-Africa Movements, 1890-1910* (New Haven: Yale University Press, 1969), p. 21.

62. Earle Anderson, *Liberia: America's Friend* (Chapel Hill: The University of North Carolina Press, 1952), pp. 285-286.

63. Dumas Malone and Basil Rauch, *American Origins to 1789* (New York: Appleton-Century-Crofts, 1960), p. 44.

64. Richard C. Wade, *The Negro in American Life* (Boston: Houghton-Mifflin Company, 1965), p. 11.

65. John R. Spears, *The American Slave Trade* (New York: Charles Scribner's Sons, 1900), p. 71.

66. Daniel P. Mannix, *Black Cargoes: A History of the Atlantic Slave Trade, 1518-1855* (New York: The Viking Press, 1963), p. 58.

67. Frank Tannenbaum, *Slave and Citizen: The Negro in the Americas* (New York: Vintage Books, 1963), pp. 28-29.

68. Milton Meltzer, *In Their Own Words: A History of the American Negro, 1619-1865* (New York: Thomas Y. Crowell Co., 1964), pp. 8-9.

69. From *Seventy Negro Spirituals*, edited by William Arms Fisher, page vii. Copyright 1926, Oliver Ditson Company. Used by permission.
70. Work, p. 480.
71. William Sidney Drewry, *The Southampton Insurrection* (Washington: The Neale Company, 1900), p. 31. Reprinted by Johnson Publishing, 1968.
72. Lerone Bennett, Jr., *Before the Mayflower: A History of Black America* (New York: Johnson Publishing Company, 1961, 1969), pp. 124-125.
73. Meltzer, pp. 124-125.
74. 19 How. 393, 15 L. E. D., 691 (1857).
75. See Appendix for text of Proclamation.
76. Editorial, *Chicago Tribune*, August 1, 1863. Reprinted courtesy of the *Chicago Tribune*.
77. Quoted by Harold Schoen in "The Free Negro in Texas," *Southwestern Historical Quarterly*, XXXIX, (April 1936), p. 301. Used by permission of the Texas State Historical Association.
78. Ibid., p. 305.
79. H. P. N. Gammel, editor, *Laws of Texas*, I (Austin, Texas: The Gammel Book Company, 1898), 30.
80. Harold Schoen, "The Free Negro in the Republic of Texas," *Southwestern Historical Quarterly*, XL (July 1936), p. 26. Used by permission of the Texas State Historical Association.
81. Ibid., p. 27.
82. Harold Schoen, "The Free Negro in the Republic of Texas," *Southwestern Historical Quarterly*, III (January 1937), p. 178.
83. Sallie Glasscock, *Dreams of an Empire: The Story of Stephen Fuller Austin and his Colony in Texas* (San Antonio: The Naylor Company, 1951), p. 155.
84. Walter Lord, *A Time to Stand* (New York: Harper and Brothers, 1961), p. 153.
85. Quoted in Schoen, XL (July 1936), p. 33.
86. Gammel, *The Law of Texas*, II, p. 326.
87. William Loren Katz, *Teachers Guide to American Negro History*, p. 66. Reprinted by permission of Quadrangle Books Copyright 1968, 1971 by the Anti-Defamation League of B'nai B'rith., p. 66.
88. Work, p. 257.
89. Jack Greenberg, *Race Relations and American Law* (New York: Columbia University Press, 1962), p. 139.
90. Maurice Evans, *Black and White in the Southern States* (London: Longmans, Green and Company, 1915), p. 151.
91. *Guinn v. United States*, 238, US 347.
92. Beverly W. Bond, Jr., *The Civilization of the Old Northwest: A Study of Political, Social, and Economic Development, 1788-1812* (New York: _____, 1934), p. 133.
93. John D. Barnhart, *Valley of Democracy: The Frontier Versus the Plantation in the Ohio Valley, 1775-1818* (Bloomington: _____, 1953), p. 157.
94. Carter G. Woodson, *A Century of Negro Migration* (New York, 1918), p. 52.
95. Ibid., p. 57.

96. *An Act Extending the Right of Suffrage in the Indiana Territory*, February 26, 1808, Carter, Territorial Papers of the United States, Indiana, VIII, 526.
97. Ibid., VIII, 111.
98. David Dodge, "Free Negroes of North Carolina," *Atlantic Monthly*, LVIII (January 1866), 21.
99. Ibid., p. 22.
100. *The Liberator*, August 20, 1831.
101. Revised Statutes of Arkansas, 1838, pp. 584-585, as quoted in Orville W. Taylor, *Negro Slavery in Arkansas* (Durham: _____, 1958), p. 245.
102. From Oregon Provisional Government, Copy of the Oregon Laws, 1844, as printed in E. E. Rich, editor, *The Letters of John McLoughlin from Fort Vancouver to the Governor and Committee, Third Series, 1844-46.* (Toronto: Champlain Society, and London: Hudson's Bay Record Society, 1944), p. 233.
103. *American Travelers Guide to Black History* (Garden City, New York: Doubleday & Company, Inc., 1956), pp. 8, 9. See also Langston Hughes and Meltzer Milton, *A Pictorial History of the Negro in America* (New York: Crown Pub., 1956, p. 81.
104. William S. Willis, "Divide and Rule; Red, White, and Black in the South East," *Journal of Negro History*, XLVIII (July 1963), pp. 157-176.
105. William S. Willis, Jr., James C. Curtis and Lewis L. Gould, eds., *Black Experience in America: Selected Essays* (Austin: University of Texas Press, 1970), p. 43.
106. William H. Leckie, *The Buffalo Soldiers: A Narrative of the Negro Cavalry in the West* (The University of Oklahoma Press, 1967), p. 81.
107. Philip Ashton Rollins, *The Cowboy* (New York: Charles Scribner's Sons, 1922), p. 22.
108. "Shaded Heroes," in *Time*, LXXXV (February 26, 1965), p. 103. Reprinted by permission from *Time*. Copyright Time Inc., 1965.
109. Phillip Durham, "Negro Cowboys," *American Quarterly*, VII (Fall, 1955), p. 103.
110. "Slaves on Horseback," *Pacific Review*, p. 409.
111. Phillip Durham and Everett L. Jones, *The Negro Cowboy* (New York: Dodd, Mead and Company, 1965), pp. 17-18.
112. Durham and Jones, quoted in Charles Wynes, ed., *The Negro in the South Since 1865* (New York and Evanston: Harper & Row, Publishers, 1968), p. 223.
113. Ibid., p. 293.
114. Charles A. Siringo, *Riata and Spurs* (Boston: Houghton Mifflin Company, 1931), p. 18.
115. *U.S. Statutes at Large*, Vol. XIV, p. 27 ff.
116. Dumas Malone and Basil Rauch, *The New Nation, 1865-1917* (New York: Appleton-Century-Crofts, 1960), p. 159.
117. C. Vann Woodward, *the Burden of Southern History*, pp. 55, 72. By permission of Louisiana State University Press.
118. C. Vann Woodward, "Tom Watson and the Negro in Agrarian Politics," *The Journal of Southern History*, IV (February 1938), quoted in Charles E. Wynes,

ed., *The Negro in the South Since 1865* (New York: Harper & Row, Publishers, 1965), p. 48.

119. Arthur M. Schlesinger, *Political and Social Growth of the American People, 1865-1940* (New York: Macmillan Publishing Co., Inc, 1941), p. 228.

120. C. Vann Woodward, *The Strange Career of Jim Crow* (New York: Oxford University Press, 1974, p. 36.

121. Oscar Handlin, *The History of the United States*, Vol. 2 (New York: Holt, Rinehart and Winston, 1968), p. 17.

122. C. Vann Woodward, *The Burden...*, p. __.

123. Booker T. Washington, "The Atlanta Exposition Address," in Harvey Wish, ed., *The Negroes in Emancipation* (Englewood Cliffs, New Jersey: Prentice Hall, 1964), p. 41.

124. John A. Garraty, *The American Nation: A History of the United States* (New York: Harper & Row, Publishers, 1966), p. 571.

125. Saunders Redding, *They Came In Chains* (New York: J. B. Lippincott Company, 1969), p. 197.

126. Booker T. Washington, *Up From Slavery* (New York: Sun Dial Press, Inc., 1937), p. 316.

127. Gunnar Myrdal, *An American Dilemma*, Vol. II (New York: Harper & Row, Publishers, 1944), p. 815.

128. W. E. B. DuBois, *The Souls of Black Folk* (New York: Fawcett Press, 1903), p. 46.

129. "Ten Most Dramatic Effects in American History," *Ebony*, XVIII (September 1963), p. 34.

130. W. E. B. DuBois, *The Souls of Black Folk* (Chicago: A. C. McClung Publishing, 1903), pp. 50-59.

131. W. E. B. DuBois, quoted in S. F. Fullinwinder, *The Mind and Mood of Black America* (Homewood, Illinois: The Dorsey Press, 1969), pp. 63-64.

132. John Hope Franklin, *From Slavery to Freedom: A History of Negro Americans* (New York: Vintage Books, 1969), p. 490.

133. Willhelmena S. Robinson, *Historical Negro Biographies*, International Library of Negro Life and History, p. 194. Reprinted by permission of the Association for the Study of Negro Life and History, Washington, D.C., 1967.

134. Marcus Garvey, "The Negro's Greatest Enemy," *Current History*, XVIII (September 1923), pp. 951-957.

135. Saunders, p. 260.

136. Ibid., p. 225.

137. Gustave Anguizola, "Negroes in the Building of the Panama Canal," *Phylon*, XXIX (Winter 1969), pp. 351, 359.

138. Langston Hughes and Anna Bontemps, eds., *The Poetry of the Negro, 1746-1949* (New York: Doubleday & Company, Inc., 1949), pp. 32-33.

139. Henry F. Pringle, *Theodore Roosevelt: A Biography* (New York: Harcourt Brace Jovanovich, Inc., 1931), p. 458.

140. Joseph Bucklin Bishop, *Theodore Roosevelt and His Time: Shown in His Own Letters* (New York: Charles Scribner's Sons, 1920), pp. 27-29.

141. George E. Mowry, *The Era of Theodore and His Time: Shown in His Own Letters* (New York: Harper & Row, Publishers, 1958), p. 212.
142. George Wallace Chessman, *Theodore Roosevelt and the Politics of Power* (Boston: Little, Brown & Co., 1969), p. 145.
143. Ibid., p. 146.
144. Pringle, Op. Cit., p. 462.
145. Saunders, p. 225.
146. *Survey Graphic*, XXXI (November 1942), pp. 488-489.
147. Roy Cook, *Leaders of Labor* (New York: L. B. Lipincott Co., 1966), p. 146.
148. Robert M. Lewin, "Retirement of A. Phillip Randolph—End of an Era," *Fort Worth Star-Telegram* (September 4, 1968), p. 7A.
149. James Hope Franklin, *From Slavery to Freedom: A History of Negro Americans* (New York: Random House, 1967), p. 561.
150. Harvey Wish, ed., *The Negro Since Emancipation* (Englewood Cliffs, New Jersey: Prentice-Hall, Inc., 1964), p. 170.
151. *The Autobiography of Malcolm X* (New York: Grove Press, Inc., 1966), p. 221.
152. "Malcolm X," quoted in *Britannica Book of the Year*, 1964, p. 241.
153. Eldridge Cleaver, from *Soul on Ice*, pp. 82-83. Copyright 1968 by Eldridge Cleaver. Used with permission of McGraw-Hill Book Company.
154. Ibid., p. 56.
155. Ibid., p. 61.
156. For a detailed discussion of the Strategy of Protest, see Chapter IV of Lewis M. Killian, *The Impossible Revolution? Black Power and the American Dream* (New York: Random House, 1968).
157. Martin Luther King, Jr., "I Have a Dream." Copyright 1963 by Martin Luther King, Jr. Reprinted by permission of Mrs. Dorothy Rudo and Joan Daves.
158. From *Life* magazine (December 13, 1968), p. 4. Copyright 1968, Time Inc.
159. Adapted from Whitney Young Jr., *To Be Equal* (New York: McGraw-Hill Book Company, 1964), pp. 38-41.
160. "Other Voices, Other Strategies," in *Time* (Special Issue, April 6, 1970). Reprinted by permission from Time, The Weekly Newsmagazine. Copyright 1970, Time Inc.
161. David Llorens, "Julian Bond," *Ebony*, Vol. XXIV, No. 7 (May 1969), p. 60. By permission of Julian Bond.
162. From *Life* Magazine (December 13, 1968), p. 9. Copyright 1968, Time, Inc.
163. Gunnar Myrdal, *An American Dilemma: The Negro Problem and Modern Democracy*, Vol. II (New York: Harper & Row, Publishers, 1944), p. 834.
164. Roy Wilkins, *Today's Education*, Vol. III (Washington: National Educational Association, 1969), p. 32.
165. From Kenneth Weinberg, *Black Victory*, p. 67. Copyright 1968 by Kenneth G. Weinberg. Reprinted by permission of Quadrangle Books.
166. Ibid., pp. 238-239.
167. James F. Barnes, *Carl Stokes: Crisis, Challenge and Dilemma*. Quoted in William G. Shade and Roy C. Herrenkohl, *Seven on Black: Reflections on the Negro Experience in America* (New York: J. B. Lippincott Company, 1969), p.

127.

168. Carl B. Stokes, "My First Year in Office," *Ebony*, Vol. XXIV, No. 3 (January 1969), p. 118.

169. Prince Hall, "A Charge Delivered to the African Lodge, June 24, 1797," in Thomas R. Frazier, ed., *Afro-American History: Primary Sources* (New York: Harcourt, Brace and Jovanovich, Inc., 1970), p. 49.

170. John Stacks, "The Powell Factor," *Time* (July 10, 1995), p. 25.

171. Editorial, *Fort Worth Star-Telegram*, May 27, 1970.

PART II
THE BLACK THREAD
OF TEXAS HISTORY

Nature smiled with favor on the wide exotic regions of Texas and created a reservoir of minerals and natural resources that have facilitated growth and development unparalleled in the Western Hemisphere. This land of opportunity, whose longitudinal arcs extend some 800 miles from the Panhandle to the rippling waters of the Gulf of Mexico and whose latitudinal breadth ranges some 800 miles from the piney woods of east Texas to El Paso, is also a land of diversity which was settled by diversified people.

Nomadic Indian tribes roamed the plains of Texas and temporarily deterred the advance of European and American pioneers who looked to this part of Spanish territory for settlement and a new way of life. Once the hostile Indians were subdued, floods of immigrants came to the frontier and played significant roles in the development of Texas. The great variety of geographic and other features attracted the major migratory currents of westward expansion which included some twenty-five or more distinct groups. The gradual weaving of these ethnic polyglots into a motley cultural pattern has resulted in a populace which distinguishes itself as Texan.

One thread in the colorful fabric has been scantily noted in the past and little studied in the present. This ignored contributor to Texas history is the black man. Slave and free, he has made worthwhile contributions to the cultural development of Texas.

REBY CARY ELECTED TO FT. WORTH SCHOOL BOARD, 1974-1978

Secretary of the Board

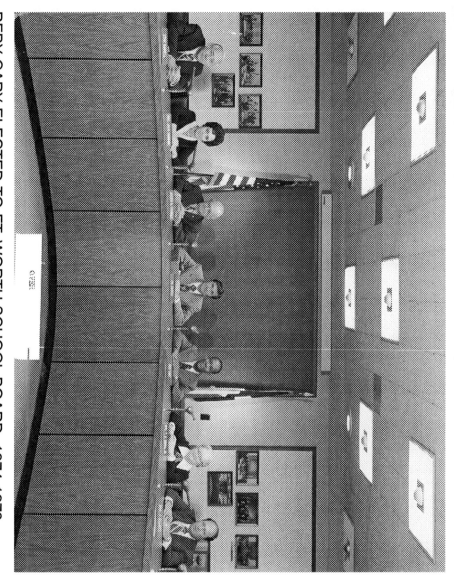

EXPLORATION

Blacks were with most of the early explorers who adventurously pushed out and penetrated this new wilderness. In a number of instances, blacks were used as guides for meandering Spanish expeditions which emanated from the already established settlements of Central and South America.

One of the most colorful black personalities in the annals of Texas lore is that of Estevanico, an Arab Moor from the town of Azamor on the Atlantic coast of Morroco.[1] This adventurer was one of the victims of Portuguese conquest of the small city in 1513 and was one of those Muslims captured by Christian zealots carrying the banner of the cross.[2]

Estevanico sailed with Narvaez's fleet from San Lucas de Barameda, Spain, June 17, 1527, and survived the ill-fated expedition, which was buffeted by the fury of Antillean winds and destroyed on the coast of Tampa, Florida. Some 242 survivors attempted to get from Florida to Mexico in crudely constructed boats, and again the elements of nature rose up in indomitable fury and smashed their crafts at Galveston or Matagorda Bay in November 1528. Estevanico, Nuñez Cabeza de Vaca, Alonso del Castillo, and Andres Dorantes were the survivors whose exploits would arouse the interest of other explorers.

The shipwrecked explorers initiated one of the longest walks of mankind. Their circuitous trip through the American Southwest began somewhere west of the Sabine River in Texas. The black explorer Estevanico learned the sign language of the hostile Indians in east Texas and practiced ritualistic medicine to appease and placate the Karankawas, who held Cabeza de Vaca and his companions prisoners for a long time. When the Spanish leader miraculously removed an arrow from the heart of one of the Indians and he survived, they believed the Spaniards were supernatural beings. The surviving explorers were able then to move from village to village, practicing their pseudo-witchcraft, and thus they traversed the mountainous region of central Texas along the Brazos River.

The remnants of the Narvaez expedition followed the setting sun with undaunted courage in an effort to find the shore of Mexico. They crossed the Pecos River near its junction with the Rio Grande and continued over the uplands to the mouth of the Rio Conchos, and thence to the Rio Grande.[3] As the quartet reached the lower California Valley, they met some Spanish slave-runners who led them to Mexico.

Estevanico's exploration challenged the imagination of other conquistadors and was significant in facilitating subsequent explorations and discoveries. Because of his knowledge, Estevanico was chosen in 1539 by Viceroy Antonio de Mendoza to guide the expedition in search of the legendary Seven Cities of Cibola, alleged to be in Zuni Territory. The viceroy ordered Estevanico to obey the orders of Friar Marcos de Niza or be severely punished. There was constant discard between Estevanico and Friar Marcos because the guide acquired turquoise and was a promiscuous seducer of Indian women.[4]

Estevanico was instructed to send crosses back with the Indian who accompanied him as a symbol of his progress. The explorer always managed to stay out of range of Friar Marcos and "proceeded on his way with all the assumption of authority of which he believed himself entitled as an envoy of Viceroy Mendoza."[5] His overconfidence and lack of complete knowledge of the ways of the Indian led to his death. As he advanced into the Zuni country, Estevanico sent gourds by messengers ahead of him as symbols of authority to command obedience. The chiefs disregarded the signs and demanded Estevanico's removal from the land. Estevanico ignored the warning and was subsequently killed.

Estevanico is remembered as a man of courage and daring who caught the Spanish fever of discovery and exploration. He became an early symbol of the development of this state and figures in the first pages of the history of Texas. His exploits helped stimulate European interest in settling this part of the Southwest.

At first the lure of gold and the fabled Cities of Cibola kept the Spanish from settling permanently in Texas. France, the traditional enemy of Spain, took advantage of Spain's apparently averted attention and preceded her in attempting to secure Texas. As La Salle looked for the source of the Mississippi River, he established, by a navigational miscalculation, the first settlement in Texas in 1685 at Matagorda Bay. The French claim to Texas was later nullified in the French and Indian War and by the Paris Peace Treaty of 1763 which concluded that conflict. It divided the Western world between Spain and England: all the land east of the Mississippi belonged to England, and all land west of the big river to Spain.

Continuous conflict in Europe continued to weaken Spanish control in the Western Hemisphere. But the American Revolution temporarily revitalized Spain's declining empire. Spain saw an advantage in assisting the colonies to throw off the English yoke, and her reward came with the Treaty of Paris, 1783, which gave her virtually complete control of the territory adjacent to the Gulf of Mexico. But this control, which represented the colonists' western boundary, precipitated a new struggle between the United States and Spain.

The French Revolution also had its effect on Spanish possessions west of the Mississippi. In 1793 Spain joined England in an alliance against the French. Spain proved incapable of defending its empire in the Western Hemisphere. The inability to defend her western lands was glaringly evident in the difficulties Spain showed in coping with American surprise attacks. Philip Nolan, an Irish equestrian-entrepreneur, repeatedly conducted clandestine forays into Texas and defied Spanish authorities' orders to desist from removing horses from the Texas savannas. On one of his last raids in 1801, there were two black men with him: one whose name is recorded as "Cesar" (Caesar) and the other as "Robert."[6] When the Comanche Indians stole some horses from the American hunting party, Philip Nolan, Robert Ashley, Joseph Reed, David Fero, and Cesar volunteered to pursue the Indians and recover their horses. This they soon did without resistance from the Indians.

However, their trouble came from other quarters. Miguel Musquiz came from the Spanish fort at Nacogdoches with 150 men and attacked the Americans. In the fighting that followed, Nolan was mortally wounded by a musketball. The remnants of the Americans regrouped and made a pledge to fight to the finish. Cesar carried the surplus gunpowder, but he and the entire party were captured. Funeral rites were conducted for Nolan at the Spanish stockade, and Cesar and a companion dug the grave in which the notorious fighter was laid to rest.[7]

Cesar's life was spared after he was forced to give damaging testimony against his comrades to the Spanish government. His chancy career in the early settlement of North American ended presumably rather quietly as a servant to Juan Pedro Walker, an American expatriate and adventurer in the service of Spain.

Spain finally conceded that it could not defend the territory west of the Mississippi and in 1800 the Treaty of San Ildefonso ceded the territory to France. But the French Revolution inspired the restless in the Western Hemisphere. Toussaint L 'Ouverture, Black Napoleon of Haiti, defeated the Corsican Napoleon's colonial forces under the General Charles Leclerc and indirectly forced Napoleon to sell the Louisiana Territory to the United States in 1803. However, Napoleon left the Texas boundary a vague and indefinite span of land; this land was dispute until the Adams-Onis Treaty of 1819 set the boundaries beyond the Sabine.

Indignation over that treaty with Spain resulted in a filibustering expedition by James Long whereby in which he captured Nacogdoches and set up a Texas republic. The Spanish again sent superior forces to run the Americans out. There were other Americans who realized that filibustering into the Spanish provinces would not succeed, so they employed legal measures to facilitate the colonization of Texas.

Black Migration and Colonization

The panic of 1819 impelled many debt-ridden Americans to move westward for a new lease on life. The impulse of freedom followed these pioneers into Texas, and the hoe and plough changed a fallow and unproductive wilderness into a productive enterprise. The restrictive land policy of the United States and a new liberal land policy of the Spanish government attracted Moses Austin to request permission to enter Texas. According to Lester B. Bughee's "Slavery in Early Texas," "No mention was made of slavery in either the petition or the grant."[8] Generous grants of land were given as part of a new plan to help protect the frontier from Indians by encouraging the development of settlements.

Moses Austin was accompanied to Texas by his black body servant, who remained with him until his death in 1821. In the same year, Mexico won its independence from Spain and Stephen F. Austin inaugurated plans to continue his father's enterprise along the Brazos River. When Stephen F. Austin assumed the mantle of his father as leader of the colony at San Felipe in 1821, he brought blacks with him.

Blacks came to the Texas frontier for reasons different from most other migrants in this period. They fled from the oppressive tyranny of southern slavery to Texas seeking an opportunity to enjoy a life free from the shackles of the peculiar institution which they had not experienced in the Mississippi and Atlantic coastal regions. They attempted to shed the chains of slavery without shedding the blood of their oppressors. This biracial movement westward was a spontaneous and individualized phenomena motivated by the desire for land and a new way of life. George Woolfolk explains that "Hundreds of Blacks were inspired by the Latin-Catholic's thrust of equality into the frontier and continued to come with hope after the Anglo-Protestant cultural thrust clashed with the Latin-Catholic in the open cockpit of Texas."[9]

Spain had joined England in promulgating her policy of prohibiting slavery in her colonies. A royal cedula was circulated in Texas and Coahuila prohibiting the purchase of Negroes on the coast of Africa, under severe penalties.[10] This policy encouraged blacks to seek refuge in Spanish territories. However, the law was ineffective and not too vigorously enforced because of the distance of provinces from the capital. Vessels from Martinique, the slave citadel of the Caribbean, where often observed landing their human cargo at Velasco and on the Sabine River without fear of arrest by Spanish or Mexican authorities,[11] who continuously practiced a policy of salutary neglect.

After independence from Spain, continuing incentives for black migration were Mexican laws which prohibited slavery. In 1824 the Mexican government continued Spanish policy and incorporated a colonization law which prohibited the commerce and traffic in slaves and mandated that all slaves brought into Mexico were automatically free once they touched Mexican soil. Runaway ads in newspapers dramatized the allure of Mexico. An ad in the *Commercial*, October 28, 1843, offered a $350 reward for slaves who "ran away from the subscriber on the 13th of August, seven likely Negro men, five of them from about twenty to twenty-five years of age, the other two between forty and forty-five…it has been ascertained that their intention was to go to Mexico. Two Negro men, John and Abe or Abram…. They are likely making their way to Mexico or to the Indians…. $50 [each]."[12]

Equality for peoples of color was a dynamic centripetal force which drew large numbers of runaway slaves to Mexican soil, attracting blacks but acting as a deterrent to white slaveholders who would not come without free labor to help carve out the Texas wilderness. A census taken in 1825 showed that the Austin colony's population was about 1,800, including 443 slaves.

Despite its illegality under Mexican law, proliferation of the slave trade began in 1825 when the father of Texas agriculture, Jared Groce, introduced hundreds of slaves to cultivate cotton on the Brazos. His operation of the Antillean model was almost completely self-sufficient. The success of this enterprise encouraged others to develop similar plantations, and Texas began to align itself economically with the interests of the Deep South. That interest created new demands for more slaves. In 1836 there were an estimated 5,000 blacks in Texas. Overall, the total slave population in this state through 1860 was 182,000, a relatively small number compared to other slave states.

The influence of the Central European element in Texas was a deterrent to slave labor. Most Germans were skilled artisans or small farmers, rather than plantation owners, who took pride in doing their own work and thus were not enthusiastic about using slave labor; they were also mindful of their experience of oppression under Prussian tyranny. However, as fast as some acquired more affluence, "they followed the customs of the country and purchased slaves like other whites."[13]

An increasing number of blacks had been entering through Galveston, the principal slave-portal of Texas, in spite of repeated efforts by the European powers to stem the flow from Africa to the Western Hemisphere. The human cargo of slave-runners putting into Texas ports, in violation of the admiralty laws, was confiscated and held at Galveston. Slaves were then sent to the adjacent territory of Louisiana for distribution. Galveston became the supply house for Louisiana and the commercial emporium of Texas; those buyers who wanted to inspect their purchase personally could do so at the seaport.

A special note should be made that in order to commemorate the preponderance and impact of slavery in Texas, the Waller County Commissioners voted in December 2000 to build a monument at the courthouse to honor the slaves in Hempstead, Texas.[14]

The famous Jim Bowie and his brother Rezin accumulated enormous wealth by purchasing slaves smuggled into Texas. They made a deal with the pirate Jean Lafitte to buy slaves at one dollar per pound (average $140 each). Then Jim would inform customs agents of the whereabouts of the smuggled blacks, knowing that the law provided that half of the profits from such sale went to the informer; this gave Bowie legal title to the slaves at half price. He later sold them in Mississippi for $1,000 each.[15]

Between 1845 and 1860 it was generally felt that slaves fared better in Galveston because of the social climate in this cosmopolitan cultural center of Texas. Its prestigious gentility not only tried to outdo its neighbors with material things but also with the quality of its slaves. Consequently, Galveston slaves ate and dressed better than their counterparts on the mainland.[16]

All blacks who came to Texas were not slaves; some were free men. Hendricks Arnold was one of the first free blacks with the Austin colony. His father was among Austin's original three hundred settlers who came in the early 1820s from Mississippi. Arnold later fought in the Texas Revolution. In 1849 he fell victim to the cholera which raged in Bexar County.

Two other blacks were among the pioneering families Austin accepted as colonists and to whom he granted land. Lewis H. Jones, a farmer, came to Texas in 1826 from Mississippi but never received title to his land. Greenbury Logan, a blacksmith, came in 1831 from Missouri and opened a boarding house in Brazoria. After Goliad, he answered Austin's call for volunteers to march on Bexar.

Occasionally blacks formulated plans to settle free blacks in Texas. In April 1834, Nicholas Drouett, a mulatto and a retired Mexican Army officer, came to Texas seeking the privilege of introducing five hundred black families from New Orleans. The project of free blacks had become a reality in Texas, and they were barred from acquiring land in a white society.[17]

Stephen F. Austin continued to invite white settlers to Texas, but in order to attract enough settlers, Austin had to lay aside his moral integrity and succumb to the demeaning and inhuman practice of allowing settlers to introduce slavery to Texas.[18] Many Americans felt that if the Mexican restrictions were lifted, great multitudes would flock to this new corner of the Southwest.[19] Austin's pragmatic acquiescence and justification for permitting slaves to be brought to Texas gave rise to some doubt about the genuineness of his vocalized opposition to slavery after 1840. The influence of the United States' morality in regards to slavery soon passed to Texas and its American founder.

Stephen F. Austin owned only one slave, a forty-year-old black woman named Fatima whom he purchased February 26, 1828, at San Felipe de Austin.[20] From time to time he would lease the number of slaves necessary to do a particular job. The availability of slaves in Texas had been guaranteed by the Congress of Coahuila and Texas in a decree issued May 5, 1828, which attempted to disguise continuing slavery as contract labor. Blacks were forced to sign a bond promising to serve for ninety-nine years.[21]

Again in 1829, Austin supported the slaveholding interest when the Mexican government issued its decree to abolish slavery completely. The father of Texas assured the settlers that as a Mexican citizen he would seek constitutional guarantees that their right to hold their property in slaves be protected.[22] The Mexican government interpreted its law so that it did not apply to slaves brought in before the deadline of September 15, 1829.

Austin's public attitude toward blacks wavered between antislavery and proslavery. Prior to the Texas Revolution and the annexation of Texas, Austin's position became fixed. He wrote his brother, Henry Austin, that he was adamantly "opposed to a union with the United States unless we first receive some guarantees, amongst them I should insist on the perpetual exclusion of slavery from this country."[23] He wanted to keep out vagabonds, outlaws, and redundant prisoners who were indentured from European prisons. Austin contended that "union with the United States would bring Negro slavery— that curse of curses, and worst of reproaches on civilized men, that unanswerable, inconsistency of free and liberal republicans."[24] Through persuasion and special interpretation of the Mexican laws, Austin and the settlers managed to circumvent the laws of Mexico and finally gained support from the United States to throw off the yoke of Mexican rule by revolution and gain independence.

The Texas Revolution

Support for the American settlers came primarily from land speculators and slaveholders in the Deep South. Many of the settlers were those who made up a class of landless or the dispossessed who, as Benjamin Lundy wrote, "sought a new theater where they might press their claims to public favor and political distinction."[25] They were to share in the continued acquisition of land given as grants to land companies (speculators) and agree to promote settlement in Texas. Consequently, the land speculators of New York controlled most of Coahuila and Texas and the Territory of Santa Fe. However, they soon were in danger of these claims being disavowed by the new Mexican government.

On September 15, 1829, President Guerrero issued a decree totally and immediately abolishing slavery throughout the republic. This decree made revolution imperative to the slaveholders, whose main desire was to "reestablish the system of slavery, to open a vast and profitable slave market therein, and ultimately annex it to the United States."[26]

Migration was accelerated in order to have more Americans as nationals. Inducements and overtures were made to the United States for support. A binding agreement was made with Southern legislators that "in case the independence of Texas shall be established all grants and claims...are to be legalized, (particularly if the claimants take an active part in the revolution); the system of slavery is to be re-established upon firm constitutional basis, and every facility will be given to the introduction of slaves from the United States, Cuba, and Africa."[27]

The American settlers took advantage of the Mexican upheavals of 1832, which brought Santa Ana to power, and united with the victors to oppose the Central government and demand separation of Coahuila from Texas. The Mexican government refused, declared martial law, and sent military forces to disarm and regain control of its provinces. Fighting flared at Anahuac, Velasco, and other parts of South Texas. The revolution was underway.

The black man's contribution to Texas independence is noteworthy because it indicated his ultimate desire for liberty. To some it seems ironic that men would fight for rights denied them by other whites, yet blacks sacrificed their lives for the apparently impossible dream. When the Texas Revolution broke out, black men were still willing to shed their blood for liberty in spite of being bound by the laws of slavery. However, some enlisted in the Mexican army to ensure their continued freedom, perhaps not suspecting that Santa Ana planned to use slave revolt as a strategy of his military campaign, as a letter by Benjamin Milan of July 1835 suggests.[28] Slave insurrection was a continuing source of fear and apprehension for white Texans; and indeed, the first slave insurrection of any consequence occurred during the initial stages of the revolution.

Sam McCullough, Jr., legally a free man, wounded near Montagorda Bay in October 1835, became the first free black to fight and give his blood for the independence of Texas against Mexico. As a result of his wounds, McCullough was an invalid for life.[29]

After the war, he desired to acquire land to support his family but found that the laws of the Republic of Texas, for which he had fought and bled, deprived him of citizenship by reason of his African blood.[30] President Sam Houston gave formal recognition to the veteran's heroic gallantry and later granted him permanent residence, but he still rejected his plea for land and citizenship.

After the dramatic siege and heroic defense of the Alamo, which ended on March 6, 1836, five survivors and Joe, Travis' slave, witnessed the tragedy of the slaughter in the fortress.[31] This twenty-three-year-old black man had been a constant companion to Travis and was a full-fledged member of the American garrison. During the attack on the former mission by the Mexican army, Joe fought alongside Travis until his master's death. The black defender of the Alamo went into hiding. Santa Ana's soldiers discovered Joe and hurriedly brought him before the victorious Mexican general, who attempted to persuade the former slave that his life was not in jeopardy. Joe did not trust the Mexicans, however, and left with another survivor, Mrs. Almeron Dickinson, who was on her way to Gonzales. No known records indicate the surname of the black survivor of the Alamo, but the name of "Joe" must be recorded in the annals of Texas history as one of the heroic defenders of the Alamo.

Thirteen days later the Mexicans massacred three hundred Americans who were under the leadership of Colonel James Fannin at Goliad. Peter Allen, a black musician from Pennsylvania, died with his own "impress of individuality."[32]

Stephen F. Austin employed blacks at many of the social functions where they were able to display their creative musical skills. At one function, "the music was furnished by three Negroes, one used the clevis pin, another scooped or banged on a cotton chopping hoe with a case knife, and a third sang at the top of his voice."[33] In many skirmishes of the Texas Revolution, black musicians inspired the colonists to resist the enemy.

As the fighting between the Texans and Mexicans intensified, blacks answered the call for volunteers in every instance. When Stephen F. Austin became commander-in-chief on October 10, 1835, Greenbury Logan, the free black blacksmith from Missouri, marched with him in his attack on Bexar. Later, under General Houston, when Texans were rallying under the battle cry of "Remember the Alamo" at the Battle of San Jacinto, April 26, 1836, another black man, Dick the Drummer, distinguished himself at the battle whereby Texas won its independence. According to one observer, "this gray-headed descendant of Ham carried consternation into the ranks of Santa Ana's Myrmidons."[34]

But independence came only to whites. When General Houston negotiated the Treaty of Velasco with Santa Ana in May 1836, it provided that all private property captured by the Mexican army, including horses, cattle, Negro slaves, or indentured persons of any color, should be restored to Texas. The constitution for the new Republic of Texas in 1836 further relegated blacks to a life of serfdom. It provided that "all Negroes still in bondage, who had been held in bondage, who had been in slavery prior to the removal of their masters to Texas, should remain in that state."[35]

Free blacks, who enjoyed extraordinary privileges not accorded slaves, were soon to feel the rod of oppression, especially those blacks who had helped the Texans during their uncertain and anxiety-filled days prior to independence. William Goyens, Jr. is a classic example of the dilemma of those blacks who came to Texas and lived as free persons.

Goyens had come to Texas from Moore County, North Carolina, where he was born in 1794. He and his eight brothers and sisters had been free persons because of the service their father had rendered to the colonists during the American Revolution. However, because of the negative racial attitudes toward blacks, life and freedom in North Carolina was severely limited.

The insatiable spirit of freedom and heralded opportunities of Texas, as a Mexican province, attracted William Goyens, Jr. to come to Nacogdoches in 1820 by way of New Orleans. This east Texas town was a focal point of continued Mexican and American hostilities. The Adams-Onis Treaty of 1819 had resulted in a short-lived coup d'etat. Dr. James Long, incensed over the United States' granting all the territory west of the Sabine to Spain, which included Texas, besieged Texas and declared it an independent state. Nacogdoches was the scene of the battle in which the rebellion was put down. Goyens heard about Nacogdoches from fleeing remnants of Long's men.[36] When Hayden Edwards engineered the Fredonian Rebellion in 1825 in an attempt to confiscate the land, Goyens assisted the Texans in preserving their land holdings. He was a blacksmith and gunsmith, serving Mexican, Spanish, and American pioneers, but he also became a freighter, which added immensely to his wealth.

In 1832 Goyens married Mary Sibley, a white woman from Georgia. It is interesting to note that both enjoyed good family relationships in spite of prevailing attitudes. He was also a most hospitable host to travelers through Texas and entertained Benjamin Lundy when he came to Texas in an endeavor to set up a colony of free blacks. It was Lundy's mission to "demonstrate that the cultivation of sugar, cotton and rice could be engaged in profitably by the use of free labor."[37] This plan never materialized because of opposition from land-hungry settlers and the adjacent slave state of Louisiana.

When Nacogdoches was left in ruins by Long's Rebellion, the Mexican government in January 1833 attempted to attract more settlers and legislated a new colonization law. Goyens was the benefactor of this act which made him one of the wealthiest men in Texas. It gave 177 acres to the farmers and not less than 4,428 acres to each stock raiser; settlers also had to be Catholic. Goyens, obligingly, became a Catholic and finally came to own 3,818 acres of land in Nacogdoches County and 9,056 acres in Houston, Cherokee, and Angelina Counties.

In spite of Goyens' affluence, he always lived in fear of being returned to slavery by fugitive slave catchers or whites who claimed runaway slaves. But the prestige and respect which Goyens had, gave him the paternal and fraternal protection of his white neighbors and friends of the Republic.

Goyens' most worthy contribution was probably his diplomatic service to the young republic in dealing with foreign relations. At the time, Texas was being threatened by a possible Indian-Mexican coalition, and Goyens was chosen to assist Houston in negotiating with the Cherokee Indians. Goyens was an excellent interpreter and had the respect and confidence of the Indians that they would be treated fairly.[38] As a result of the consultation at San Felipe, definite boundaries were established for the Indians in exchange for their agreement to remain at peace during the Texas Revolution. Texas never sustained this treaty, however; in 1837 it was rejected by the Senate. The military, under Secretary of War Johnston, continued to wage war on the Cherokees until on July 17,

1839, the Indians were decisively defeated. Houston's and Goyens' honor was at stake and both expressed their sorrow and dismay over the broken promises.

Goyens died in June 1856 at the age of sixty-two and was buried in a Mexican cemetery. In 1936 the state of Texas placed a historical marker on Goyens' grave, five miles west of Nacogdoches.

By 1840 blacks in Texas experienced another drastic legal setback to their anticipated enjoyment of the fruits of their participation in the Texas Revolution. Texans, yielding to the pressure of the "peculiar institution," passed the Definitive Act of February 5, 1840,[39] which made it mandatory for all free blacks in Texas to leave the state within two years or be returned to slavery. A few years earlier, in 1836, the republic became alarmed at the large number of free blacks who were aligning with the Mexican government. Most alarming were the escapades of Nat Turner and Denmark Vesey, who led insurrections. This act precluded the annexation of Texas, clouded blacks' future as free men in Texas, and made further sojourn in the wilderness untenable. Being black, free, or a foreign citizen was enough to warrant enslavement. On several occasions the British recovered from the crews of British vessels blacks who had unlawfully been brought to Texas by being sold.[40]

In spite of the severity of the act excluding free blacks from Texas, many were allowed to remain by special efforts of friends or by those who had compassion for the oppressed. An article in *Southwestern Historical Quarterly* tells how Augustine M. Tomkins, a slaveholder, "successfully defended a group of free Negroes (in court) who were charged with violating the laws of the country by remaining in Texas."[41]

One of the most prominent blacks who was granted special permission to remain in Texas was Aaron Ashworth. He came to Texas in 1833 and eventually owned the largest ranch in what are now Orange and Jefferson Counties; he also owned 27,500 head of cattle. His affluence enabled him to purchase slaves and hire tutors for his children. He became one of the most influential ranchers in all of east Texas and was a staunch supporter and a generous contributor of funds and property in support of the Texans' struggle for independence. As a result of his outstanding service, Ashworth was recognized as a prominent citizen so much so that when the Definitive Act of 1840 was passed by the Texas legislature, requiring all Blacks to leave Texas, Ashworth's neighbors interceded. A special act by the Texas Congress permitted Ashworth to remain in Texas and retain ownership of his land.[42]

The Definitive Act of 1840 became the political barometer which forecast an intensification of sectional rivalry between the slaveholding and non-slaveholding states. The United States had played a vital role in helping American settlers revolt successfully against Mexico, and, by Texas legislating against free blacks remaining within its borders, validated its proslavery leaning. Southern expansionists, who had political and economic interest in the new republic, risked a major war with Mexico by annexing Texas.

War came with Mexico in 1845 as dominant Southern congressmen attempted to extend the United States' western territorial corral for the expansion of slavery. The Americans emerged victorious and the Treaty of Guadalupe Hidalgo, 1848, which ended the war, dampened black hopes of achieving liberty and freedom in Texas. The American tradition of freedom was submerged in the despotism of slave power and land speculators who were determined to revive the slave trade and extend and perpetuate involuntary servitude.

Plantations demanded black slave labor. Thus, as Earl Wesley Farnell explains in his book on the Galveston era, "when the State Democratic Convention opened in Houston on May 4, 1859, the issue of the slave trade was the dominating factor."[43] Ferdinand Flake, publisher of *Die Union*, called the Democrats State Rights Clubs, Slave Clubs.[44]

Civil War and Reconstruction

In Texas, black men were the principal but nonparticipating actors in the divisive drama which tore the nation asunder in 1860. Very little fighting was done on Texas soil. With the exception of Sibley's expedition into New Mexico in 1861, the capture of Galveston by Union forces, 1862-63, and the repulse of United States forces at Sabine Pass, 1863, there was no fighting in this part of the Southwest.

Occasionally blacks were victims of impressment and were forced to serve with Confederate soldiers in labor battalions. Searches were often made in the Big Wood settlement in east Texas for blacks who were coming through this state, and those captured were impressed to cut wood for Confederate steamers.[45] Others were used as teamsters. Prominent planters who were liable for military duty furnished black drivers in exchange for exemption from military service.[46] None of the blacks would volunteer to fight on the side of those who were doing their utmost to destroy the fabric of union and who fought for their continued enslavement. Blacks lingered in the shadow of hope, waiting for deliverance to come by a victorious Union army. "Flight became the most effective means of resistance,"[47] Wendell Addington says in his article "Slave Insurrections in Texas," and many joined the Union soldiers to tip the military scales against their claimants and aid in attaining their own freedom.

Others participated with sympathetic whites in planning general insurrections such as occurred in Brenham, Texas, August 6, 1860. Several blacks and whites were taken into custody by the Washington County Vigilance Committee on suspicion of conspiring to take over the town.[48] What action was taken by the vigilantes remains unknown.

Incendiary plots by white abolitionists and blacks were widespread in 1860. On July 17, 1860, a white man, William H. Crawford, was lynched in Fort Worth on suspicion of being an abolitionist conspirator,[49] and the Reverend Anthony Beweley was lynched near the Jacksboro Highway, north of Fort Worth, because he was accused of tampering with the slaves. Most plots were politically motivated by Texans who were disenchanted with the Republican Party's national platform and conspired to create havoc on Election Day, August 1860. Some blacks testified that poison "was to be administered in the food at breakfast and deposited in the wells and springs."[50] Fire and devastation was to reduce and paralyze northern Texas and culminate in a general revolt of slaves.[51]

On July 8, 1860, arsonists destroyed the entire northwestern section of Dallas, Texas; one half-hour later incendiary fires began in Denton, Texas, and then in Pilot Point, Denton County; Ladonia, Fannin County; and Milford, Ellis County. The continuous threat of slave revolts and divisiveness between slaveholders and Republicans inspired abolitionists, who kept tensions high and created a schism which plagued military unity in this sectional conflict.

The Texans on the frontier did not wholeheartedly support the South, and as soon as military reverses became commonplace for Confederate soldiers, they deserted in large numbers. "The number of citizens disloyal to the Confederacy along the frontier was astonishingly high[52]...on one occasion eighty-eight of Dellure's regiment, near Crockett, deserted in a body."[53] Confederate forces capitulated with the surrender of Lee to Grant at Appomattox on April 9, and by May 10, Jefferson Davis was a prisoner of war. "Although the war was over, the 62nd U.S. Colored Infantry engaged in a minor skirmish in Texas on May 13, with recalcitrant rebels. Sergeant Crockett, a Negro, is believed to have been the last man to shed blood in the Civil War."[54] The surrender of General Kirby Smith on June 2, 1865, signaled the end of the War of Secession for Texas and the beginning of a slow process of gradual liberation for blacks.

Lincoln issued his Emancipation Proclamation on January 1, 1863, declaring all slaves to be freed. Because of intentional delays and poor communications, blacks in Texas did not receive the official notice until June 19, 1865, when General Granger proclaimed it upon his arrival at the port of Galveston. This historic day, now called Juneteenth, that ended the depersonalized economic traffic in human beings and set in motion a social upheaval in American society is still celebrated by blacks in Texas. This was a festive occasion and many white farmers excused black laborers from work and provided cattle and hogs for big community barbecues. For many years in Fort Worth, the Armour and Swift packing companies sponsored picnics in all-black Greenway Park. Later on, blacks were permitted to use the facilities of Forest Park for celebration on this one day.

Brenham, Texas, once held the biggest Juneteenth celebration in the state; railroad excursions from Fort Worth and Dallas were the vogue of the day. From 1950 to 1960 the biggest excitement was in Limestone County, Commanche Crossing, Mexia, Texas which became the mecca for blacks all over the United States who thronged to this small community to commemorate the day of liberation. Church services, oratories, dancing, drinking, barbecuing, all were part of the panorama of liberation and freedom.

In the 1970s a large number of blacks in north Texas were attracted to the Texas State Fair Juneteenth Jamboree in Dallas, and all over Texas blacks commemorated this Black Jubilee. But the most spectacular is the revitalized observance in Fort Worth. In 1974 more than 10,000 blacks thronged into Sycamore Park in observance of Juneteenth. The Economic Development Board, headed by the Reverend Henry Masters, laid elaborate plans for the celebration and highlighted by a parade, speeches, and exhibits; it was a tremendous success.

Plans were begun immediately to expand the activities, and in 1975 more than 18,000 persons milled in the same park and created traffic jams far into the night. This sudden surge of interest is the result of black pride, engendered by new dimensions of historical awareness and perspectives reaffirmed in the civil rights movement of the 1970s.

A special historical note should be made at this point that in 1980, State Representative Al Edwards of Houston successfully passed a bill which made Juneteenth (Emancipation Day) one of the four official state holidays. This author was one of the principal supporters of its passage in the black caucus. This legislation rekindled the flame of freedom and etched on the stone of memory the historic presence of American aspirations and freedom.

Why the long delay in notifying the slaves in Texas about their freedom? Most whites anticipated vindictive retaliation for their previous condition of servitude from the newly freed blacks and were apprehensive about freeing them. Intensified racial unrest remained unabated throughout the war, as was evident along the Brazos River.

At the close of the war in July 1865, Brenham, Texas, was made a military post. Black troops stationed at Camptown, "from which circumstances this colored addition to Brenham derives its name,"[55] were viewed as a threat to racial peace. The white citizenry were incensed over blacks wearing guns and having the authority of the U.S. army behind them.

A major incident broke out on the evening of September 6, 1866. Black soldiers, accompanied by black women, entered a ballroom where a dance was in progress. The Southerners resented the blacks entering the dance hall and a fight ensued. Two federal soldiers were wounded and one was killed. The entire block in which the dance hall was located was burned to the ground by the drunken black soldiers.

In anticipation of the chaos and confusion that would follow in the wake of the newly freed blacks being emancipated, a Bureau of Refugees, Freedmen and Abandoned Land had been established by President Andrew Johnson through a general court order of the War Department. On September 21, 1865, at Galveston, Texas, General E. M. Gregory became the assistant commissioner for the Freedmen's Bureau in Texas. Other under-commissioners were stationed at Marshall, Austin, Victoria, Brenham, Columbia, Hempstead, Anderson, Courtney, Woodville, Millican, Leona, Inianda, Wilson County, and Wharton. All commissioners were ordered to publicize the Emancipation Proclamation.

White resentment and overt resistance to the activities of the Bureau increased in magnitude until the organization was unable to effectively help blacks on a large scale make the transformation into the majority of American society. Former slaveholders were most antagonistic to Bureau commissioners who attempted to protect the freedom from peonage through quasi-legal contracts. They took advantage of the illiterate blacks who were in many cases coerced into signing perpetual contracts of labor that recapitulated their former condition of servitude. Even then, after working, they received no pay for their labor. William E. Strong, Inspector General of the Freedmen's Bureau, reported on January 1, 1866, that, "two-thirds of the freedmen in the section of the country through which [I have] passed [Texas and all the Southwest] [have] not been paid one cent in wages since they were set free."[56] To intimidate and compel blacks to work without compensation, they were "beaten daily and shot at will by gangs of cutthroats that infested the country.... The freedmen were held down by the shotgun and six-shooter."[57]

An ironic twist to this type of activity is that in spite of hostilities toward blacks, many of them had used the shotgun and six-shooter to protect white frontiersmen against marauding Indians. While the Civil War was raging, Indians in the West took advantage of the preoccupation of federal troops with putting down the rebellion of the South and conducted a number of sorties to reclaim large segments of land previously taken by white settlers. To resist this threatening offensive by the Indians, Congress passed legislation in July 1866 reorganizing the army to include black soldiers who had fought valiantly in the War Between the States. The act stipulated that white officers could be in command of the black regiments and a policy developed where these ebony soldiers would be assigned to duty in the West. This would provide a safety valve for the racial tension that inevitably developed whenever blacks were armed and given authority.

By 1867 a full-scale Indian war was taking place. It took black men of the Ninth Cavalry stationed at Brownsville, Texas, and the Tenth Cavalry in central Kansas to help quell the Indian uprising. These Buffalo Soldiers assisted in achieving peaceful settlement of the Central Plains…West Texas, and Rio Grande Valley.[58] They provided reasonably safe passage to the stagecoaches and wagon trains transversing the canyon of the Davis Mountains, gateway to New Mexico and California. Fort Davis was manned for many years by the tough Buffalo Soldiers who kept the Apaches in check by patrolling western overland routes and helped the white man in the war of extermination of the Indians.[59] Some of these soldiers later became cowboys on the western ranges.

The saga of the black cowboy must not go unnoticed in the history of Texas. Those blacks who played dramatic and unheralded roles in the territory beyond the continental divide were from the Lone Star State. They all began their trade as slaves when their masters moved to Texas and acquired cattle. Valuable skills in riding, roping, and handling cattle were learned from the Native Americans and Mexicans. Jim Kelly, a black who worked for the Olive family, is credited with being one of the best horse trainers in the state. He was typical of the black cowboys who had a "disciplined sense of equality and pride of race."[60]

An article in a 1968 issue of *Ebony* asserted that "The Negro buckaroo, the rider and roper and wrangler was as good—and as bad—as the white cowboy."[61] Occasionally, when blacks are recognized as cowboys, they are stereotyped as being house servants and cooks. In truth, most cooks on the range were ex-cowboys of any nationality who were unable to do hard riding because of injury or age.

After the Civil War, "the Negro cowboy moved out across the Plains to play a significant role in the development of the cattle industry and became a part of the Spirit of the West…a spirit which demanded a conscience but cared little for color."[62] His survival lay in his equestrian skill and his quickness with the gun. In some areas of the West there were two kinds of people—the quick and the dead.

It was in Loraine, Texas, that "80 John" became a black legend in his time and an example of the West's occasional disregard of the stigma of color. The fratricidal conflict over slavery was reaching the boiling point when Webster Wallace was born September 15, 1860. His mother was purchased as chattel in Missouri and brought to Victoria County, Texas. By age 15, Wallace had been thoroughly schooled in the ways of the frontier. He was an excellent wrangler and cowhand and was exposed to the complex operation of a ranch by working for Clay Mann in New Mexico and Texas. He established habits of thrift: while the other wranglers were going on gambling and drinking sprees in the saloons, Wallace would go back to camp and save his money.

When Clay Mann decided to settle in the present site of Colorado City, Texas, his cattle were branded with a huge "80" on their sides. From this brand Wallace acquired the name "80 John," by which he was known throughout the cattle ranges of Texas.[63]

This black man of the sage witnessed the laying of the rails which brought the Texas and Pacific to Colorado City. Land adjacent to the railroads was offered for sale and 80 John purchased two sections of land that would represent the beginning of his enterprise.

Because John was well respected by many ranchers, he became a member of the Texas Southwestern Association.[64]

Investing in land and cattle, 80 John became one of the wealthiest ranchmen in West Texas. He died in 1939, leaving more than 10,000 acres of land to his heirs.

Other blacks who were freed or born when Big John was born were not so fortunate. Their ability to make reasonable progress after the war diminished because of the hatred engendered by the Civil War and the sudden emancipation of the slaves which deprived whites of free labor. So traumatic was emancipation that many masters suffered racial psychosis. Anne Multer, a newly freed black, witnessed the mental anguish of her master shortly before he committed suicide. He raved and screamed that he "would not live in a country in which blacks were free."[65]

Discontent intensified in Texas because the army would not provide plantation owners and small farmers with a supply of black labor.[66] In spite of local opposition, the army was able to gradually establish schools for the freedmen, and some of these institutions have survived until this century. Schools for freedmen were not established where the army was not present;[67] the Bureau left Texas in 1868. Most rural and poor whites did not educate their children and resented the newly freed blacks' exposure to education.[68]

Blacks Enter the
National Political Arena

Meshack Roberts had served his master faithfully in a community near Gilmer during the Civil War, producing sufficient food to take care of his master's family for the duration. Roberts was granted his freedom because of his meritorious service. He accepted his new freedom by assuming responsibility for organizing black participation in the political life of the community.

Texas was readmitted to the Union on March 30, 1870, after the legislature ratified the thirteenth, fourteenth, and fifteenth amendments. The Union League came into Texas in 1871 as the political arm of the Republican Party; its primary purpose was to "master" the votes from a total of 253,475 black citizens. Northern politicians utilized the freedmen's enfranchisement to remain in power, but in the former Confederate states, blacks broke the all-white pattern of state and local government. On January 14, 1873, Meshack Roberts was sworn in as one of five men of color elected to the thirteenth legislature.[69] His ephemeral participation came to an end in the same year with the defeat of Governor Davis by Governor Coke. This signified the end of Reconstruction and carpetbag rule in Texas.

The Ku Klux Klan then became the extra-legal law of the land. Blacks were threatened, whipped, and killed in order to make them virtually slaves once again. The wrath of the Klan was turned on Roberts and he fled to Marshall, Texas.

Marshall, Texas, had been the citadel of Confederate strength in eastern Texas during the Civil War. The headquarters of the Trans-Mississippi Department of the Confederacy of Blacks sought protection of the victorious United States Army under the watchful eye of the Freedmen's Bureau. When Meshack Roberts fled to Marshall, he had time to reflect on the basic needs of the newly freed slaves, which were, in fact, his own needs. He had not had the advantages of education, and the ex-Senator could neither read nor write.[70] He influenced the Freedmen's Aid Society to provide the only advanced school to train blacks for the ministry for the Methodist Episcopal Church[71] and played a significant role in the initial organization of Wiley College in 1873.[72] The school was later chartered by the Freedmen's Aid Society in 1882.

Another black who was interested in education was Norris Wright Cuney. He used politics and business to carve a cultural niche for blacks in Texas. His boyhood was spent along the Brazos, the oasis of black culture. Cuney was born May 12, 1864, at Sunnyvale Plantation (Waller County), which was owned by his father, Colonel Philip Cuney. The young lad attended school in Pittsburgh, Pennsylvania, until the Civil War interrupted his education in 1861.

After the war, the Cuney family returned to Galveston, and the young Cuney was appointed first Assistant Sergeant-at-Arms of the twelfth Texas Legislature[73] and used his influence in the furtherance of educational opportunities for blacks. He helped sponsor a bill which led to the establishment of Prairie View State Normal and Industrial Institute on Colonel Kirby's plantation near Hempstead, Texas. When the legislature was not in session, Cuney served as one of the school directors for Galveston County, a position to which he was appointed in 1871.

But Cuney's interest was in the political rank and file of the Republican Party. In 1875 he was nominated for Mayor of Galveston but lost to the Democratic nominee, R. L. Fulton. Undaunted by this defeat, his prestige served to restore harmony to Galveston when the city was plagued by racial tension. When Galveston was faced with a serious confrontation between white and black strikers in 1876, Cuney became the prime mediator between the two groups. He urged the blacks to disperse and the strike came to a peaceful end.

In 1880 Cuney was elected a delegate to the Republican National Convention in Chicago, in which he supported the unsuccessful candidature of James C. Blaine. At the state convention, which met August 23 to 24, Wright Cuney and Dick Allen were named as the persons to unite the Republicans in Texas.[74] The former was a likely choice because in 1879 he held the dike against the flood of blacks who were joining the Republican Party. In that same year Cuney became a candidate for the 66th District (Galveston, Brazoria, Matagorda, and Wharton counties) and again was not successful. This loss made Cuney turn his attention to a business venture.

Cuney entered the stevedore business in 1883. He employed some five hundred Negro men and later organized an association of longshoremen, which drew the ire of white longshoremen. Blacks were used as "scabs" when white longshoremen struck against the Mallory Lines in Galveston. Mobs threatened the life of Cuney and other blacks. Hatred and prejudice directed toward blacks had become a way of life, to keep them economically and politically subordinated. A meeting decrying the servile status of blacks was held July 10, 1883, in Houston to deal with the growing and menacing problem to black workers.[75]

Through the persistent efforts of Cuney, law and order miraculously prevailed in the Mallory strike, and a compromise was agreed upon whereby black longshoremen would unload two vessels per week and white longshoremen of the Knights of Labor, two per week. There was a gradual lessening of bitterness on both sides and a disposition to return to more just and peaceful methods was secured.

With each successful settling of the problems in Galveston, the prestige of Cuney skyrocketed in the estimations of both black and white citizens. After an Alderman's election filled with fraudulent manipulation of votes, Cuney was elected on the Citizen's ticket, April 29, 1885. He was a key supporter of a special charter amendment that altered the structure of Galveston's government. The city was divided into six wards, with one alderman elected from each ward and six from the city at large. This was a progressive plan and one adopted and modified by several cities.

By 1886 the immutable roar of racism spread like wildfire across the plains of Texas. An eighteen-year-old Negro was lynched in Comanche, Texas, for the murder of a Mrs. Ben Stephens of that city. While the heat of racial passion flowed high, agitators vented their hostilities on the blacks and ordered all of them to get out of town in ten days or be killed.[76] Blacks left the west Texas town and as late as 1970 no blacks were listed in the census,[77] a source of lily-white pride for some of the citizens of Comanche[78]. In Richmond, Texas, organized mobs took possession of the town and thoroughly intimidated the colored people who remained.[79] This signaled the beginning of organized resistance to the political ambitions of blacks. Cuney was quickly recognized as the black leader to be reckoned with, and a concerted attempt was made by the opposition to strip Cuney of his influence in Texas.

Racial prejudice worked successfully in keeping Cuney from being elected to local office, but he maintained his standing with the national party. Cuney was invited to the inauguration of Benjamin Harrison in 1889, to the chagrin of many white Texans. The next year, when President Harrison came to Texas, the black leader occupied a conspicuous place of honor in the festivities honoring the president. Galveston harvested political fruit and that city was given appropriations for river, naval, and harbor improvements. A customs house was built and Norris Wright Cuney was appointed its first collector. General Clarkson persuaded Harrison that Cuney was a worthy person and endorsed by the businessmen of Galveston.[80] This sentiment was expressed again in 1893 when Grover Cleveland was elected and petitioned by citizens of Galveston for Cuney to remain as collector. Nevertheless, he was replaced by a Democrat.

Cuney's influence began to decline in 1890 when an interracial phenomena erupted within the Republican Party. White Republicans balked at the idea of being led by black men, and this divisiveness strengthened the Democrats in Texas;[81] later, in 1896, Cuney's dwindling power was dealt a death blow by the national Republicans when he supported the nomination of William R. Allison of Iowa against that of William McKinley. Mark Hanna despaired of winning Cuney over to the McKinley camp and through manipulations of the credentials committee at the national convention in St. Louis, Missouri, refused to seat the Allison-Read Texas delegation of which Cuney was a member.

The true character of Cuney comes to the surface at this time in his political life: his unyielding stand for the principles he believed in, in spite of monetary and prestigious gains he could have had by "jumping on the bandwagon"; instead he remained loyal to the Republican Party and sustained fidelity to his friends in Texas. Most of his life had been spent in fearlessly championing the cause of racial equality and human rights. As an article on Cuney explains, "He departed from partisanship when a matter of rights was involved."[82]

In 1897 Cuney died. In an eulogy of the leader, William H. McDonald said, "The Negro race looked for and needed a man worthy to lead them—looked for a man who was a ripe student, who had the audacity of genius, and was a good combination of heart, conscience and brain."[83]

What William McDonald saw in Cuney also alluded to himself. He was born on the threshold of Reconstruction to ex-slave parents, June 22, 1866, at College Mound, sixteen miles east of Kaufman, Kaufman County. McDonald's mother died when he was five years old. His father later remarried and the young lad began his education by attending a three-month school. At eight years of age he became a houseboy and court courier to attorney Captain A. T. Adams. His experience in court was a very early contribution to the lively mind which took from all and gave more back than it took.

William McDonald graduated at the top of his class in the spring of 1884, delivered the valedictory speech, and immediately was hired as principal of a school in Forney, Texas. After deciding to leave the teaching profession, William McDonald wrote "Thesis on Moral Philosophy" and in 1905 was awarded the degree of Doctor of Philosophy by Paul Quinn College in Waco, Texas.[84]

A highlight of McDonald's career was his leadership in the organization of the "Texas Colored State Fair Association, the first State Fair in the Lone Star State."[85] This fair was designed to provide an agricultural showcase for the farmers' products and culinary and sewing works of art. This appealed to whites and blacks alike and many cities competed to host the spectacular event. The first one was held in Fort Worth, October 15, 1887. The Honorable S. L. Ross, governor of Texas, escorted by the Texas Colored Militia, was the outstanding dignitary who formally opened the fair. Permanent location of the fair was made in Marshall, Texas, in 1889 and McDonald remained superintendent of the association until he turned his attention to politics, which occupied a major part of his interest.

McDonald vaulted into political power in 1888 when he became the guiding hand behind the political campaign of E. H. R. Green, a publicity-seeker aspiring to a position as national committeeman.[86] Green was the son of Hetty Green, "the witch of Wall Street," a railroad magnate who sent her son to manage the Texas-Midland Railroad.

In 1890 McDonald was appointed county chairman of the Republican Party, which had its strongest support in east and south Texas. He endeavored to forestall racial division of the party and heroically fought the "lily white" movement in Texas. So persistent were his efforts that he attracted the attention of his constituents and they elected him as delegate from Kaufman County to the Republican state convention in Dallas, April 12, 1892. He was also among the 120 black delegates to the Republican national convention in Minneapolis in the same year. According to William Oliver Bundy, "In 1894 McDonald was made State Chairman and from that time to 1912, a period of eighteen years, was the foremost Republican leader of the great commonwealth of Texas."[87]

During the state elections of 1896, McDonald switched his political support to Governor Culberson, a Democrat, because, in his opinion, blacks would receive more benefits from Culberson. They did benefit, because when Culberson took office, he donated 50,000 acres of land for a Negro state university. A. W. Jackson asserts that McDonald "looked beyond the emoluments of office and served his state for the good of humanity."[88] He rejected a coalition with the populists and was responsible for their demise in Texas.

At the GOP National Convention in St. Louis in 1896, a nickname was given to William Madison McDonald by a reporter. The reporter wrote, "There is a colored man here from Kaufman, Texas, by the name of McDonald. He has an Irish name, but is a kind of goose-necked Negro, evidently, as smart as a whip."[89] Time proved that "Gooseneck Bill" was a shrewd businessman, a crafty politician, and a believer in black self-help.

In 1921 he established the Fraternal Bank and Trust Company, which was the depository for the 22,334 blacks in Fort Worth and the large number of Negro Masonic Lodges throughout the state of Texas. These lodges developed out of a basic socioeconomic need of blacks to provide for themselves interrelated social amusement, religious solidarity, and benevolent economic stability which they did not have in the post-Civil War period.

McDonald was elected in 1899 as the Grand Secretary of the Masonic Lodges and held that office until 1925 because of his ability to make the lodges financially sound.[90] He always admonished blacks that if they wanted stores, "go establish such stores," if they wished for black editors, "go and establish a black paper," if they wanted to manage great business concerns and great enterprises, "go establish them."[91] When McDonald died on July 4, 1950, his estate was valued in excess of $100,000. McDonald is buried in the black section of Oakwood Cemetery, which opened in 1879 and was donated by the pioneer and civic leader John Peter Smith. McDonald has the tallest monument, a fifty-five-foot granite spire, a symbol of segregation to the last breadth.

In his eulogy of McDonald, Reverend S. R. Prince, pastor of the Mt. Pisgah Baptist Church of Fort Worth, lamented the fact that the deceased had also been trained as a minister but was well known for his invectives against the men of the cloth, whom he thought were grafters and not high honorable men.[92] Consequently, he chose not to preach and had turned to business and politics.

Political leadership in Texas of the kind exemplified by McDonald had been sporadic in nature, but the most consistent leadership has been that of the black minister. Freedmen and slaves brought to Texas from the Deep South institutionalized religious concepts and experiences which they used to ease the hardships endured in their chattel condition.

The phalanx of ministers who have helped blacks bridge the chasm of second-class citizenship is too numerous to enumerate, but several pioneer contributions must not go unnoticed. One is that of the Reverend Lacey K. Williams. The migratory instinct and the intrepid spirit of the parents of Lacey Kirk Williams moved them from Alabama to Texas. Williams' father, Levi, became a black impresario and, despite severe hardships, sailed from Algiers, Alabama, to Galveston, Texas, and thence traveled overland to Bryan and the Brazos Bottom.

The land here was rich and productive, but ownership of the land was withheld from the freedmen so that the new immigrants had to become sharecroppers. Ronald Walters writes, "In the South, whites resisted the drives by the Freedmen's Bureau to make small farmers out of thousands of Blacks. They were willing to see the emphasis placed on Black labor, not on Black ownership."[93] In this environment, Levi initiated the move to organize a church and school for the sharecroppers. In 1880 the River Lane Public School was established in Burleson County.

Lacey left the Brazos and went to Waco, Texas, which was already a thriving city. There he found employment and later an opportunity to teach. He passed the Burleson County Board teacher's examination and was awarded a certificate to teach the second grade. In spite of his zeal for teaching, Lacey felt a deeper passion for the ministry, and he became licensed to preach in December 1894. As a licensed preacher, Lacey became the acclaim of Texas; those who heard him requested his services. This demand soon took its toll of Lacey's physical well being. He spent three months in Colorado Springs for meditation and to recover his health. Lacey returned to Temple, Texas, the black center of Bell County, just as an epidemic of smallpox swept the county, and Lacey again succumbed to illness.

When Lacey recuperated from his illness, he turned his mind to the furtherance of his education and in 1902 matriculated at Bishop College, Marshall, Texas, and was called to the pastorate of Mount Gilead Baptist Church of Fort Worth in 1910. He became a bishop in 1912. In Fort Worth Lacey expanded Mount Gilead into one of the finest sanctuaries in all of north Texas. He also became leader of the largest body of black churches in Texas, the Texas Baptist Foreign Mission Convention. His outstanding leadership ability became distinctive as Williams worked very closely with the (white) Southern Baptist Convention in promoting racial harmony and goodwill between the races.

The voice of this exponent of racial harmony and religious messages was articulated in two newspapers edited and published by Williams, the *Dallas Express* and *Western Star*. He was most vociferous in his denunciation of the liquor traffic and became one of the leading prohibitionists in Texas.

When L. K. Williams launched a new building program for Mount Gilead, he met resistance from white property-owners downtown and was warned not to build. He offered the whites the building site for $20,000. No one took the offer and the Mount Gilead Baptist Church was built in the downtown section and remains there to this very day at 600 Grove Street. It is a symbol of the courage, devotion, and faith of a black minister who had an uncompromising faith in God. The magnificent edifice built on Fifth and Grove streets attracted white residents to the Sunday services, and Williams' influence continued to promote racial harmony in this city. This lasted until 1916, when Williams was called to the Olivet Baptist Church in Chicago, Illinois, and finally to be president of the National Baptist Convention.

The year that Norris Cuney died and Bill McDonald had reached the zenith of his career, a significant change in black-white relations seemed to have taken place in Texas and the entire United States. The U.S. Supreme Court tempered its judgment in its historic "separate but equal doctrine" in *Plessy v. Ferguson* and gave legal sanction to a partial elevation of human rights. Mark Hanna and President William McKinley directed this nation's interest to Cuba and the Philippines to share in the economic sphere of influence dominated by the major European powers. Some black observers, like James Weldon Johnson, felt that the subsequent Spanish-American War reflected national concern about people of color who were victims of oppression. Blacks such as Hugh McElroy, a Texan, played important roles at San Juan Hill and in bringing the conflict o a victorious ending.[94] But it was evident that after the war this racial concern was not genuine and did not extend to the blacks in Texas.

The Brownsville affray was an event which alienated the black community from Theodore Roosevelt and was the prelude to things to come, where white supremacy would remain the basic tenet for America. The ever-present racism which overshadows the American nation came to the forefront in August 1906 when Theodore Roosevelt flexed his domestic "Big Stick" and without civil or military trial summarily court-martialed three companies of black soldiers at Fort Brown (Brownsville, Texas) who comprised the Twenty-fifth Infantry.

Animosity of white citizens had been rekindled on August 1, 1906, when the black infantrymen arrived in Brownsville from duty at Niobrara, Nebraska. The local citizenry resented armed black soldiers and set out to demonstrate their opposition, hostility, and displeasure. An inspector of customs, Mr. Tate, struck Corporal Newton, a soldier, on the head with a revolver when the black trooper didn't get out of his way quickly enough. Sergeant Reed and another soldier were knocked in a ditch for apparently no reason at all. And, to add to the tension, on August 12, a white girl claimed she had been intimidated by black soldiers.[95]

Even though Major Charles Penrose, commander of the fort, had restricted all but two of his men to their quarters and all had answered the roll calls, local authorities reported that from nine to twenty soldiers had slipped out of the fort about midnight and attacked the town. An unsubstantiated report also stated that

> they went through the town, shooting whomsoever they saw moving and firing into houses wherever they saw lights. They fired upon and hit in the arm the lieutenant of police...fired also at two policemen, killed one bartender man in a saloon and wounded another, and came very near to killing several women and children.[96]

No one actually saw the black soldiers return to camp, but white witnesses and circumstantial evidence convinced army investigators that some of the blacks must have participated.[97]

The prosecution was unable to verify by ballistic tests the rifles used by the soldiers and a grand jury in Brownsville, Texas, failed to find true bills against the prisoners.[98] Relying on reports by Texas Ranger Captain Bill McDonald and Major August P. Blocksom, Roosevelt ordered a summary court martial of all the black soldiers regardless of their involvement. He did not concern himself with the rights of blacks but maintained that "there can be nothing more important than for the United States Army in all its membership, to understand that its arms cannot be turned with impunity against the peace and order of the civil community."[99] These men were denied due process of law and never tried before the appropriate tribunal or, of course, a civil court.

To offset the political impact his handling of the situation at Brownsville would have on the congressional election on November 6, Roosevelt signed the Discharge Without Honor order on November 5 and held it until the day after the election. The northern black vote was crucial to many Republican congressmen who would have to face the ire of the black electorate over a Republican president who had turned his back on blacks in the United States.

Outrage continued unabated at the court-martial, and the incident was kept vociferously in focus by Senators Tillman and Foraker. They introduced a resolution in 1908 demanding an investigation of the episode and persisted so ably that the president in 1909 accepted a compromise measure setting up a special military court to hear those denying any implication in the incident.[100] Foraker offered impressive facts in support of the theory that the shooting had been the work of residents of Brownsville, who then placed the blame on the Twenty-fifth Infantry.[101] Of the eighty-four soldiers who testified before the tribunal, fourteen were finally declared eligible for reinstatement in the army.

One black soldier lived to see his name vindicated. Justice came sixty-six years later on his eighty-seventh birthday to Dorsie W. Willis, the only known living soldier who was a member of D Company, First Battalion, Twenty-fifth Infantry. He lived in Minneapolis, Minnesota, and shined shoes as a means of livelihood for fifty-nine years. Secretary of the Army Robert Forehke called the Brownsville case a "gross injustice" and ordered the discharges changed to honorable. During special services at the Zion Baptist Church on Sunday, February 11, 1973, Major-General DeWitt Smith and Lieutenant Colonel William Baker of the United States Army delivered Willis his honorable discharge certificate, which was back-dated to November 25, 1906.

The Brownsville episode clearly demonstrated that the black man had not gained political status in 1906 to guarantee him equal justice where whites were involved. Neither could he receive protection from local authorities from racial predators who objected to blacks organizing any kind of organization.

Longview, Texas, was the center of the most volatile racial confrontation in 1919. A black doctor, C. P. Davis, had organized the Negro Businessmen's League, and whites suspected that the motivation for the organization was a result of articles in an issue of the *Chicago Defender* newspaper. This paper carried stories of atrocities and urged black organization and resistance.

When a story appeared in one of its issues that a black youth who had been lynched for rape had actually had the consent of the girl and that they had been amorous in their affections for each other, the white residents, inflamed and armed, beat the writer of the story to a pulp, while the police looked on with approval and then ordered him to leave town. Later the mob went to the black section of Longview to do further harm but instead were met with gunfire; they retreated but returned in larger numbers and set fire to the black community. The police arrested six League members and sent out an all-points bulletin for the arrest of Dr. Davis. They also ordered every copy of the *Chicago Defender* destroyed and tried to arrest the father of the author of the original story. The violence continued until an outside militia came to Longview and peace was restored.

Blacks in Texas Politics

The black man's struggle for political equity in Texas has been a long and tedious one. From 1840 to the post-Reconstruction period, blacks lost considerable economic and political ground in this state. Texas broke its political affinity with the national Republicans in 1860 because local leaders did not support the principle of the abolition of slavery, the principal plank in the Republican platform. The North won the ensuing sectional struggle and the victory insured Republican domination for at least four more years. Simultaneously the black man had an opportunity to become an active participant in the politics of the state. Blacks constituted a new entity; they emerged from the nadir of slavery into a new arena of political opportunity. Before the Civil War, iron shackles adorned their hands; once the war came to an end, those hands held ballots.

Blacks wielded unusual influence in the Texas Republican Party during Reconstruction. They adhered to and gave allegiance to the party that mandated their emancipation. The state Republicans capitalized on the distrust blacks had for their former masters and organized the Union League in 1867 at Houston, Texas, as an adjunct to the Republican Party, to control the new group of freed blacks. There were 78,629 black voters in the state in 1885.[102] They benefited from the military rule imposed on Texas and other Southern states who refused to accept the Fourteenth Amendment as a condition of restoration to the Union. Too, overt acts of violence and lack of governmental protection of the blacks gave added incentives to radicals to inaugurate the vindictive congressional plan that placed Texas in the fifth Military District under General Philip Sheridan. The authorities in the military districts were to enroll all qualified voters, including blacks, and provide for a convention to draw up a state constitution.

When the state constitutional convention met in 1868, the radical Republicans named G. T. Ruby, one of the black delegates, permanent chairman of the convention. Ruby was a newspaper journalist from Haiti who had migrated to Texas in 1866 and had been elected a delegate to the convention. His political prowess and past activities as president of the state council of the Union League qualified him to attract the black votes.[103] He and Matt Gaines continued as the two leading black senators in the Texas legislature until 1870. However, the newly enfranchised freemen continued to play a subservient role in the political machine and never were able to elect blacks to top positions in the state government. A common practice was the use of a compiled delinquent tax list, from which lawyers sued blacks for a five-dollar poll tax. Democratic landowners who used elected officials to harass and intimidate blacks diminished their potential voting power. The threat of nocturnal visits from the Ku Klux Klan and the loss of property discouraged many blacks from voting. Coercive violence was the rule of law during 1870. Historians say that the trouble in Texas during this period of Reconstruction was due to the struggle between conservatives and radicals. It might be noted that these labels were misnomers to blacks. To them the conservatives were the radicals who maintained control by extra-legal means, including murder.

By 1870 Texas led the nation in homicides, with 323 deaths. Governor Edmond J. Davis sought permission and created a state police to help quell the lawlessness throughout Texas. A separate committee on lawlessness was appointed by Davis in 1868 and it was from subsequent reports from the committee that he created a military force and state police.[104] Much opposition was made to the proposal of Governor Davis because the State Police was to be racially integrated and included a large number of blacks. Whites resented blacks being used to keep the peace. The State Police was abolished in 1873 because of racial bias.[105]

The Klan became most active in the state election of December 1873 and elected as governor Richard Coke of Waco. He was backed solidly by the Ku Klux Klan, who were in the vanguard of the Democratic Party; they nullified the black vote in Texas. W. C. Nunn writes, "Radicals and freedmen declared that the Democrats were planning to re-enslave the Negro."[106]

Ed Davis received 42,663 votes and refused to recognize the final tabulation of 85,549 votes favoring Coke; neither would he vacate the seat of Governor of Texas in 1874. In *Ex Parte Rodriquez*, the Texas Supreme Court invalidated the election due to apparent fraud. The Democrats ignored the court's ruling and the Capitol building became an arsenal as Davis and Coke refused to give ground. President Grant refused to send troops to enforce compliances with the court order. Davis finally capitulated and allowed Coke to occupy the governor's seat.

Blacks felt the wrath of a government that supported and legalized white suppression of them throughout Texas. Coke continued in office another two years after being reelected in 1876.

Between 1874 and 1900, coalition groups developed with the Greenbacks, independents, and populists, who also attracted large numbers of blacks. They were especially active in Navasota, the cotton capital of Grimes County. The county census in 1890 revealed a total population of 21,312, of which 11,664 were black. Most of these blacks still retained their Republican allegiance, and local power though the Democrats had regained control of the state government. Grimes County blacks sent a succession of black legislators to Austin for the next decade.[107] In 1879 as many as eight black members were elected to the sixteenth legislature of Texas and local offices in predominantly black counties.

The vacillating pendulum then went the other way. Two years later black political power was almost nil; only one senator and four representatives in the seventeenth legislature were black. In 1884 the lily-white movement gained impetus and crystallized white political rejection of blacks. The Populist Party making substantial gains in state and county elections stimulated this rejection. Low-income white farmers who aligned themselves with blacks dominated the people's movement. The poll tax had been adopted in an attempt to minimize the effect of poor agrarian whites. The moneyed interest became alarmed at the black-white coalitions in the Populist Party, reunited around the banner of racism, and dethroned Cuney, who had gained political control of the political machinery in 1883.

Blacks attempted to help themselves and retaliated by becoming more involved in the

Granger movement. *The Book of Texas* states that "An alliance for Negroes was organized at Lovelady, Texas, in 1886 by R. M. Humphrey and spread through the South until it had a membership of more than a million...."[108] However, many of the benevolent groups were opposed to involving themselves in politics. R. S. Stout, the Grand Master of the Association for the Colored Farmer, said in an editorial that "we care for the sick, bury the dead, and care for the widows and orphans...nothing of that kind [politics] shall ever be brought into the Mutual Alliance Association of Texas."[109]

In the continuing struggle for political participation and power, black involvement invariably added a new dimension to the black-white relationship. Whenever a surge of black votes formed a distinct pattern of concentration as a potential balancer of power, whites laid aside their differences and took coercive and nonlegal methods to negate this power by disfranchising blacks. Disfranchisement was a mutual "white gentlemen's" agreement that neither of the political opponents would use the Negro's support against the other.[110] The Republicans in Texas finally defected and the Democrats, with consent of liberal white Republicans, emerged in 1899 as the dominant party in the political struggle in this state. This victory brought to a successful climax the efforts of the Jaybirds (regular Democrats) to end the influence of political black Republicans. They attempted to exclude blacks by duplicating the election process that nullified the purpose of the Fifteenth Amendment.

Occasionally, outstanding statesmen in Texas exemplified a high moral spirit of fair play and justice toward blacks, instead of a framework of degenerative political expediency. In 1890 James Stephen Hogg, a product of the Progressive Movement, noted for his fair play and opposition to lawlessness in any form, was elected governor of Texas. He advocated the cessation of lynching, equal educational opportunities, and enfranchisement of blacks long before Senator Roscoe Conklin proposed the Fourteenth Amendment to give blacks equal protection of the law.

Hogg often ignored the attempts of radical politicians to inject the race issue and maintained that "Negroes were in the country to stay....[E]conomic and political justice were their immediate concern rather than social equality."[111] Hogg's popularity among blacks soared to such an extent that Negro Hogg Clubs were organized. In spite of his liberal-conservative attitude toward blacks, however, Hogg could not stem the tide of racism that permeated this state.

In the white man's union, in the Texas legislature, a big controversy had developed in 1903 which had to do with the rights of blacks to vote under the Terrell Election Law. Some counties wanted them to be qualified to vote, while others were adamantly against blacks exercising the right of suffrage. Blacks were systematically relegated to nonvoting citizens, and by 1905 the Democrats had completed the political paralysis that blacks experienced prior to the Civil War.

From 1905 to 1944, black participation in politics remained stagnant. Southern Democrats continued the exclusion of blacks from party politics. They had the constitutional sanction of the state legislature that made the primary election the exclusive domain of whites. The legislature passed a bill signed by Governor James V. Allred that denied the eligibility of blacks to participate in a democratic election in this state. It provided that "in no event shall a Negro be eligible to participate in a Democratic primary election in the State of Texas, and should a Negro vote in a Democratic primary election, such ballot shall be void and election officials are herein directed to throw out such ballot and not count the same."[112]

This discriminatory legislation was challenged in 1924 by Dr. L. A. Nixon of *El Paso v. Herndon*, an election judge. The Supreme Court ruled that the act was in violation of the equal protection clause of the Fourteenth Amendment.[113] Undaunted by the court's action, Texas invalidated its unconstitutional statute and made a valiant effort to circumvent the decision by authorizing the State Executive Committee of the county Democratic convention in Dallas, Travis, and Harris counties.[114]

Homer P. Rainey, a former president of the University of Texas at Austin and a candidate in the primary election, slanted his "Little New Deal" platform toward the black community. This platform was attractive to many blacks, including the powerful Carter Wesley, who was one of the most influential blacks in the state. Wesley gave editorial support in his chain of newspapers to Rainey because he considered him a liberal candidate. But strained relations developed when the gubernatorial candidate suggested segregated polling places for black and white voters. Wesley suggested, "Blacks go fishing."

Many, however, did take advantage of the opportunity to vote. This was the first time that blacks voted in the democratic primary in Texas, and they were not going to neglect this opportunity. From a total of 1.5 million votes, it was estimated that 50,000 to 90,000 were black votes, and Rainey carried 85 percent of that vote.[115] Nevertheless, Beauford Jester, his opponent, who also campaigned vigorously in the black community, was victorious. He won 1,366,146 to Rainey's 233,235.

The new overtures of whites and black votes were ephemeral attempts to guarantee success at the polls. White politicians enticed the so-called black leaders in the major cities to initiate the leadership in their communities.

Black leadership came primarily from the ministers, who had weekly contact with their parishioners and addressed captivated or ready-made audiences each Sunday. But the influence on the party has remained passively ineffective because of the lack of cohesive unanimity among blacks to compensate for their small demographic ratio to the white population. Too, black organizations are not financially self-sustaining; they tend to become pawns of white groups who can pour more money into black coffers and direct black leadership the way they want. A case in point is that of Valmo Bellinger of San Antonio, who has been part of the maverick machine for the past decade and has been able to deliver black votes.

A large segment of whites was unrelenting in its efforts to disengage blacks from the political machine of the Democratic Party in Texas. The ultraconservatives renewed their effort to nullify the political power of blacks by resorting to the pre-primary.[116] The Jaybirds, a county political organization, had used this procedure since 1889 in Fort Bend County, Texas. The names of the nominees who ran under the auspices of the Jaybirds were automatically placed on the state primary ballot; thus, only whites participated in this exclusive elective process.

The process was immediately challenged, and the High Tribunal ruled in 1953 that Texas' pact with the Jaybirds was invalid. It maintained that a state cannot approve an "electoral process in a form which permits a private organization to practice racial discrimination in the election."[117]

In 1952 Coke Stevenson capitalized on the availability of black voters by adopting a low-key civil rights position and consequently earned 90 percent of black votes. He changed his civil rights position again in 1956 to the conservative traditionalism of Texas and his appeal to blacks diminished considerably.[118] The rural concentration of blacks in east Texas who voted for Stevenson was vulnerable to the political manipulations of white politicians. The rural sections of Texas neutralized black political power by making it ineffective.

Typical of this situation is Marion County, where blacks constitute more than 50 percent of the population. The majority of them are in the older age bracket and accept the paternalism of whites as a way of life. They are not as demanding as the young blacks, who continuously migrate to the urban centers. Political aspirations are channeled within the dominant political party and the economic needs of blacks are used as a basis of manipulation keeping them powerless.[119]

Occasionally, blacks have organized on a statewide basis in an attempt to influence the politics of this state. In 1962 the United Political Organization held a conclave in Austin, Texas, under the aegis of M. J. Anderson to support John Connally for governor. This was a group of precinct workers and black leaders from the major cities of the state who took advantage of the political gestures of the Democratic nominee and made plans to reinforce black political power throughout the state. Most participants were caught up in the move in this state toward liberalism, which found labor more sophisticated, and the Latinos and blacks finally beginning to wield organized minority power.[120] They had the opportunity to become full partners and participate in the affairs of every political subdivision of the states. From the smallest hamlet to the larger metropolitan communities, blacks were influencing the history of the state.

The election of the Reverend Zan W. Holmes, Jr. to the Texas state legislature in 1968 marked the beginning of blacks in North Texas making significant inroads into the economic and political arenas of this state. He succeeded state representative Joseph Lockridge, the first black elected to the legislature from Dallas in 1967 and killed in a plane crash May 3, 1968. Reverend Holmes was the first pastor of Hamilton Park United Methodist Church from 1958 to 1968 in the upscale, planned-housing community for middle-class blacks in Richardson in North Dallas County, and was well known in all the black communities in Dallas.

Reverend Holmes was born in 1935 in San Angelo, Texas, and his family moved to Austin, where he graduated in 1952 from Anderson High School. He received his Bachelor of Arts degree from Huston-Tillotson College in 1956. Being a student who believed in "scholarship and love for all mankind," the scholar became affiliated with Alpha Phi Alpha Fraternity, the first and oldest black fraternity in the United States. Responding to his call to the ministry, Reverend Holmes received his Bachelor of Divinity in 1959 and a Master of Sacred Theology in 1968 from Southern Methodist University in Dallas, Texas. He also received an Honorary Doctor of Law degree from Dillard University, New Orleans, and an Honorary Doctor of Divinity degree from Huston-Tilloston.

This outstanding minister has served as district superintendent for Dallas Central District North Texas Conference and presently serves as the senior pastor of the St. Luke Community United Methodist Church. He chose not to seek reelection to the Texas House of Representatives, but he remains active in the religious, educational, and political activities of the state of Texas. In 1974 he was appointed by Governor Dolph Briscoe as Chairman of the Legislative Committee of the Constitutional Revision Commission. Reverend Zan Holmes was the first African-American elected president of the Dallas Pastors Association in 1963 and the first man of color to be selected a member of the Dallas Foundation.

Reverend Zan W. Holmes, Jr. has been an adjunct professor of preaching since 1978 at the Perkins School of Theology at Southern Methodist University and has authored several religious publications. In 1990 he was awarded the Peace Maker Award by the Dallas Peace Center. Whenever racial friction arose in the city of Dallas, this spiritual leader could always be counted on to help restore peace and harmony. Pastor Holmes developed the St. Luke congregation into a prominent religious component of community service and involvement in the affairs of the city and state that affected members in their everyday lives.

Even in the year 2001, when the evil forces in the community attempted to mar the St. Luke Community Methodist Church with swastikas and Rebel Confederate symbols, some legislative benefits accrued to the black community by this action that enhanced the passage of the Hate Crime Bill that was being held up in the Senate. This bill had been sponsored in the House of Representatives by Rep. Senfronia Thompson, and in the Senate by Senators Rodney Ellis and Royce West. The hatemongers picked on the wrong church. They chose one that had many political leader members of that congregation, such as Ron Kirk, Mayor of Dallas; John Wiley Price, County Commissioner; Helen Giddings, State Representative; and Reverend Zan Holmes, Senior Pastor. State senators changed their minds, voted passage, and Governor Rick Perry signed the legislation into law. Reverend Holmes' influence epitomizes the fulfillment of the Davidic prophesy that "Princes shall come out of Egypt" (and Texas and Dallas?).

Athletics in a small rural Texas town seemed to transcend racial heritage and break traditional mores and folkways which excluded blacks from elected offices. It certainly was out of the ordinary when Dennis Rundles was elected mayor of Detroit, Texas, a town in Red River County with an estimated population of 789. In April 1971 he won by a vote of 94 to 80, after a recount, against councilman Wayne Blanton. A white majority must have elected Rundles, because he only received thirteen votes from his black constituents. One of the first conciliatory acts the black mayor did was to recommend his opponent to be the assistant mayor; that recommendation was approved by the city council.

Most citizens of Detroit, Texas, agreed that Rundles' record as a basketball coach had influenced their appreciation and respect for him. He had grown up in Annona, Texas, and finished high school in Clarksville; he matriculated at Texas College in Tyler. Later he played professional baseball with the Kansas City Monarchs. Rundles returned to Annona in 1942 and spent ten years as a basketball coach in Detroit. An item in the *Dallas Morning News* stated, "His teams have put Detroit on the sports map. The 1960 Negro team, playing its home games on a dirt floor, had a perfect 40-0 season and went to the state Interscholastic League, Class B finals against Colorado City."[121] His basketball teams made several trips to the Texas Interscholastic League in Austin, and in 1969 his team won third place in the competition.

Being a member of the Detroit, Texas, Lions Club gave Dennis B. Rundles an added boost when he made the decision to run for mayor. He still operates the only television repair shop and is a partner in the Detroit Furniture and Hardware Company. He continues to give this town leadership in developing new streets, federally sponsored affordable housing, and a volunteer fire department. Mayor Rundles is a Baptist minister who is pastor of the Solid Rock Baptist Church, Paris, Texas. He governs by the content of his character and not the color of his skin.

The same racial tenet may have been true in some cities in Tarrant County. In Arlington, Texas, Elzie Odom, a 1987 postal inspector retiree, who had served the postal community for a number of years, decided that Arlington's middle-class voters needed representation on the city council. Odom was born in Burkeville, Newton County, Texas and received his college education at Prairie View A&M College. He moved to Arlington in the spring of 1979.

Elzie Odom threw his hat in the election ring in 1989 and lost. Undaunted, he ran again in 1990 and beat an Arlington Chamber of Commerce officer by sixteen votes in a runoff. Elzie Odom was the city's first African-American councilman who was elected at large. In 1994 the city of Arlington had changed to elections for single-member districts and Odom's election parameters were reduced and he won handily the councilman of the northern district.

In 1997 Elzie Odom was elected Mayor of Arlington to succeed Richard Greene, who had decided not to seek reelection; he won against Paula Hightower without a runoff. Odom had support from the incumbent and the business community, verifying this author's basic hypothesis that "the businessmen run this country and use the political machinery to stay in power." Odom became the first Afro-American elected mayor of a major city in Tarrant County. In 1999 Elzie Odom had no opposition in the mayor's race. At this writing, he had won his third term as Mayor of Arlington and still has a major problem: Arlington, Texas is the nation's largest city without a public transit system.

The larger the city, the more difficult it is for black candidates to win the top leadership positions. A pioneer for political inclusion in the Dallas community was Lucy Phelps Patterson, the first black female elected to the Dallas City Council. She was born in Dallas and graduated from Booker T. Washington High School. Lucy Patterson received her Bachelor of Science degree from Howard University and a Master's degree from the University of Denver. She was elected to City Council in 1973 and served until 1977. In 1982 Lucy Patterson sought to advance the political status of blacks by running as a candidate for the U.S. Congress but lost. If she could have generated more support from the downtown business establishment, her outcome might have been different.

Whenever blacks have the support of the downtown businesses, history can be made. A classic example of that premise is what happened in Dallas with the election of Ronald Kirk. The top of the political pinnacle was reached in Dallas in 1997 when Ronald Kirk was elected mayor. Governor Ann Richards appointed him as the ninety-eighth Secretary of State and he served as a legislative aide to U.S. Senator Lloyd Bentsen.

Ronald Kirk had a natural alliance with the business community, but this was a major problem for some of the black activists in Dallas who felt he was too closely aligned with the leading businessmen in the city. This opposition was quickly reduced by the mayor's outstanding leadership in the economic and social programs of his administration. He led the 1998 Capital Bond Drive, a successful drive in lowering city taxes, which helped many sections of Dallas, and a campaign in support of a new downtown arena for the Dallas Mavericks and Dallas Stars Hockey team. On May 1, 1999, Ronald Kirk was elected to his second term as the fifty-fifth mayor of Dallas with over 74 percent of the popular vote, including the largest Afro-American support for a conservative black elected official.

Before his term expired, Mayor Kirk had set his goal of becoming a United States senator in the vacancy created when Senator Phil Gramm decided not to seek reelection. On Wednesday, November 7, 2001, Mayor Kirk formally announced his resignation as mayor and his candidacy for the United States Senate. His ambition included being the first Afro-American elected to that position from Texas. As evidenced during his tenure as mayor of Dallas, Mayor Kirk's extraordinary political talent of coalition-building could be an asset. However, he faced a predictable and insurmountable dilemma in the primary election because he had to campaign over the entire state and was not well known in other parts of Texas. Too, five Democratic candidates were vying for the same position. Victor Morales and Dan Morales would attract most of the Hispanic votes, and Ken Bentsen was already a congressman and well known all over Texas.

Recently the political selection trend from blacks seem to have been modified; the larger the city, the better the prospect for an Afro-American to become mayor, if he has the support of the business community and a strong base of minority voters. In 1997 Lee Brown was elected and became the first black mayor of Houston on January 2, 1998; he had the support of former mayors Kathy Whitmire and Bob Lanier. This son of migrant farm workers was born in Oklahoma and lived there until he was five years of age, when his family moved to California. Lee P. Brown received his Master's in sociology from San Jose State College in California and a Ph.D. in criminology from the University of California at Berkeley.

Brown was Chief of Police in Houston from 1982 to 1990 and helped break down an insurmountable racial barrier in this Gulf port city. Previously he had had an outstanding career in law enforcement in Portland, Atlanta, New York City, and Washington, D.C.; President Bill Clinton appointed Brown as drug czar during his administration. Being a Democrat, Lee Brown was reluctant in defending Houston during the presidential campaign in 2000 against democrats who maligned Houston's air quality when they attacked the Republican candidate, George Bush. This non-defense of Houston caused Lee Brown to lose some essential bipartisan support when he sought a third term. In the state primary, Mayor Brown was forced into a run-off election.

A changing ethnological division was a major factor in Brown's mayoral run-off election; Hispanics, a fast-growing segment of the city's population, are on the verge of becoming a dominant political bloc all over the state of Texas. An ironic and legal contradiction is that according to the Texas constitution, Hispanics are still classified as white. Prior to World War II, Hispanics were classified as "white persons" with Spanish surnames. Texans wanted to maintain a "divide and conquer" strategy and keep blacks and

Hispanics from joining together in economic and political unity. Hispanics became a self-imposed minority after watching blacks pursue the civil rights agenda in the 1960s. Hispanic leaders have initiated a statewide movement to get changes in the redistricting process so more of their leaders can be elected to higher offices at all levels of government. In Houston they tried to complement their success in Austin, where they recently elected a Hispanic mayor, Gus Garcia.

Usually City Council elections are non-partisan, but this one varied from the norm. The demographic changes and political tread of blacks, whites, and Hispanics have ushered in political problems for the dominant economic and political hierarchy. Incumbent Lee Brown, a Democrat, was challenged in 2001 by Orlando Sanchez, a Republican, who wanted to be the first Hispanic mayor of that city. It was predicted that many Hispanics would defect from the Democratic Party and join white conservatives in electing Sanchez. Lee Brown would be supported by liberal Democrats and a large percentage of black voters. Plus, he would receive special help as a reward for his administration's success in Houston's being selected as one of the possible sites for the Olympics. He also benefited tremendously from the endorsement of Chris Bell, who ran third with 16 percent of the votes in the primary. Lee Brown defeated Orlando Sanchez, gaining 52 percent (165,865) of the votes to Sanchez's 48 percent (155,164). Lee Brown immediately appealed for unity between black and Hispanic voters, but the stage was already set for further conflict between these two political forces. Without some semblance of racial cohesiveness, both groups stand to lose the ability to elect more of their constituents to higher offices.

Small cities still provide blacks unusual and equal opportunities for winning elections. In many cases race is not a problem. As redistricting plans conform to multicolored demographic changes, black candidates can't win solely on black issues but must campaign on the basis of their qualifications, not the color of their skin. During the May 5, 2001 election, Kenneth Cary (no relationship to this writer) had an overwhelming victory in Watauga. This newcomer to north Texas is vice president of business development for Citigroup and formerly lived in Niagara Falls and Buffalo, New York. He garnered 76 percent of the vote and became the first black councilman in northeast Tarrant County. In The Colony, a city in the 26,000 population range on the eastern shore of Lewisville Lake in Denton County, Bernetta Henville-Shannon became the first black mayor in this city. She is a business leader in the north Texas area.

Barbara Jordan, a lawyer on the other end of the political spectrum, was a reflection of a new enlightenment permeating Texas society. Ms. Jordan was the daughter of Mrs. Arlyne Pattern and the Reverend Benjamin Meredith Jordan, a warehouse clerk, who suffered a heart attack on the day his daughter was sworn in as a member of the Texas legislature. His timely passing seems related to that of Simeon: "Lord, now lettest thou thy servant depart in peace, according to thy words. For mine eyes have seen thy salvation."[122] Rev. Jordan's daughter was the first black elected to the legislature since Reconstruction.

The distinguished congresswoman was born February 21, 1926, in Houston. She attended Phillis Wheatly High School in that city and graduated magna cum laude in 1956 with a degree in political science from Texas Southern University, an all-black university in Houston's Third Ward. She then matriculated at Boston University pursuing a LIB degree. Upon graduation in 1959, the Congresswoman gained legal experience by working for Bill Elliott, a Houston judge.

Miss Jordan made her political debut by actively campaigning and supporting the John F. Kennedy-Lyndon Johnson ticket in 1960. She tried her own wings by running for the Texas legislature in 1962 and 1964 but lost both races. In 1967 the Supreme Court ordered the reapportionment of legislature seats and the Sixtieth Legislature redistricted the legislature; Houston gained ten additional seats with several of them in predominantly black areas.

Part of Ms. Jordan's success was attributed to the support of her by whites who abandoned their old racial clichés. Her platform was low-keyed to state minimum wages, industrial accident laws and lower auto insurance rates, which blue-collar workers and middle-class employees would be concerned with. She won 30 to 50 percent of the ballots in black precincts, and 25 to 40 percent in the white precincts.[123] Barbara Jordan won a seat in the state legislature and was voted the outstanding freshman senator of that year.

Her six years as a state senator were most impressive. In a special session during March 1972, the Texas Senate unanimously (29-0) elected Ms. Jordan as its President Pro-Tempore. Lieutenant Governor Ben Barnes said, "She is the first black woman ever elected to preside over any state senate or house in the nation."[124] This legislative body reflected a changing mood in white attitudes towards blacks in Texas. Charles Sanders of *Ebony* explained that "To pick Ms. Jordan the body rose above two waning but still common prejudices—prejudice against blacks and against promoting women to places of authority."[125]

The one-man vote ruling by the Supreme Court was a political bonanza for blacks in Texas and the rest of the nation. The single-member district realignment set the stage for Barbara Jordan to gyrate to the national legislature. In November 1972 she ran for Congress from the 18th District and received 81 percent of the votes from the heavily populated black and Mexican-American communities.

The principal political asset and credentials Jordan carried to Washington was that she was one of Lyndon Baines Johnson's protégées. This astute politician and former president helped her win appointment to the House Judiciary Committee. It was here that she crystallized her prestige and influence not only in Congress but throughout the nation. Her performance was spectacular in the Watergate impeachment proceedings. As a 1991 article in the *Fort Worth Star-Telegram* reported, "It was she who helped bring down President Nixon by holding the mirror of the Constitution up to his deeds and allowing—through perhaps the clearest explanations by any of the 38 Judiciary Committee members who conducted the Grand Inquest of the nation—a nationwide television audience to understand how the very system of government was subverted."[126]

Houston continues to provide outstanding leadership to the Texas State Legislature and thus to the United States Congress. At age thirty-four, George Thomas (Mickey) Leland was the United States Congressman representing the 18th Congressional District of Texas. He was born in Lubbock, Texas, November 27, 1944, and moved to Houston at an early age. He graduated from Wheatley High School in 1962. Mickey Leland (his adopted name) was a 1970 graduate of Texas Southern University, receiving a Bachelor of Science in Pharmacy and remaining there as an instructor of clinical pharmacy for one year.

Mickey Leland was elected to the Texas House of Representatives in 1972 and served until 1979. He served on many committees but was outstanding on the powerful House Appropriations Committee and the Legislative Budget Board. Leland was very active with the Texas State Democratic Party and the Texas Democratic Black Caucus; in 1978, he also organized the National Black/Hispanic Democratic Coalition, which he cochaired. Upon Barbara Jordan's retirement, Leland was elected to the United States Congress in 1978.

In Washington, D.C., in 1979, this legislator was elected Freshman Whip of the Ninety-sixth Congress and served on the Committee on Interstate and Foreign Commerce, Committee on Post Office and Civil Service, and the Committee on the District of Columbia. Mickey Leland was chairman of the Select Committee on World Hunger and was killed in an aircraft crash, August 7, 1989, while on his way to a United Nations refugee camp in the vicinity of the Sudanese-Ethiopian border. In 1990 Ethiopian-born Americans in Dallas led the movement to establish a Children's Home in Ethiopia in memory of U.S. Representative Mickey Leland of Houston, Texas.

Upon the death of U.S. Congressman Mickey Leland, Leland's Chief of Staff, Rodney Ellis, modified and accelerated his own priorities to bring to fruition many of the community goals he and Mickey Leland had in common. Rodney Ellis has a multiplicity of talents and experience; he was a graduate of Texas Southern University with a Bachelor of Arts degree, his Master's degree from the Lyndon Baines Johnson School of Public Affairs, and his Juris Doctor's degree from the University of Texas Law School. He served three terms on the Houston City Council and was an astute entrepreneur as a cofounder of Ap Securities, Inc., an investment banking entity. He also served on the Texas Law School Foundation Board.

Since his election in 1990 to the Texas State Senate, Senator Ellis has made outstanding contributions to his constituents in District 13, parts of Harris and Fort Bend counties, and the entire judicial process. Recognition of his competence and high-caliber leadership was shown from 1999 to 2001 when he served as President Pro Tem of the Texas Senate and an unprecedented performance when he served as Acting Governor for fifty days. When Rick Perry was sworn in as governor, Senator Ellis automatically became the Lieutenant Governor by virtue of his serving as President of the Senate. Many who had known Rodney Ellis conclude that because of his many achievements, he is well qualified to become the first black elected governor of the state of Texas, especially after he authored and passed a portion of a bill this author had tried unsuccessfully when I served in the House of Representatives. Ellis' 1995 Texas Workforce Commission consolidated job training and employment activities under one unit at state and local levels. It gave local areas more control so they could provide realistic job training for specific industries in their jurisdiction.

Senator Ellis' $340 million Texas Grants Program that provides free college tuition to qualifying students, and his Texas Legislative Internship Program administered by the Mickey Leland Center on World Hunger and Peace at Texas Southern University, illustrate his high priority for educating youth. The latter provided for undergraduate and graduate students to serve as interns in the Texas legislature and other local and state agencies. His support of the Texas Hate Crime Bill illustrates his ability to build coalitions on a complex racial issue.

Many black voters who supported and held Reverend Zan Holmes in high esteem were disappointed when he did not seek reelection in 1972. However, the quality of legislative leadership would not be diminished: Eddie Bernice Johnson filed and became the first Afro-American female from Dallas elected to the Texas legislature. She also had the honor of being the first black female to chair the House Committee on Labor.

Eddie Bernice Johnson was born December 3, 1935, in Waco, Texas. She received a diploma in nursing at St. Mary's in 1955, a Bachelor of Science in Nursing from Texas Christian University in 1967, and a Master's degree from Southern Methodist University in 1976. In 1997 she resigned from the state legislature to accept employment as Regional Director of Health, Education and Welfare in Dallas; later she was appointed an executive assistant to the Administrator of Health Services, Washington, D.C.

When Governor Bill Clements vetoed the Redistricting Bill in 1979 because it did not include a potential seat for the black community in Dallas, he enabled Eddie Bernice Johnson to refocus her interest on the Texas legislature. In 1986 she won a seat in the Texas Senate, a seat she held until 1993 and which was really to her advantage. The 1990 census highlighted the fact that blacks in Dallas should have a congressional seat. The Texas legislature was required to submit a plan for redistricting to the United States Justice Department for approval and Lieutenant Governor Bob Bullock appointed her chairlady of the Senate Sub-Committee on Redistricting, against the wishes of many Democrats who vigorously opposed the creation of the new district. Fred Blair, Chairman of the Black Legislative Caucus in Austin; John Wiley Price, Dallas County Commissioner; and Alphonso Jackson, Dallas Housing Authority accused the Democrat-controlled House of diluting the voting strength of blacks to ensure the reelection of whites. Ironically, Republicans and black leaders worked together to create a predominately Afro-American congressional district in Dallas.

State Senator Eddie Bernice Johnson engineered the shape of Congressional District 30, but sacrificed and diluted black voters in Tarrant County so Martin Frost could keep a district he was losing in Dallas to herself and John Bryant. Judge Maryellen Hicks of Fort Worth argued that "we shouldn't be sacrificed to save anybody's job," and State Representative Fred Blair of Dallas, a member of the Redistricting Committee, said, "Blacks should be up in arms...we're going to get it here or we're going to get it in court."[127] Nevertheless, Eddie Bernice Johnson prevailed and was elected to the United States House of Representatives in the 1992-93 election, becoming the second black female from Texas to hold this position, and successor to the legendary Barbara Jordan. At this writing she is the chairlady of the Black Caucus in Washington and was one of the chief critics of then-Governor George Bush. During the new president's inaugural speech before both houses during the certification of the Electoral College vote, Eddie Bernice led the Black Caucus in a walk-out protest in support of some black leaders who maintained that "he is not our president."

Dallas appears to have an abundance of qualified blacks who are competent and willing to represent their constituents. When Eddie Bernice Johnson left the Texas Senate to assume her new position in the United States Congress, no void existed in quality of representation. Royce West was elected senator of Dallas' District 23 to replace her. He has functioned many years in a leadership role. When this writer was an Associate Dean of Student Affairs at the University of Texas at Arlington, Royce West was the first Afro-American elected president of the student union at that institution. He graduated from UTA with a Bachelor of Science and Master's degree. He earned his Doctorate of Jurisprudence from the University of Houston. Royce West is licensed as an attorney and counselor-at-law by the state of Texas.

Attorney Royce West made an unsuccessful bid for the Dallas County District Attorney position, failing to face the political reality that, at the time, no black Democrat could win a county-wide elected office in Dallas or Tarrant County. He should have noticed the changing trend in 1986 when Judge Larry Baraka ran on the Republican ticket and became the first black to win a countywide seat in Dallas County. Royce was elected to the Texas Senate in November 1992 and continues to serve at this time. In January 1999 Senator West was presented with the Martin Luther King, Jr. Justice Award by Mayor Ron Kirk of Dallas, who was the recipient of the award in 1998. While the state legislature was in session in 2001, Senator Royce West was successful in bringing one of his primary goals to fruition, the establishment of a four-year state university in south Dallas.

Senator Royce West's attendance at the University of Texas at Arlington came on the heels of an institutional, state, and national racial problem associated with the image of the Rebel flag that was the athletic symbol of that school in Arlington, Texas. The Rebel Rousers, a recognized student organization at UTA, would often drive a red fire truck, decked with a large number of Confederate flags, through the black community located in a ten-block-square area north of the campus and Division Street bounded by Cooper and Center streets. Disruption was continuous; black students in the school band were harassed by the playing of "Dixie," and other blacks objected to the playing of the song because they felt it was a symbol of Southern whites longing for the old days marked by slavery and defiance to the federal government by asserting that "the South will rise again."

While an assistant professor of history at Tarrant County Junior College (South Campus), this writer was invited to speak at UTA in February 1969 at the students' observance of Black History Month. I was assigned a subject: Castration of the Black Man's Masculine Image. In my deliberation, I attracted the attention of President Harrison and the black students who had confronted the university with twenty-one demands that included the hiring of a black professor and expansion of the curriculum to include black studies. I admonished the black students to seek improvement in their academic grade points instead of marching and demonstrating against the Rebel flag. I challenged the administration to react with understanding, meet the legitimate grievances, and help end the many years of discrimination in the state of Texas. A few days later, Dr. Charles McDowell and a group of students visited me and asked me to accept a position at UTA; on September 1, 1969, I was appointed the first Afro-American full faculty member at that university as an assistant professor of history and the Associate Dean of Student Life. However, most of my time was spent trying to keep racial hostilities from exploding. On Wednesday, October 15, 1969, a confrontation between members of CAP (Collegians for

Afro-American Progress) and Phi Gamma Delta Fraternity took place in the SUB. Theodore Smith and other black students attempted to remove an obnoxious drawing that depicted a Polynesian with a bone in his hair, painted in dark purple and draped with a Rebel flag. Tempers finally subsided with an agreement to have a hearing on the matter.

Two days later on October 17, 1969, members of Kappa Alpha Fraternity deliberately displayed the Rebel flag in front of the Student Center. CAP members demanded the removal of the flag and the white students refused; a scuffle broke out and I was able to stop the confrontation. I had taught one of CAP's leaders, Bernice Smith, at Dunbar High School, and those black students knew that I would stand up and defend them when I thought they were right. My influence prevailed.

After student confrontations at the football games and other conflicts in front of the Student Center, I persuaded Attorney Jenkins Garrett, a member of the Texas University System Board of Directors, to ask the regents to outlaw the flag because the sporadic racial confrontations could get out of hand and someone killed. The Board of Regents responded favorably and the Rebel theme was discarded. By a vote of the student body, the athletic teams' name was changed to the University of Texas at Arlington Mavericks.

I then turned my attention to the establishment of a Tri-Ethnic Center in the UTA Library. I established the undergraduate Zeta Chi Chapter of Alpha Phi Alpha Fraternity, Inc., of which I am a Life Member. This was the first black fraternity on UTA's campus that is an auxiliary of the first and oldest black fraternity, Alpha Phi Alpha, established in the United States in 1906. I also sponsored the Zeta Psi Chapter of Alpha Phi Alpha Fraternity, Inc., on the campus at Texas Christian University, and the Omega Psi Phi Fraternity at the University of Texas at Arlington in April 1971. Each year, Zeta Chi members joined the Collegians for Afro-American Progress in sponsoring the observance of Afro-American History Month at UTA.

In May 1972, I asked John Hudson, Head Librarian at UTA, about the possibility of developing in the library a special collection of materials dealing with the problems of black Americans. A committee was formed and the concept was expanded to include Chicanos and American Indians. On September 10, 1972, on the first floor of the University of Texas at Arlington library, the first tri-ethnic minorities cultural center opened, the first of its kind in the southwest and perhaps the nation. Lass Estrellas de Jalisco, a mariachi band, played for the opening ceremonies. This opening coincided with the beginning of La Raza Week, sponsored by the Mexican-American students at UTA, which featured Chicano films, Chicano speakers, and a march in sympathy of farm workers. Later the cultural center was moved to the sixth floor of the library.

While the University of Texas at Arlington was trying to accelerate the cultural heritage and appreciation of ethnic groups in Texas, racist groups were trying to turn back the clock on blacks and Jews in this state. I left the University of Texas at Arlington in 1978 because I was elected to the Texas House of Representatives for District 95 in Tarrant County. The Rebel flag just wouldn't go away, nor would the Ku Klux Klan. On Saturday, June 16, 1979, the KKK held a cross-burning in a field on the outskirts of Euless, Texas, in northern Tarrant County. An estimated two hundred gun-toting Klansmen showed up dressed in Army fatigues, white robes, and carrying modified M-16 rifles, 45-caliber pistols, and bayonets. Klan leader John Davis of Hurst; David Duke, Grand Wizard; and Lewis Bean, Great Titan of the KKK, all denigrated blacks, Jews, gays and lesbians. This reflected the bigotry and ethnic obscenities that are basic in the Klan's political posture. Many Euless policemen were in attendance and socializing with this racist organization.

The hands-off attitude of state and local peace officers was an affront to many black citizens. However, many agreed that since the site wasn't in the Euless or Fort Worth city limits, the Tarrant County sheriff's department was responsible for security. Sheriff Lon Evans maintained that the Klan was within the scope of the law and had the right to hold such demonstrations. So, on June 22, 1979, I addressed a letter to Attorney General Mark White, in which I asked, "Since there are members of black organizations planning the same type of activity, I'm writing you to see if they have the same constitutional guarantees and rights as the members of the Ku Klux Klan outside of Euless on Saturday, June 16, 1979 and at other times throughout this state." Mark White did not respond, but John W. Fainter, Jr., First Assistant Attorney General, replied in a letter dated July 13, 1979, that: "Mark White does not condone activities by any group for whatever purpose if those activities are in violation of the law. Further, General White will at all times use his lawful authority to ensure that all citizens of the State receive equal treatment and guarantees under the law." This assertion was not clear to State Representative Wilhelmania Delco and the Texas Legislative Black Caucus.

Attorney General Mark White had been dodging issues important to blacks for a long time. The first black elected State Representative for District 37 inTravis County, Wilhelmania Delco, Chairwoman of the House Committee on Higher Education, had been asking him for specific rulings for two years. This dynamic and articulate legislator was a graduate of Fisk University, Nashville, Tennessee, with a degree in sociology and minors in economics and business administration. In 1968 she was elected to the Austin Independent School District Board of Trustees, where she gained invaluable experience in the problems confronting our public schools. She was a proud member of the Alpha Kappa Alpha sorority and was well respected all over Texas and the nation for her legislative expertise. Her legislative cohorts elected her Vice-President of the National Black Caucus of State Legislators.

Always a "Socratic questioner," Representative Delco raised the question of whether Prairie View A&M University was entitled to share directly in the Permanent University Fund (PUF), and more specifically, if Prairie View wasn't the college or branch university "for the instruction of Colored youth" specified in the Texas Constitution of 1876.

Article VII, section 10 of the 1876 constitution made provisions for the establishment of a "university of the first class and styled The University of Texas." Section 13 mandated that the Agricultural and Mechanical College of Texas be made a branch of the University of Texas and subject to its jurisdiction. The Act of 1876 also called for separate schools, and Prairie View was the "school for colored." In 1879 and 1881, the legislature authorized $600,000 annually from the Available University Fund (AUF), income from the interest on the PUF. But in 1882 the Comptroller of Public Accounts, W. M. Brown, arbitrarily refused further payments to Prairie View; this action resulted in Prairie View being placed under the jurisdiction of Texas A&M, denying this school its right to the PUF. Mark White didn't want to rule because of the strong political pressure of the A&M alumni and he needed many of the black voters for his forthcoming electoral campaign for governor against Bill Clements.

Representative Delco organized statewide support for Prairie View and fought valiantly in demanding that Prairie View be a constitutional branch of the University of Texas system. She also introduced House Bill 658, which sought to give Prairie View one-sixth of the PUF. A compromise was finally made that gave Prairie View six million dollars for ten years, and in exchange Representative Delco and the Black Caucus would not hold Texas in violation of the Civil Rights Act and seek judicial remedy in the Federal Courts. This author opposed the compromise because the funding was a temporary one. Today Prairie View is still getting "crumbs" from the PUF, and many of the alumni from that institution still feel that Texas A&M is getting the bulk of the funds that rightfully belong to Prairie View.

The Negro Chamber of Commerce Movement in Texas

Many scholars, philosophers, and laymen have contended that a basic solution to black problems is one of economics. It's long been recognized that the businessmen run this country, and they use the political machinery to stay in power. Black entrepreneurs also hold the keys to independence and more self-determination, minus dependence on welfare and other handouts.

Blacks in America are becoming more organization-conscious with each succeeding generation. A large number of organizations are founded as a means of protest against certain evils which blacks believe should be combated through group activity. Others are formed for social, religious, political, or economic improvement and have become a distinct and component part of American heritage. However, it is interesting to note how blacks have patterned certain organizations after those of whites and merely prefixed or suffixed the name of the group or organization with the word "Black" or "Negro." It is with this imitated phase of institutional organizations that one takes cognizance of the events and conditions instrumental in the development of the Negro Chamber of Commerce movement in Texas.

There is a direct relationship between the transition of certain factions and elements of the population and the development and expansion of businesses, which in turn create an atmosphere for the emergence of a chamber of commerce. The desires, aspirations, and previous experience of migrants moving into a new community add to the cultural, institutional, and economic development of any city. Consequently, this "New Negro" moving into the larger cities of Texas with a zeal to improve his conditions, economically, educationally, and politically, undertook through organization the realization of his needs and ambitious. Since he was not accepted as an integral part of the white organizations, so he aped the white chambers of commerce and other civic organizations, which in many instances are endorsed and encouraged by the white chambers of commerce in his city.

Chambers of commerce in the United States represent a composite body of businessmen who directly or indirectly regulate the conduct and activities of their communities. These are the men who shape and formulate the local, state, and national community policies. Members of the "entrepreneur cell" occupy positions and memberships in every important movement or organization in their particular locales. As such, they have consolidated these varied interests and influences into a centralized, organized group, defined as a chamber of commerce. From this center flows the expression of the people as determined by the businessmen.

The establishment of the National Negro Business League played a significant part in the development and organizational scheme of Negro economic improvement institutions throughout the United States. The founding of such an organization was due largely to the profound thinking and works of the eminent educator Booker T. Washington. As

Washington traveled the country and studied the economic conditions of the Negro people, he sensed a deep need for a clear-cut analysis of their status and possible solutions for the alleviation or mitigation of their varied problems. Along this line of thinking, he deemed it expedient to call together the leading Negro men then engaged in successful business pursuits and to discuss pertinent problems and then feasible solutions, thus enhancing the growth and development of their individual businesses. Booker T. Washington describes the formation of the National Negro Business League as follows:

> In the summer of 1900, with the assistance of such prominent Coloured Men as Mr. T. Fortune, who has always upheld my hand in every effort, I organized the National Negro Business League, which held its first meeting in Boston, and brought together for the first time a large number of the coloured men who are engaged in various lines of trade or business in different parts of the United States. Thirty states were represented at our first meeting. Out of this national meeting grew state and local business leagues.[128]

The purpose of the Business League from the onset was the promotion of industrial and commercial achievement whereby the influence of the race could be increased and enabled to maintain a position of influence in the American economy and eventually obtain economic freedom. Thus, as Negroes continued to leave the rurals and go to the cities, and as businessmen began to develop and grow, offspring of the first National Negro Business League in the form of chambers of commerce and similar bodies sprung up all over the United States and especially in Texas.

The history of the Negro Chamber of Commerce of Dallas is significant in that it represents the establishment of the first Negro Chamber in Texas, and a change in the common identity from a business group with a business developmental program to a group that would represent the interests of all the people and on all matters and issues which affected their lives. This transition is typical of other chambers, which had a peculiar and familiar setting in a dispute between two factions as to who would represent the Negro businessmen of Dallas at the 1926 convention of the National Negro Business League in Chicago, Illinois.[129] The difference arose between Lawyer Wells and Professor T. W. Pratt. By a vote of the body then in session, Professor Pratt won the privilege of being the delegate to the convention by a 2:1 vote. But because of the lack of finances in the treasury, Lawyer Wells elected to represent the Business League of Dallas at his own expense. This widened the gap of disharmony within the Dallas League's ranks, and on November 26, 1926, Professor T. W. Pratt summoned a group of men together and accordingly organized the first Negro chamber of commerce in Texas. E. J. Crawford, owner of a leading funeral home, was chosen president by the assembled group and thus, under his guidance, the Negro Chamber of Commerce of Dallas was launched. The significant factor in this change was that the founders, in setting up this new organization, thought the league too conservative in its scope and activity. They wanted something more dynamic, and they did not think the league had reached a cross-section of all the citizens well enough. While organization included only business and professional men, the proposed Negro chamber of commerce would go out to reach everyone.[130]

One of the professionals and black Chamber board member was Marecellus Clayton Cooper, the first black dentist in Dallas, Texas. His grade-school education was in Little Egypt, a segregated community in North Dallas; his family moved and he graduated from a high school in Springfield, Missouri. Later he attended Meharry Medical School, Nashville, Tennessee, and began his dental practice in 1896 in Dallas. He was one of the pioneering forces in the Negro Chamber in that city.

From 1926 to 1935, the Dallas Negro Chamber of Commerce struggled for survival as a community clearing house for Negro problems, but in 1933 the organization brought to its rank a leader who reactivated and made this unit span all opposition and competition by other elements and produced the most progressive and dominating chamber in Texas. On January 1, 1933, A. Maceo Smith, organizer of Western Mutual Life Insurance Company, "reorganized the Dallas Negro Chamber of Commerce and placed it on a sound financial basis with a full-time paid executive staff and a permanent program."[131] Currently, Reginald Gates is the executive director, and Dallas is still one of the leaders in the chamber movement.

This reactivating leadership, as exemplified by Antonio Maceo Smith, is a general racial phenomenon which is found to be true and necessary in most of the Negro chambers of commerce in Texas because of the instability of these units. Houston, having no Negro organization strong enough to represent and assist in the economic uplifting of its Negro citizens, found in the formation of a chamber of commerce organization a leader in the person of J. W. Robinson, who was a member of the Noon-Day Luncheon Club. This club was composed of a group of businessmen who met once a week to discuss problems common to all of them. Mr. Robinson felt that some organization was needed to stimulate the economic consciousness of the Negro citizens, so he initiated a meeting for that purpose and became the leader responsible for the founding of the Houston Negro Chamber of Commerce. However, the first year was not dominated by any outstanding achievement but merely molded public opinion as to the purpose and status of such an organization in the community.[132]

The need for a person to make the Houston Negro Chamber of Commerce a dynamic and prominent organization was recognized and its members found the answer in Ollie King Manning. As executive secretary and because of his excellent leadership qualities, Houston's Negro Chamber of Commerce became nationally known and Manning was elected Executive Secretary of the National Negro Business League. He died October 10, 1947.

Another phase of leadership which has proven significant to the chamber of commerce movement is leadership that is inspired by the white chambers. In several instances white chambers have brought the idea to the Negro groups. Joe S. Moore, manager of the Montgomery County Chamber of Commerce, writes, "This organization does endorse the Negro Chamber of Commerce in Conroe. Some three years ago, Mr. Fred Yates, who as then manager, affected the organization of the Negro Chamber of Commerce, feeling that this group needed a vehicle to promote civic pride and improvement.[133]

In Navasota, a representative of the East Texas (white) Chamber of commerce was sent to encourage the setting up of a Negro Chamber of Commerce. Owen R. Smith, Manager of Navasota and Grimes Counties Chamber of Commerce, asserted that "the Chamber of Commerce was instrumental in helping the colored citizens get their present chamber organized—it is the only civic organization by which the colored business leaders and other colored citizens can analyze and solve their community problems."

Other Prominent Black Texans

Quite often it takes a national emergency to focus on discriminatory problems and inequities in American society. When the Japanese invoked the Day of Infamy at Pearl Harbor in 1941, blacks could only enlist and serve in the kitchens of the United States Navy. When the attack took place, DORIS MILLER came out of the kitchen of the battleship, *U.S.S. Virginia*, pulled the mortally wounded captain to a safer spot, and shot down three Japanese fighter planes. Then he returned to his kitchen duties.

Miller was named after the midwife who delivered him. He constantly rejected the nickname "Dorie," which many of his friends and Navy personnel used to "masculinize" his name. He was an outstanding fullback at Moore's High School in Waco, Texas, and at the age of twenty enlisted in the United States Navy as a Mess Attendant, Third Class. Blacks could not enlist in any other categories in the Navy. Doris Miller was the first Afro-American to receive the Navy Cross, the highest honor for armed combat heroics; it was presented by Admiral Chester Nimitz. Two years later, in 1943, he was killed in another military action on the *U.S.S. Liscome Bay* when it was hit and sunk by a Japanese torpedo.

In honor of Doris Miller, a park, a cemetery, and a YMCA in the black community of Waco were named after him. An auditorium in Austin and the enlisted men's quarters at the Great Lakes Naval Base are also dedicated to his memory.

The military accolades of the 99th Pursuit Squadron in World War II changed the minds of many Americans who held the racist assumption that blacks were innately inferior to whites and not qualified to fight in the emerging aeronautic age. Blacks proved their military prowess by being an essential part of America's military superiority and helping to achieve victory in the European and Pacific theaters. But the aviation quality they attained could not have been possible without a corresponding group of well-qualified instructors. One native of Fort Worth who had outstanding teaching ability was a 1936 graduate of I. M. Terrell High School, CLAUDE PLATT; he matriculated at Tuskegee University in the fall after high school graduation. Many black students were attracted to that historic university because of the reputation of its founder, Booker T. Washington. Jim Crow and segregation were more pronounced there in Alabama than in many other states, but black students still chose Tuskegee to further their education.

In 1939 congressional legislation authorized the Civil Aeronautics Authority to sanction the Civilian Pilot Training Program. Encouraged by his mother, Marie Platt, an eminently good elementary school teacher in Fort Worth, Claude Platt pursued his childhood dream of becoming a pilot and entered the program at Tuskegee. The presidential election of 1940 led to the removal of the segregation requirements of the armed forces and the admission of blacks on an equal footing with white servicemen. Franklin Roosevelt needed the black vote against Wendell Wilkins and he used this issue to gain black support. Roosevelt lived up to his promise. Subsequently, this author was one of the first blacks in Fort Worth to enlist in the United States Coast Guard as an apprentice seaman, and yet I was still required to ride in a separate coach on the trains that carried me to my Coast Guard assignments. For years, the only positions blacks could hold were cooks and stewards. Claude Platt became one of the first black cadets to receive his pilot training by the Air Force. His training took place from 1939 to 1945 and then because of his superior flying capabilities of the PT-17 aircraft, he was selected to teach airmen at Tuskegee from 1941 to 1945, including members of the 99th Pursuit Squadron. One student, Colonel Benjamin O. Davis, Jr., etched himself further in the annals of history as he commanded the 99th Pursuit Squadron in Tunisia. Upon his return to the United States, he organized the 332nd Fighter Group which flew more than 3,000 missions in Europe and destroyed almost 300 enemy planes.

After the war, Claude Platt was employed as a machinist at Menasco AeroSystem in Arlington in 1962, and after a short stint there, he worked at Bell Helicopter Plant until he retired in 1991.

Speaking of flying and outstanding aeronautic achievement, the University of Houston and its alumni must be elated over the achievement of one of its graduates, DR. BERNARD A. HARRIS, JR., M.D. He has many outstanding accomplishments, but his exploration in outer space stands out above many others; he was the first African-American to walk in space as a medical doctor mission specialist. Astronaut Bernard Harris had the honor of also serving with Eileen Collins, the first woman to pilot a space shuttle mission. Their mission on February 3, 1995 was a part of the international cooperation program the United States has with the Russian Space Station, MIR. The astronauts' flight was designed to improve efficiency in communication while spaceships are in orbit by developing operational flexibility in video switch and digital television downlink.

Dr. Bernard A. Harris is a graduate of the University of Houston. He is a clinical professor and Associate Professor of Internal Medicine at the University of Texas Branch; Assistant Professor at the Baylor School of Medicine; and Vice-Chairman of the Board of Regents for Texas Tech University Health Science Center in Lubbock, Texas. Dr. Harris is the Vice-President of Business Development for SPACEHAB, a subsidiary of Space Media. In 1998 he was appointed to the National Deafness and Other Communication Disorders Advisory Committee.

If there has ever been a princely leader who helped Texas and had an enormous impact on the entire United States, it has to be HEMAN MARION SWEATT. The Texas Constitution mandated segregated schools, and the dual school system applied to blacks anywhere in this state. The "separate but equal" policy was concurrently unequal.

Heman Sweatt grew up in the Third Ward district in Houston. He was a graduate of Wiley College, Marshall, Texas, and wanted to get an advanced degree. In 1946 Sweatt attempted to matriculate at the University of Texas Law School but was refused admission. He filed a lawsuit, which really put him and Texas on the map. Attorneys W. J. Durham, James Nabrit, Jr., and Carter Wesley, who also owned two black newspapers, the *Dallas Express* and the *Houston Informer*, were the legal authorities for Sweatt. Dr. J. Frank Dobie, a white English professor at the University of Texas, also helped the plaintiff in his effort to be accepted at the University Law School. Sweatt exploded into the news media, got pro and con support, and was even threatened with death.

Travis County Judge Roy Archer ruled that Texas should come up with a law school for blacks. The state made a makeshift school, rented some classrooms in Houston, hired two black lawyers, and named the school Prairie View Law School. This school was the only state-supported school for blacks and was forty-five miles from Houston. The school had no trained faculty, nor an adequate law library. Sweatt maintained that he couldn't get an education in the basement of a building that in no way could duplicate the facilities at the University of Texas at Austin. After four years of litigation, Chief Justice Warren decreed in his ruling that the law of separate but equal in *Plessy v. Ferguson* in 1896 was unconstitutional. He decreed that separate educational facilities are unequal, and "Therefore, we hold the plaintiffs are deprived of the equal protection of the laws guaranteed by the Fourteenth Amendment."[134]

In September 1950, Sweatt was admitted to the University Texas Law School but withdrew in 1952 because of academic deficiency. At the invitation of Whitney Young of the Urban League, Sweatt went to Atlanta University School of Social Work on a full scholarship. He earned a Master's degree in the field of community organization and went on to do social research for the Cleveland Urban League for the next eight years.[135]

Heman Sweatt had effectively eliminated the court edict of separate but equal and moved equality in Texas and the nation closer to reality. The Supreme Court followed up with its mandated integration of public schools in 1954 in its ruling in *Brown v. the Board of Education*. A prince had come out of Egypt and Texas. Heman Sweatt could not practice law in Texas, but black America was doubly rewarded in March 2001. Racial diversity and the inclusion of blacks has been a long time coming to this state; Governor Rick Perry broke that impasse when he appointed Attorney Wallace Jefferson as the first black to the Texas Supreme Court. He replaced another minority, Judge Al Gonzales, who resigned his seat on the Texas Supreme Court to work as a counselor to President George W. Bush. Jefferson had just been approved by the Texas Senate to be a member of the State Commission on Judicial Conduct.

WALLACE JEFFERSON graduated from high school in San Antonio, Texas, and attended Michigan State University, where he received his degree in 1985; he also graduated from the University of Texas School of Law and was admitted to the state bar in 1988. Jefferson worked as a civil attorney and argued effectively several cases before the State Supreme Court. In 1996, in *Brown v. Bryan County*, Jefferson won the court's approval in a 5-4 vote that the Sheriff's Department was not liable for a deputy who used excessive force. In 1998, by the same count, he defended Texas' Lago Vista School District by asserting that it was not responsible for a teacher who had had an off-campus sexual relationship with a fifteen-year-old student. As he reflected on his achievements, Wallace Jefferson went back three generations through the eventful past and found his blood ties with his grandfather, Shredick Willis, who was once owned by State District Court Judge Nicholas Battle. At age thirty-seven, Wallace Jefferson had certainly made worthwhile and notable achievements his ancestors dreamed of but never experienced.

If princes are to continue to come out of Texas or anywhere, it must be with a basic educational component, reading. Even at age 103, GEORGE DAWSON is an extraordinary example of one continuing the goal of mastery of reading in the sunset of one's life. This grandson of slaves from Harrison County, where Marshall is the county seat, was born in 1898. His early experience in Marshall, Texas, was typical of the institutionalized racial hostility superimposed on blacks throughout the South and other parts of America. In that city, blacks were not permitted on the courthouse property except as supervised laborers or the main feature of a lynching to "keep blacks in their subordinated places." In his memoirs George Dawson relates the impact of a lynching of an African-American with the consent of the sheriff and other leading citizens. It must be noted again that the United States Supreme Court had ruled two years before Dawson was born, in *Plessy v. Ferguson*, that "Blacks had no rights that whites were bound to respect." He witnessed this American tenet and it left an indelible imprint on his life.

At eight years of age, George Dawson followed the rule for all young black boys: since he could not attend public school, he had to work full-time for white farmers at the rate of $1.50 per week. Later he worked in the building of the railroad from Kaufman to Dallas, and for the city of Dallas as a member of a road crew. However, Dawson could not read and decided to take steps to correct this deficiency. On January 4, 1996, he enrolled in a literacy class under the tutelage of Carl Henry at Lincoln High School, and in two years, by January 17, 1998, Dawson was reading at a third-grade level. Recognition and fame came his way at ninety-eight years of age.

School trustees in the Carroll School District in Southlake will name the new school George Dawson Middle School in honor of the achievement of this Afro-American. Thirteen-year-old Robs Lawrence suggested the name to his father, Jerry Lawrence, a trustee on the Carroll School Board, and it passed by a 4-3 vote. This is a historical first for this part of north Texas, to have a school named in honor of a black in a district which is 95 percent white; this is some tribute. Blessings continue to flow for Dawson because on May 11, 2001, Texas Wesleyan University gave him an Honorary Doctorate of Humane Letters in absentia. His reading instructor, Carl Henry, accepted it for him because he was ill and unable to attend. George Dawson died July 5, 2001 at age 103 and left an immortal legacy of literacy.

At the time citizens of Dallas were eulogizing George Dawson at his funeral services, members of the American Legion Post 838 in Fort Worth were still celebrating and honoring 105-year-old BENNIE (BEN) COLLIER for his service in the United States Army. In a miraculous physical health, he can still read without the use of eyeglasses. Bennie Collier was born in Granger, Texas (Williamson County), and came to Fort Worth at the age of four. When World War I began, he joined the United States Army and served in the quartermaster and work battalion. Afro-American soldiers were segregated in the armed forces and limited to menial duties in supply and work units. After the war, Bennie Collier was employed for twenty-eight years by the College Avenue Baptist Church in Fort Worth.

When President-Elect George Bush began his Washington, D.C. presidential trek to his swearing in, Midland, Texas was glamorized by the news media as the focal starting point. It was designated in Texas as "midway" between Fort Worth and El Paso. But for Afro-Americans in Texas, this western center for the oil industry was equally gratifying in importance: the highest-ranking black elected official in Texas, MICHAEL WILLIAMS, Railroad Commissioner, also had his roots in Midland. He was a former prosecutor and assistant district attorney in that city.

In 1990 Michael Williams was appointed by President George (Herbert Walker) Bush the Assistant Secretary for Civil Rights in the U.S. Department of Education. When Carole Keeton Rylander was elected comptroller, she vacated her position as railroad commissioner and Governor George W. Bush appointed Michael Williams to finish her unexpired term. In the 2000 general election, Michael Williams received unprecedented majority support from the Republican leadership and voters in Texas. Today he is the only Afro-American statewide elected official and the first to serve on the three-member panel of the State Railroad Commission. In 1999 he was elected chairman of that body. Michael Williams has also served as Chairman, Texas Juvenile Probation Commission and Alternative Fuels Council.

Many black citizens and scholars in Texas have hypothesized the importance of business to any community or city. They are still firm believers that economic self-help development in the inner city was the key to independence and improving the quality of life. This supposition came to fruition when COMER COTTRELL decided to come to Dallas. He was an ex-sales manager for Sears and Roebuck in Los Angeles, California, and he had a vision to start his own company. On January 5, 1970, he formed the Pro Line Corporation with $600 and a borrowed typewriter in a small office-warehouse. His military experience in the United States Air Force as a PX Manager gave him invaluable insight on the hair products black consumers required. Cottrell marketed "black cosmetics" in military exchanges and in two years had a very lucrative and profitable business.

In 1973 Comer J. Cottrell and his younger brother, James Cottrell, hit the million-dollar mark in sales and bought their first manufacturing plant in Gardena, California. Hair Food, a gel-type hair conditioner, and "Kiddie Kit," a product to make the hair more manageable, doubled their sales and in three years they relocated to a 35,000-square-foot facility in Carson, California.

After a trip to Africa with Mayor Tom Bradley of Los Angeles in January 1979, the Cottrells opened a foreign market potential. PRO-LINE products are being manufactured and sold in Nigeria, Kenya, the Ivory Coast, islands of the Caribbean, and Taiwan. In 1980 the entrepreneurs marketed an at-home kit, Curly Kit, which made their sales skyrocket and caused them to look toward Texas for a greater share of the market. Pro Line found a 127,000-square-foot complex on I-30 in Dallas and it became the largest black-owned manufacturing facility in the southwest.

What did Comer Cottrell bring to Texas? He set an example for many young people that if you think you can succeed, you can. His philanthropic influence stands out vividly as he helped to maintain an educational institution for the benefit of blacks and other minorities. When Bishop College was being forced to close in Dallas, Comer Cottrell stepped in, purchased the property, and enabled Paul Quinn College to move from Waco to the Bishop College site; he serves on that board.

Being a shrewd businessman, Comer Cottrell acquired and sold interest in the Texas Rangers baseball team along with Governor George W. Bush. He serves on the boards of Chase Bank of Texas and the Better Business Bureau. He is a former president of the Dallas Black Chamber of Commerce and the Dallas/Fort Worth International Airport.

Another black who learned very early the importance of being a business owner was DUMAS M. SIMEUS, who was born in Haiti. He also realized that if he was not going to stay in poverty the rest of his life he had to get an education, so he used his visa to study electrical engineering at Howard University in Washington, D.C. Simeus did postgraduate work at the University of Chicago, where he received a Master's degree in Business Administration.

Simeus was vice-president of Atari, Inc., international game maker, and worked at Bendx and Hartz Pet Food. In 1972 he decided to own his own company. "Today, under the umbrella of Simeus Foods International, Inc., Mr. Simeus owns two food processing plants that employ more than 750 people including 400 in Mansfield, Texas." He has more than eighty different products and does food processing for other large corporations such as Denny's, Hardee's, T.G.I. Friday's, Taco Cabana, and the Olive Garden. His revenue for year 2000 exceeds $200 million.

Blacks in Texas have always had a knack for being connoisseurs of exotic and soul food, but they have an equal passion for having the best automobile with outstanding class status. Such is the contribution and notable achievement of DAVID STEPHENS. His early childhood was spent in Washington, Louisiana, where he worked with his family raising cattle and farming corn, cotton, and potatoes. David Stephens matriculated at Southern University in Baton Rogue and earned a degree in marketing in 1974. His interest had always been in automobiles and in 1977 he went to Atlanta for an internship. This was the beginning of his phenomenal automobile entrepreneurial achievement.

In 1992 David Stephens assumed the position of manager of a Mercury dealer in Texas City, Texas, but in May 1993 he initiated his ownership of a Lincoln-Mercury dealership in Wichita Falls. He became successful after about nine months of operation, and this profitable development put him on the threshold of a monumental success in this endeavor, in addition to his varied experiences in the past twelve years with Ford Motor Company in Texas City, Austin, and Houston.

When the Jaguar Corporation sought to conform to the equal opportunity statutes in vogue in the United States in 1998, they set as their immediate goal the appointment of its first African-American dealer in the United States. David Stephens submitted his impressive resume, and in May 1998 the special honor was given him as the first black Jaguar dealer in the United States. He sold his dealership in Wichita Falls and moved to Plano. With his wife, Delores Stephens, creating the interior design of this new business consortium, David Stephens opened his Millennium Automotive Group on the West Plano Parkway. Why Plano? This multi-industrial center of northeast Texas in Collin County and partly in Denton County has many luxurious amenities that keep it as the economic center of north Texas. David Stephens' Millennium Group, with its sophisticated, state-of-the-art Jaguar, complements this upscale environment and caters to those for whom cost is not a problem and who desire the ultra and exotic technology found in the Jaguar.

The most notable indication that David Stephens is a top businessman was his paying off the million-dollar loan from Ford Motor Company in five months, an unusually short period for repayment of any loan of that magnitude. This employer makes it a point to hire skilled and reliable personnel who demonstrate high ethical and moral values. His sales in 2000 netted more than 48 million dollars.

One doesn't have to be born in Texas to be claimed and acclaimed as a true Texan. BISHOP T. D. JAKES, Pentecostal minister, was born and reared in South Charleston, West Virginia. He relocated his ministry in 1996 from West Virginia to Dallas and electrified people all over America with his presentation of the Gospel. He makes the Bible a therapeutic and living organism that can help people with many of their personal problems, whether they be related to finances, drugs, marriage, children, or imprisonment. What appears to attract many converts and Christians is his attempt to bring them into the reality of the world we live in. Many ministers preach the inevitability of poverty and say that everything will be in the "other world." In the early 1940s I remember many black ministers stopped singing one of the favorite songs, "You Many Have All This World, But Give Me Jesus." Bishop Jakes believes that God wants his children to enjoy life while on this side. He maintains that individuals must put forth educational, economic, and political efforts to enhance their lives while they live.

The Potter's House has food and clothing ministries for the poor and homeless, special services and seminars for those in prison, and is currently undertaking the construction of a 231-acre rehabilitation and jobs complex in the long-neglected black community in south Dallas. Further, Bishop Jakes attempts to motivate individuals and groups with a sense of self-help. The membership appears to be imbued with a basic tenet of Isaiah, the prophet: "Thou art our Father; we are the clay, and thou our Potter; and we all are the work of thy hand."

It is an indication of dynamic leadership when a minister can take a small membership and develop it into one of the largest congregations in the southwest, with some 28,000 members. The Potter's House at 6777 West Kiest in Dallas was expanded and enlarged in August 2000 and has the latest technology for the propagation of the Gospel. The main auditorium can seat 8,000 congregants; it has two 20' x 26' video screens, power and data terminals for laptop computers, and a foreign language center that enables six simultaneous translations.

When you hear other ministers criticizing the enormous growth as being more secular than religious, and that there is no quality in "bulk," you know something is taking place. Critics claim that in Bishop T. D. Jakes' metaphorical interpretations of the Bible, he distorts the scripture for his own personal benefit and borders on being a heretic. Bishop Jakes doesn't have to depend on the church's finances to live in a million-dollar palatial home in the Dallas-White Rock Lake area and support his upscale life style: he has authored some twenty-six books, including the best seller *Woman Thou Art Loosed*, and generates income from record royalties and speaking honoraria. He also broadcasts on several radio stations and TV stations such as BET (Black Entertainment Television) and TBN (Trinity Broadcasting Network). His spiritual charisma attracts people from all ethnic and educational backgrounds. Recently President George W. Bush invited him to help in the prayers for the victims of the September 11, 2001 terrorist attacks on New York and the Pentagon. What better example could we have of the prophetic pronouncement of David that "Princes shall come out of Egypt, and Ethiopia would lift its hands to God" than in Bishop T. D. Jakes?

But that prediction will fail to come to fruition if we don't become more attuned to the realities of our opportunities in America today and stop making excuses and blaming others for our economic and social ills. Blacks must aggressively seek educational opportunities so they will be able to live in a dynamic and changing society. Every child should have a motto of determination: "I will prepare myself, and some day my chance will come." Blacks must seek economic independence through work skills and business development so we won't always have our hands out for perpetual care. This brings me to an ex-slave's account in *Lay My Burden Down: A History of Slavery* (Ben Botkin, 1945).

It appears in the chapter "You Been Set Free."

> When freedom came, my mama said Old Master called all of 'em to his house, and he said, 'You all free, we ain't got nothing to do with you no more. Go on away. We don't whup you no more, go on your way.' My mama said they go on off, then they come back and stand around, just looking at him and Old Mistress. They give 'em something to eat and he say, 'Go on away, you don't belong to us no more. YOU BEEN FREED.' They go away and they kept coming back. They didn't have no place to go and nothing to eat. From what she said, they had a terrible time. She said it was bad times. Some took sick and had no 'tention and died. Seemed like it was four or five years before they got to places they could live. They all got scattered...Old Master every time they go back and say, 'You all go on away. YOU BEEN SET FREE. YOU HAVE TO LOOK OUT FOR YOURSELVES NOW.

NOTES, PART II

1. *The Journey of Alvar Nunez Cabeza de Vaca*, translated from his own narrative by Fanny Bandelier (Chicago: The Rio Grande Press, Inc., 1905), p. xxvii.

2. John Bartlett Brebner, *The Explorers of North America* (New York: Meridian Books, The World Publishing Company, 1933), p. 70.

3. John Fiske, *The Discovery of America*, Vol. IV (Boston: Houghton Mifflin and Company, 1892), p. 502.

4. George Parker Winshop, The Coronado Expedition, 1540-1542 (Chicago: The Rio Grande Press, Inc., 1964), p. 29.

5. Woodbury Lowery, *The Spanish Settlements, 1513-1561* (New York: Russell and Russell, Inc., 1959), p. 278.

6. Papers of Mirabeau Buonaparte Lamar, "Early Settlement of Texas," IV, edited from the original papers in the Texas State Library by Charles Adams Gulick, Jr. (Austin: A. C. Baldwin and Sons, 1922), p. 439.

7. Bennet Lay, *The Lives of Ellis P. Bean* (Austin: University of Texas Press, 1960), p. 22.

8. Lester B. Bughee, "Slavery in Early Texas," *Political Science Quarterly* (Vol. XIII, September 1898), p. 390.

9. George R. Woolfolk, "Turner's Safety Valve and Free Negroes' Westward Migration," *The Journal of Negro History* (July 1965), p. 185.

10. *The Letters of Antonio Martinez: Last Spanish Governor of Texas, 1817-1822*, translated and edited by Virginia H. Taylor and Juanita Hammons (Austin: Texas State Library, 1957), p. 157.

11. E. M. Davis, *The Story of Texas Under Six Flags* (Boston, Guinn & Co., 1897), p. 13.

12. The *Commercial*, October 28, 1843.

13. E. C. Barker, "The African Slave Trade in Texas," *Texas State Historical Association Quarterly* (Vol. VI, July 1902), pp. 146, 149.

14. Art Chapman, "Texas at Large," *Fort Worth Star Telegram* (December 19, 2000), p. 3B.

15. Jack Maguire, "Talk of Texas," *Austin Statesman* (March 4, 1979).

16. Earl Wesley Fornell, *The Galveston Era: The Texas Crescent on the Eve of Secession* (Austin: University of Texas Press, 1962), p. 117.

17. Quoted by Harold Schoen in "The Free Negro in Texas," *Southwestern Historical Quarterly* (Vol. XXXIX, April 1936), p. 305.

18. Austin to Lucas Alamon, May 18, 1830, *Annual Report of the American Historical Association for the Year 1922, The Austin Papers* II, edited by Eugene C. Barker, II (Washington: United States Government Printing Office, 1928), p. 385.

19. Henry S. Brown to Austin from New Orleans, March 21, 1828, ibid., p. 27.

20. John Gibson to Austin, Bill of Sale Agent, ibid., p. 289.

21. Cited in Ernest Wallace and David M. Vigness, *Documents of Texas History, 1528-1846* (Lubbock: Texas Technological College Library, 1960), p. 70.

22. Austin to John Durst, in Barker, ed., p. 289.

23. Austin to Henry Austin, in Barker, ed., p. 405.

24. Austin to Mary Austin Holly, Brazoria, December 29, 1831, in Barker, ed., p. 730.

25. Benjamin Lundy, *The Origin and True Causes of the Texas Insurrection*, 1835.

26. Benjamin Lundy, *The War in Texas: A Review of Facts and Circumstances* (Philadelphia: Printed for the author by Merrieio and Gunn, No. 7, *Carter's Alley*, 1836), p. 3.

27. Benjamin Lundy, *The Origin and True Causes of the Texas Insurrection*, 1835, p. 9. University of Texas Library, Austin: (Vol. XXXIX) No. 4 April 1936, p. 294.

28. Harold Schoen, "The Free Negro in the Republic of Texas," *Southwestern Historical Quarterly* (Vol. XI, July 1936), p. 26.

29. Barker, ed., p. 82.

30. Harold Schoen, "The Free Negro in the Republic of Texas," *Southwestern Historical Quarterly* (Vol. XI, No. 3, 1937), p. 178.

31. Sallie Glasscock, *Dreams of an Empire: The Story of Stephen Fuller Austin and His Colony in Texas* (San Antonio: The Naylor Co., 1951), p. 155.

32. Walter Lord, *A Time to Stand* (New York: The Naylor Co., 1961), p. 163.

33. Lota Spell, "Music in Early Southwest," *The Texas Monthly* (Vol. V, January 1920), p. 68.

34. J. A. Richards, *Famous Texans* (Dallas: Dallas Banks and Company, 1955), p. 2.

35. Harold Schoen, "The Free Negro in Texas," *Southwestern Historical Quarterly* (Vol. XL, July 1936), p. 33.

36. Ibid., p. 31.

37. Dianne Elizabeth Prince, *William Goyens, Free Negro on the Texas Frontier*, Unpublished Master's Thesis (Stephen F. Austin State College, July 1967), p. 14.

38. Senate Journal, Fourth Legislature, p. 340.

39. Gammel, *The Laws of Texas*, II, (Austin: The Gammel Book Co., 1898), p. 326.

40. J. L. Worley, "The Diplomatic Relations of England and the Republic of Texas," *Southwestern Historical Quarterly* (Vol. IX), pp. 9-10. See also: Correspondence from the British Archives Concerning Texas, 1837-1846, edited by Ephraim Douglas Adams, ibid. (Vol. 15), p. 217.

41. "Augustus M. Tomkins, Frontier Prosecutor," *Southwestern Historical Quarterly* (Vol. LIV), p. 321.

42. Durham and Everett L. Jones, *The Negro Cowboy* (New York: Dodd, Mead and Company, 1965), pp. 17-18.

43. Earl Wesley Farnell, *The Galveston Era: The Texas Presence on the Eve of Secession* (Austin: University of Texas Press, 1962), p. 224.

44. Ibid., p. 227.

45. Major C. Stafford to Captain Edmund P. Turner, quoted in *The War of the Rebellion: A Compilation of the Official Records of the Union and Confederate Armies*, Series I, Vol. XXVI, Part II (Washington: Government Printing Office, 1889), pp. 282-283.

46. F. W. Rhine, Quartermaster Agent to Major Simeon Hart, Clarksville, July 20,

1863, ibid., pp. 154-155, 193.

47. Wendell Addington, "Slave Insurrections in Texas," *Journal of Negro History* (Vol. 35, October 1950), p. 430.

48. *Brenham Inquirer*, August 11 and 25, 1860.

49. James Farker, *Fort Worth in the Civil War*, as published in the *Fort Worth Star-Telegram*, July 25, 1860 (Belton: Peter Hansborough, Bell Press, 1960), pp. 17-18.

50. *Marshall Republican*, August 18, 1860.

51. William H. White, "Texas Slave Insurrection of 1860," *Southwestern Historical Quarterly* Vol. III, January 1949), p. 262.

52. W. C. Bolden, "Frontier Defense in Texas During the Civil War," *West Texas Historical Association Year Book* (Vol. IV, June 1928), p. 29.

53. Ibid., p. 30.

54. Langston Hughes and Milton Meltzer, *Pictorial History of the Negro in America* (New York: Crown Publishers, Inc., 1956), p. 182.

55. R. E. Pennington, *The History of Brenham and Washington County* (Houston: Standard Printing and Lithography Company, 1915), p. 37.

56. Charles H. Wesley, *Negro Labor in the U.S., 1850-1925: A Study in American Economic History* (New York: Russell & Russell, 1927), p. 134.

57. Henderson H. Donald, *The Negro Freedmen: Life Conditions of the American Negro in the Early Years after Emancipation* (New York: Henry Schuman, Inc., 1925), p. 192.

58. William H. Leckie, *The Buffalo Soldiers: A Narrative of the Negro Cavalry in the West* (Norman: University of Oklahoma Press, 1961), p. 81.

59. John H. Carroll, *The Black Military Experience in the American West* (New York: Lineright, 1971).

60. Phillip Durham and Everett Jones, *The Adventure of the Negro Cowboy*, (New York, 1965), p. 36.

61. "Ride of the Century," *Ebony* (Vol. 23, February 1968), pp. 75-76.

62. Phillip Durham, "Negro Cowboys," *American Quarterly* (Vol. 7, Fall 1955), p. 103.

63. Hetlye Wallace Branch, *The Story of 80 John* (New York: Greenwich Publishers, Inc., 1960), p. 27.

64. Ibid., p. 38.

65. Eugene D. Genovese, *Roll Jordan Roll: The World the Slaves Made* (New York: Pantheon Books, 1974), p. 109.

66. Charles W. Ramsdell, "Texas From the Fall of the Confederacy to the Beginning of Reconstruction," *Texas Historical Association Quarterly* (Vol. XI), p. 219.

67. Claude Elliott, "The Freedman's Bureau in Texas," *The Southwestern Historical Quarterly* (Vol. LVI, July 1952), p. 8.

68. Ibid., p. 15.

69. E. R. Lindley, Chief Clerk of House of Representatives of 46th Legislature, *Members of the Legislature of the State of Texas from 1846 to 1939* (1939), p. 74.

70. Cyrus W. LaGrone, *History of Negro Education at Marshall, Texas*, Master's Thesis (Southern Methodist University, 1927), p. 127.

71. "Tenth Annual Report of Freedman's Aid Society," quoted in Cyrus LaGrone,

p. 43.

72. Martin Dreyer, "Tell the Truth About Texas," *Houston Chronicle Magazine* (July 7, 1968), p. 15.

73. Roscoe C. Martin, "The Greenback Party in Texas," *The Southwestern Historical Quarterly* (Vol. XXX, No. 3, January 1927), p. 171.

74. Report of the Committee on Grievances at the State Convention of Colored Men of Texas, 1883. Quoted in Thomas R. Frazier, ed., *Afro-American History: Primary Resources* (New York: Harcourt, Brace and Jovonovich, Inc., 1970), p. 178.

75. W. H. King, to John Ireland, Governor of Texas, Report of the Adjutant General 1886, *Texas Military History* (Vol. 2, No. 2, May 1962), p. 136.

76. Billy Bob Lightfoot, "The Negro Exodus from Comanche County, Texas," *Southwestern Historical Quarterly.*

77. The Sixteenth Census of the United States, Washington, 1940 (Vol. II, Population, Part VI).

78. Lightfoot, p. 415.

79. Maude Cuney Hare, *Norris Wright Cuney* (New York: The Crisis Publishing Company, 1913), p. 85.

80. Ibid., p. 121. See also: Robert C. Conter, *James Stephen Hogg: A Biography* (Austin: University of Texas Press, 1959), p. 270.

81. Robert C. Conter, *James Stephen Hogg: A Biography* (Austin: University of Texas Press, 1959), p. 218.

82. "Norris Wright Cuney: A Son of Texas," *Negro History Bulletin*, V. (Washington, D.C., The Association for the Study of Negro Life & History, Inc.), pp. 139-140.

83. Hare, p. 228.

84. William Olivier Bundy, *Life of William Madison McDonald, Ph.D., Biography* (Fort Worth: The Bunker Printing Co., Inc., 1925), p. 34.

85. Ibid., p. 84.

86. *Fort Worth Star-Telegram* (June 9, 1920).

87. Bundy, p. 112.

88. Bundy, p. 30.

89. *Fort Worth Star-Telegram* (Morning, July 6, 1950).

90. A. W. Jackson, "A Sure Foundation," *Houston Informer*, p. 120. See also: *Texas: A Guide to the Lone Star State*, compiled by workers of the Writer's Program of the Works Projects Administration in the State of Texas (New York: Hastings House Publishers, 1940), p. 262.

91. Bundy, p. 292.

92. *Fort Worth Star-Telegram* (Morning, July 10, 1950).

93. Ronald Walters, "Political Strategies of the Reconstruction," *Current History* (Vol. 57, No. 339, November 1967), p. 267.

94. "People," The University of Texas: Institute of Texas Culture at San Antonio (Vol. I, No. 16, November-December 1971), p. 8.

95. Henry F. Pringle, *Theodore Roosevelt: A Biography* (New York: Harcourt Brace, Jovanovich, Inc., 1931), p. 458.

96. Joseph Bucklin Bishop, *Theodore Roosevelt and His Time: Shown in His Own*

Letters (New York: Charles Scribner's Sons, 1920), pp. 27-29.

97. George E. Mowry, *The Era of Theodore Roosevelt and His Time: Shown in His Own Letters* (New York: Harper & Row, Publishers, 1958), p. 212.

98. George Wallace Chessman, *Theodore Roosevelt and the Politics of Power* (New York: Little, Brown & Co., 1969).

99. "Brownsville Affray," Senate Documents, 60th Congress, 1st Session, Vol. 19 (Washington: Government Printing Office, 1908), p. 4.

100. Ibid., p. 15.

101. Ibid., p. 146.

102. Lawrence D. Rice, *The Negro in Texas, 1874-1900* (Baton Rouge: Louisiana State University Press, 1971), p. 38.

103. W. C. Nunn, *Texas Under the Carpetbagger* (Austin: University of Texas Press, 1962), p. 23.

104. *Journal of the Reconstruction Convention*, 1st Session. (Austin, 1870), pp. 500-505.

105. Anne Patton Baenziger, "The Texas State Police During Reconstruction: A Reexamination," *Southern Historical Quarterly* (Vol. LXIII, No. 4, April 1969), p. 491.

106. Nunn, p. 118.

107. Quoted in J. Mason Brewer, *Negro Legislators of Texas*, p. 143.

108. H. Y. Benedict and John Lomax, *The Book of Texas* (New York: Doubleday, Page and Co., 1916), p. 136.

109. *The Standard*, Clarksville (August 6, 1886).

110. Vann Woodward, *The Strange Career of Jim Crow* (New York: Oxford University Press, 1966), pp. 9, 83.

111. Conter, p. 563.

112. *Texas Revised Civil Statutes*, Art. 3107, p. 358.

113. Nixon V. Herndon, 273 U.S. 536 (1927).

114. Donald S. Strong, "The Rise of Negro Voting in Texas," *American Political Science Review* (Vol. 42), p. 512.

115. Ibid., p. 512.

116. James MacGregor Burns and Jack Walter Peltason, *Government by the People: The Dynamics of American National Government* (Englewood Cliffs: __, 1960), p. 180.

117. Terry V. Adams, 345 U.S. 461, Supt. Ct. 809, 97 L. ED. 745.

118. *Phylon* (Vol. XXIV, Summer 1963), p. 137.

119. Harry Holleway, *The Politics of the Southern Negro: From Exclusion to Big City Organization* (New York: Random House, 1969), p. 132.

120. Harry Holloway, "Negro Political Strategy: Coalition or Independent Power Politics," *Social Science Quarterly*, (Vol. 49, December 1968), p. 539.

121. "Black Didn't Bother the Voters," Southwest Scene, *Dallas Morning News* (March 5, 1972).

122. Luke 2:29-30.

123. "Texas: A Quiet Change," *Time* (May 20, 1966), pp. 31-32.

124. *Fort Worth Star-Telegram* (March 31, 1972), p. 10.

125. Ibid., p. 10.

126. Charles Sanders, "Texas is a New Power on Capitol Hill," *Ebony*, (Vol. 30, No.

4, February 1975), p. 141.

127. "Districts," *Fort Worth Star-Telegram* (August 22, 1991), p. 1.

128. Booker T. Washington, *Up from Slavery* (New York: Sun Dial Press, 1937), p. 316.

129. Reby Cary, recorded interview with Professor T. W. Pratt, one of the founders of the Dallas Negro Chamber of Commerce (April 20, 1948).

130. Ibid.

131. *Negro City Directory*, 1941-42, Dallas, Texas, p. XII.

132. Reby Cary, recorded interview with J. E. Robinson, Houston, Texas (June 14, 1948).

133. Reby Cary, personal communication with Joe S. Moore, Manager of the Montgomery County Chamber of Commerce (June 29, 1948).

134. "The Fourteenth Annual Heman Sweatt Symposium on Civil Rights," The University of Texas at Austin (April 11-14, 2000).

135. "He Broke the Barrier," *Dallas Morning News* (May 20, 1979), p. 1A.

PART III
BLACKS IN FORT WORTH, TEXAS

STATE REPRESENTATIVE 1979-1985

Texas House of Representatives

A History of Blacks in Fort Worth, Texas

The adventurous and nomadic spirit of early Texas pioneers actuated the movement of the Western frontier from the Gulf of Mexico to the fringes of the Texas Panhandle. Texans were active participants in the historical panorama that took place in the middle part of the eighteenth century in Texas and eventually became enshrined in the history of Fort Worth. The Treaty of Guadalupe-Hidalgo, in 1848, provided for the United States' protection of Mexico from the American Indians. At the same time, gold was discovered in California and the government found it necessary to honor its treaty obligations and protect the onrush of American settlers and buffalo hunters from marauding Indians from Eagles Pass on the Rio Grande to Cook's Bend on the Red River.

On March 28, 1848, the Texas legislature passed a resolution requesting their congressional representatives "to use their influence for procuring the passage of an act establishing a chain of military posts in advance of the settlements between the Red River and the Rio Grande."[1]

Fort Worth became one of the strategic military posts established by congressional imperatives to protect the territorial confluence where migrants from the east and conquistadors from the south prepared to move westward. Transversed by the Trinity River and situated on one of its bluffs, it had been named by Major Ripley Arnold on June 6, 1849, for Major General William J. Worth. However, the fort was never fully utilized because restless immigrants kept extending the parameters of the western frontier.

Immediately after the Mexican War of 1848, plans were made to withdraw the Second Dragoons of the United States Army from "Fort Town" and use the Texas Rangers to control the Indians. The Comanche and Kiowa Indians lingered in the western hinterland of Fort Worth, and the Waco Indians around Village Creek, but neither continued to pose a serious threat. Joe B. Frantz writes that the fort "issued invitations for the restless and the questing to move into a region. Equally it issued invitations for those already present to remain."[2] Consequently, many settlers occupied the deserted fort instead of the military because it was apparently safe. Fort Town was such a tranquil place that wild game sported at will over surrounding verdant hills. The only danger was that which was exaggerated by the Dallas newspaper, that a panther came from the dense forest surrounding this township and, after being pursued, laid down in the streets. "Pantherville" became a nickname for this post.

People of all persuasions were attracted to the post. Settlers moving westward to California and drovers going north to Kansas left a residue of people who found this post to their liking. Coming from the Deep South and fleeing from the expanding tentacles of slavery, blacks also continued moving westward with undaunted spirits, seeking a land where they could be free. It is interesting to note that where the Indians were excluded from white society, blacks were tolerated, but only as quasi-free citizens. They had been moving westward ever since the Texas legislature passed the Definitive Act of February 5, 1840, which decreed that all blacks who were not out of Texas within two years would be returned to slavery.[3] This law precluded the annexation of Texas, validated its proslavery leaning, and became the barometer of changing racial attitudes in Texas. Even the Indians had been persuaded to capture and sell blacks in the Indian Territory. "The nomadic Plains Indians ordinarily recognized the Negro as a representative, along with the white man, of a hostile, encroaching culture, and treated him accordingly,"[4] says Kenneth Wiggins Porter. Being black, free, or a foreign citizen was enough to warrant enslavement.

The far western frontier had been closed to blacks by territorial fiat; they were prohibited from settling in the territories adjacent to the Rockies, and Fort Worth became a twilight zone and a shifting corral of slaves soon to be emancipated. There were not many slaves in Fort Worth and Tarrant County, because the number of plantations were not numerous; in 1850 there were 599 whites and 65 slaves. Even with the chartering of Peter's Colony, which renewed interest in the westward movement as a product of the land speculation craze during the economic calamities of the 1840s, there were few slaves brought to the area of Cooke, Grayson, Denton, Collins, Tarrant, and Dallas counties. In *The Peter's Colony of Texas*, Seymour V. Conner explains that "thirty-one families had 106 slaves or approximately three slaves per slaveholding family. Twelve slaves owned by William McKinney of Collins County were the largest holding. Sixty-one percent of the slaveholders had three or less slaves."[5]

When Captain Ephraim M. Daggett came to Fort Worth in 1852, he brought a large contingent of slaves.[6] In the same year, Lawrence Steele came with "two wagons of thirty-six slaves."[7] Estimates are without supporting data, but Colonel Middleton Tate Johnson, who built Johnson Station just northeast of Handley, is reported to have had the largest number of slaves.[8] His colleague Nathaniel Terry owned thirty slaves on his plantations.[9] Some slaves in this area were reported to have burned Randol Mill, which had been built by Archibald Leonard, in 1856.[10]

Estimates cannot be accurately conjectured as to the number of black children who were genetically related to white masters, but the descendants of one such family still live in Denton and Tarrant counties. A man named Chisholm, the cattle king of the west, bought a slave girl named Jensie for $1,400 from a family who was being attracted to California by the gold rush.

Chisholm cohabited with the beautiful mulatto and on April 13, 1857, two girls, Harriet and Almeady, were born. Such births of slaves were common occurrences because black females were construed as chattel to be used at the whims and fancies of their masters. "Meady" later met John Dalford (Bob) Jones, another slave's son, who came from Fort Smith, Arkansas, in 1862 during the great exodus from the Deep South. John married Meady in 1874, and to this union Eugie Jones Thomas, Jinks Jones, and Emery Jones were born.[11] In 1977, *The Denton Record-Chronicle* reported:

> Jinks Jones works in the Grapevine Auction center on the corner of
> Highway 114 and White Chapel Road. He has owned this business for

the past __ years. Eugie still operates a truck farm on 37 acres of the original 2,000 acres. In the 1950s the U.S. Corps of Engineers attempted to divest the "Jones" land from Eugie to expand the Grapevine Lake Reservoir; she refused to sell. Attempts to coerce her to sign documents failed and checks sent by the government were uncashed.

On September 1, 1974, Eugie Jones Thomas' home was certified by Secretary of Agriculture John C. White as a historical landmark of the Texas Family Land Heritage Program.

Slaveowners from the surrounding state proliferated the number of slaves in Tarrant County by trading them for land. Frank Lewis, in recollecting his experience in Fort Worth, stated that "my father came to Tarrant County before the close of the Civil War and traded his slaves for 264 acres southeast of where Handley is now."[12]

Other slaves were brought to Tarrant County and abandoned. James Wilson was one of 100 slaves brought by his master from Arkansas. This slaveholder attempted to sell his slaves but apparently could not find a buyer. He left the entire contingent of slaves "without food, clothes or anything."[13] Otis Isbell, who lived in White Settlement, released his 200 slaves because he couldn't afford to keep them.

The election of 1860 sounded the death knell of slavery in Fort Worth and the entire country and, as Ray Billington noted, "warned that the concept of racial equality was to be enshrined in the White House."[14] Lincoln's election was a clarion call for the South to secede from the Union. The democratic process broke down completely. Consequently, Texas joined the Confederacy as the South attempted to overthrow the federal government; blacks watched with steadfast anticipation as the fratricidal conflict took shape in 1860. They also watched with concern the violent reaction of the white populace in Fort Worth to the anticipated freeing of slaves. Most white Texans were totally disenchanted with the Republican Party's national platform because pyromaniacs had conspired to create havoc on Election Day, August 1860. Fire and devastation was to reduce and paralyze northern Texas and culminate in a general revolt of slaves.

On July 8, 1860, arsonists destroyed the entire northwestern business section of Dallas, Texas; one half-hour later incendiary fires began in Denton and Pilot Point. These series of events alarmed whites in Fort Worth and repressive acts were instituted. Nine days later, on July 17, two white men were lynched. One was William H. Crawford, a brick mason, who was hanged on a pecan tree near the banks of the Clear Fork, three-quarters of a mile west of Fort Worth.[15] Ned Purvis, a black slave, broke tradition and testified that Crawford had urged Fort Worth blacks to revolt.[16] (Testimony of blacks against whites was not acceptable.) To compound white concern, in August, "enough strychnine to fill half a barrel…was discovered in the possession of many slaves in the vicinity of Fort Worth."[17]

The other white man was a Methodist minister-abolitionist, the Reverend Anthony Bewley, who was caught on the Indian Border, returned to Fort Worth bound in rope, and lynched near the Jacksboro Highway because of "tampering with the slaves."[18] Hangings were used primarily to intimidate the black Republicans and rid Tarrant County of black sympathizers such as newspaper publisher A. B. Norton, whose antislavery editorials made him the target of the *Intellingencer*. He was one of the principal Union abolitionist editors and had previously been run out of town because of his antislavery views.

When the Civil War erupted in South Carolina in 1860, white Fort Worthians rallied to the Confederate cause after a year of indecision. Blacks lingered in the shadow of hope, waiting for deliverance to come by a victorious Union army. Victory seemed remote to Lincoln as the North experienced continued reverses on the battlefield by an inspired Southern army. Too, the South was courting the favor of England, and after the battle of Antietam, 1862, Lincoln had to placate England's new moral conscience against slavery by issuing the Emancipation Proclamation. It was to become effective January 1, 1863, but slaves in Texas did not receive the news until June 19, 1865. It set in motion a social upheaval that challenged the basic tenets of American democracy.

The nostalgia of emancipation sometimes obscures a recurring question: Why the long delay in notifying the slaves in Texas about their freedom? Slaveholders in Texas were determined to circumvent the proclamation and ignored it because the Union had no way of enforcing it while the fighting was still in progress. Most whites anticipated vindictive retaliations from the newly freed blacks because of their previous condition of servitude. Whites were afraid of the possibilities of servile insurrection and were apprehensive about freeing blacks. Most planters planned to keep blacks in quasi-involuntary servitude in order to maintain free labor. Consequently, blacks remained in legal bondage until June 19, 1865, when General Gordon Granger arrived in Galveston, Texas, to take control of this military district, which was part of Lincoln's reconstruction plan.

Social rejection and concomitant second-class citizenship mentality resulted in lackadaisical attitudes in the community. The intensity of the celebration of the emancipation of blacks has been sporadic in nature and vacillates from one generation to another. Non-Texans find it difficult to understand the significance of "Juneteenth" to blacks. It is the day of deliverance and cause for jubilee. A natural reaction to freedom is celebration. The Jewish people today still celebrate Hanukah and still attach great significance to their deliverance from Egypt and victory over the Syrians; Americans hold in high esteem the winning of independence from the tyranny and yoke of British oppression. Blacks also memorialize the gaining of their freedom from the shackles of slavery.

Juneteenth was a festive occasion and many white farmers excused black laborers from work and provided cattle and hogs for big community barbecues. For many years in Fort Worth, Armour and Swift Packing Companies sponsored picnics in all-black Greenway Park. Later on blacks were permitted to use the facilities of Forest Park for celebration on this day only.

Madeline Williams, a reporter, was assigned to cover the Juneteenth celebration in 1950 and attempted to find out why blacks were only allowed to use the city park on this one day. Because of her persistence, she asked the city attorney, Rhinehart Rover, to quote her the laws or city ordinances that prohibited blacks from using the park. He told her there were no such laws, but only custom which barred them. The subsequent story about Juneteenth made it possible for blacks to begin to use the park on days other than

Juneteenth.[19] They immediately rejected this one-day use of Forest Park, which many dubbed as a day when the city let them use it to buy a monkey for the zoo. Attendance dropped off considerably at the park.

For a while, Juneteenth became passé in the 1960s as blacks accelerated the push for integration. With the exception of a small clique, most of them did not want to be associated with "red soda water and barbecue." They opted to celebrate the Fourth of July until they realized that they were still not accepted into the total community, and they were exposed by militant blacks to Frederick Douglass' "What Is Your Fourth of July to Me?" The number of celebrants at Greenway Park had been diminishing each year, and blacks were determined to integrate all public facilities. In 1951 a contingent played golf at a white-only Worth Hills Golf Course, and the Ministerial Alliance led a boycott to keep blacks away from Forest Park on Juneteenth and pushed for use on any day.

In 1974 more than 10,000 blacks thronged into Sycamore Park in Fort Worth in observance of Juneteenth. The Economic Development Board, headed by the Reverend Henry Masters, made elaborate plans for the celebration. Highlighted by a parade, speeches, and exhibits, the celebration was a tremendous success. Plans were begun immediately to expand the activities, and in 1975 more than 18,000 persons gathered in the same park and created traffic jams way into the night. From 1976 to 1978 plans were made to conduct a week of activities. The sudden surge of interest was the result of black chauvinism inherent in new dimensions of historical awareness and perspectives reaffirmed in the civil rights movement of the 70s.

But freedom for slaves in Fort Worth and other parts of Texas was not to come to full fruition, as white Texans based their society on the labyrinth of loyal Southern custom. President Johnson's defiance of Congress created intolerable conditions for blacks and loyalists. Many Texans intimidated both elements and "expected that things were presently to go on just as if there had been no war."[20] In fact Reconstruction was fraught with white resistance which manifested itself in repression, lawlessness, and clandestine terror groups designed to keep blacks as second-class citizens subjugated to white rule. Many of these whites had left Alabama and the Deep South to escape the influence of Reconstruction radicals who were proponents of equality of the black race. Consequently, they promulgated their ideas by forming an extra-legal organization, the Ku Klux Klan, whose headquarters in Fort Worth was north of the Trinity River on Main Street.

Several prominent city leaders were members of the Klan. The most notable was J. Frank Norris, who pastored the First Baptist Church. In 1940 this church was heralded as having the largest in membership in Texas (21,000 members) and the largest Sunday School (more than 5,000 members). By night Frank Norris was a leader of the Ku Klux Klan; by day, a servant of the Lord. Needless to say, most Klansmen defended their bigoted activities as being divinely inspired. Mack Williams, reporter for *The News Tribune*, wrote, "Reverend Norris spoke frequently at Klan meetings in the Klavern on North Main Street. The large brick building burned in November 1924, a day before the curtain was to rise on a Klan fund-raising minstrel show."[21] On a Saturday afternoon, July 17, 1926, the Reverend Frank Norris shot Elliott Chips, a wealthy lumberman, whom Norris said had threatened him in the minister's study. Norris was acquitted and continued his tirades against blacks in Fort Worth.

In spite of the anti-Jewish, anti-Catholic and white-sympathizer thrust of the Klan, black men were the principal targets. Sam Kilgore, a black cement contractor in Fort Worth, remembered how the Klan burned his home and "ran the colored folks away, for no cause but just to be ornery and plunder the homes."[22] William Hamilton, an ex-slave, recounted that they would "pick out a black to whip, they did that just to keep the Negroes scared."[23]

Occasionally a black would receive white paternalistic protection and would be allowed extraordinary participation in the Fort Worth community. Because Major Van Zandt patronized and recommended other citizens to do business with John Pratt, wrote James Farber, "he held the distinction of being the city's first Negro businessman. Pratt operated a blacksmith shop at what is now Weatherford and Commerce Streets and enjoyed the patronage of practically everybody in town."[24]

Other blacks in Fort Worth didn't fare as well as Pratt. They felt the sting of racial hatred and a determination on the part of whites to refute the egalitarian objectives of radical Republicans. Vigilante committees were organized, and the *Fort Worth Democrat* reported that "two hundred sheeted riders marched through the city and county one night in 1868—trouble was here."[25]

Blacks were meted swift and arbitrary justice by hanging for crimes that others were pardoned for. The first black to be hanged in Fort Worth was Sol Bragg, who was accused of murdering Matthew Green, a white man, in 1873. Sol escaped before his trial, was recaptured, found guilty, and sentenced by Judge Hardin Hart, a one-armed judge appointed by the controversial Governor E. J. Davis.[26] Bragg was to be hanged on the first day of May 1875. In April he made an abortive attempt to escape by attempting to slug McCain, the jailer, with a bar of iron.[27] Instead the jailer subdued Sol and on the appointed day marched Sol to the gallows. Rumors prevailed that an effort would be made by a group of blacks from the west to rescue him, but this did not materialize. At the appointed hour "he ascended the scaffold…and in a calm, firm voice, addressed the crowd for about thirty minutes, protesting his innocence of the killing of Matthew Green. He maintained that Baz Moulden, another Black, had fired the shot."[28] Whether or not Bragg was guilty or not can only be conjectured. James Farber asserts, "There seems little doubt that white sheriffs, judges, and vigilantes cared little about guilt or innocence of Blacks; their concern was to keep Blacks in their places."[29] Some black had to atone for the death of a white man, and Sol was the one.

Quite frequently blacks experienced a marginal illusion of justice. A kangaroo court was held for Frank Vaughn, thirty years of age, who was accused of raping a young white girl in Fort Worth. According to the *Fort Worth Democrat*, "At a given signal he was hanged by having a box kicked from under him. A few hours later, a messenger arrived with a respite from Governor Roberts."[30] Even if the respite had arrived in time, it is doubtful that the executioners would have obeyed the law. Blacks still had no rights that whites were bound to respect.

Immediately after the cessation of the War Between the States in 1865, twenty-seven states ratified the Thirteenth Amendment to the U.S. Constitution. Acceptance of the amendment by the rebellious states, which included Texas, was one of the conditions of readmittance. The Civil Rights Bill was passed over President Andrew Johnson's veto to negate the black codes and other state policy regulations, which kept Blacks in quasi-servitude as a result of the newly adopted Civil Rights Bill. In 1872 a black man named Rucker was elected to the board of trustees in Tarrant County's first free election since 1866.[31] This election was unique in that black troops preserved law and order by guarding the polls.

The Freedmen's Bureau had been authorized by Congress as early as 1863 to protect the freedmen from capricious cruelty. Its duties were to provide schools and legal protection and to supervise and approve all work contracts between former slaves and white employers. Through patronage granted by the Republican Party, Benjamin Franklin Barkeley was appointed by General E. M. Gregory as head of the Bureau in Fort Worth. Since he lived in Birdville, he made the daily trip to Fort Worth guarded by several Negro soldiers.[32] Barkeley was an abolitionist for Kentucky who left the Deep South because he abhorred slavery. In the late 1850s, "he bought Aunt Nan, an elderly slave at an auction in order to free her and then hire her as a cook and housekeeper."[33]

Congress sought to reinforce Constitutional guarantees to blacks by passing the Civil Rights Act of 1875. This act guaranteed blacks full enjoyment and benefit of all laws and proceedings for the security of persons and property as enjoyed by white citizens. In Fort Worth, whites remained undisturbed by the law. They had relegated blacks to a subordinate position, and many blacks accepted this role with complacency.

While there was a regional outcry from the southern states, few whites expected blacks to cross accepted racial barriers in Fort Worth. The Fort Worth Democrats expressed concern about young white men who socialized with blacks, even in a religious atmosphere. The following headline appeared in the Saturday, April 17, 1875 issue of *Civil Rights*: "Disgraceful Conduct." The article said, "It is inconceivable how men with pure Caucasian blood coursing in their veins would even forget their self-respect…so as to meet socially with the colored [. A concert at the] Church at Huffman's Hall…was attended by quite a number of our citizens who were attracted together by motives of curiosity…We are informed that several young gentlemen (?) remained after the concert and exhibition was over [and] that they were promenading around the hall, each with a saddle-colored or ebony maiden (?) leaning affectionately on his arm."[34]

Maintaining racial barriers was made easier by the Republican Party's retreat from safeguarding the civil rights of blacks in the United States. According to writer Rayford Logan, "A succession of weak presidents between 1876 and 1901 facilitated the consolidation of white supremacy in the South."[35] The extension of the Texas and Pacific Railroad to Fort Worth on July 19, 1876 was a major cataclysmic force in compromising the freedom of blacks in Fort Worth. When the thundering of the iron horse broke the solemnity of the western forests, Fort Worth greeted the railroad as an economic bonanza and it became clear that the protection of blacks was less important than lucrative federal railroad subsidies acquired through legislative log-rolling. Thus the Republican Party sold blacks back into slavery when they agreed to the Compromise of 1877, in which they accepted Rutherford Hayes as the winner over Tilden in the election of 1876 in exchange for the withdrawal of federal troops.

Blacks now had no protection; mob rule intensified and the rope became the law in

Fort Worth. The local newspaper was the personification of the general attitude of whites toward blacks from 1876 to 1900. In the *Telegraphic Summary*, one byline read "More Rope Wanted: A Negro Outrages a Lady at Bremond."[35] Commenting on a lynching in Mansfield, the *Daily Democrat* stated, "The mob did right, and the sooner the red-handed and black-haired villains who are daily staining our records with the details of their hideous atrocities, learn that the people of Texas will no longer submit to their villainies, the better it will be for the country."[36]

It seems as if the editorial staff of Fort Worth's *Daily Democrat* was the principal exponents of lawlessness, mob rule, and lynching. Its editorials devoted considerable attention to advocating mob rule. A typical point is its assessment of the Lynch Law, which appeared in the editorial section on Sunday, April 14, 1848:

> On Wednesday night, a mob proceeded to the guard house at Riverside and riddled a Negro man, who was in the charge of the officers of the law, with buckshots.... The Negro was guilty of abduction of a white girl, but the laws have proved so inefficient for the punishment of crimes and have been administered with so much laxity, that blame cannot be attributed to the perpetrators of this act. In fact, the *Democrat* would greatly prefer to see a return to the old days of hempen cords and Judge Lynch.... On Tuesday, April 16, "The *Democrat* commends the action of the mob...mob law is better than none at all.... Let the people take the laws in their own hands."[37]

The awful crucibles of demagogic prejudice, oblations, and proscription were found in the reporting of activities by the *Daily Democrat*; vilifications, derogatory epithets, and racial diatribes reflected white sentiment in Fort Worth. The following typical articles were just routine and too numerous to analyze individually:

"Two spirited Negro wenches engaged in personal controversy yesterday...both were arrested and given quarters in the calaboose."[38]

Under the headline "A Bad Nigger": "A dangerous encounter in Birch Brothers Saloon on Rush Street, east of the Public Square between two Negroes. The bad Negro resisted their attempts to arrest him."[39]

"Africans at War": "Last night about 10 o'clock a fight occurred in the alley behind Bohardt's Saloon...the way those niggers gouged and hit was a caution for one to see..."[40]

Young white attitudes toward blacks were shaped by political and community permissiveness. "An Everyday Scene" was editorialized by a reporter who watched the obtrusive hatred inflicted on a black youth who joined a group of whites in gathering loose cotton from wagons going to the cotton gin. It was a practice to collect loose cotton until enough was accumulated to make a bale, which would net $40. The reporter wrote that the white boys cried, "Take that and that! ye liver color coon,"[41] as they ran the black youth from the square. Blacks, though not safe from attack anywhere in the city, nevertheless felt most protected in black communities and thus spent most of their non-working time there.

The red-light district for blacks had been ghettoized by local law. It was the center of both constructive and illicit activity. White politicians visited the area to cajole black voters because their votes could greatly influence most close elections. City councilmen made token improvements, such as building sidewalks in the black community, in exchange for black votes. In the mayoral election of 1878, Captain Day was the choice for most blacks. His organizer in black Second Ward was A. Carter, the "Boss Negro gambler,"[42] who dispensed liquor and cigars to potential voters. The patronage came to no avail because the incumbent mayor was defeated by Colonel R. E. Beckman. The victory by Beckman and the loss by Day had little effect on the social, economic, or political status of the black community. In fact, they made only slight gains.

For two years blacks had petitioned the city council to purchase a cemetery for blacks, and each time the petition was not acted on. A serious need for the cemetery materialized when the "saffon scourge" began to take its toll of black citizens. It was alleged that "the Negroes who have heretofore been considered exempt are taking the fever and dying as rapidly as whites."[43] On April 16, 1878, the petition was presented again by the black citizenry. Alderman Jackson made the formal proposal to City Council and sent reverberating shockwaves through the community by his audacity and frugality. In his desire to economize, Jackson proposed that the cemetery would not be for the exclusive use of blacks, but for whites as well. He asserted that "after death, it mattered little where a man was buried, or who happened to be his next door neighbor. He would favor the purchase of a burial ground for the use of the general public irrespective of rank or color."[44] A sum of $250 was approved by the council to purchase a Jim Crow cemetery. Finally, in 1884, the Old Settlers Trinity Cemetery on NE 28th Street was purchased for those descendants of Ham, who were forced to rest in a separate world. In life and in death, complete social rejection of blacks had crystallized in Fort Worth.

Not only was there a consensus that blacks and whites could not enter heaven through the same "Pearly Gates," but also that the children of different races should not be taught together. The school district had been established by Ordinance Number 168 on August 23, 1878, by the City Council of Fort Worth. Section five of the proposed ordinances made special provisions for a black school.[45] Attitudes had moderated concerning free schools being provided for citizens of all races in Fort Worth. In its editorial on "Free Schools," the local paper hypothesized:

> The education of the Negro is necessary that he may be prepared for the duties of his new station as a citizen. It will not let him remain in ignorance, as it will be the death of free government, or it will disease and destroy our institutions to a degree that will be far worse than intelligent despotism. Crime and pauperism are the twin off springs of illiteracy.[46]

Some blacks, with the assistance of benevolent whites, had made plans to build a school free of church denomination control. A meeting was called by Professor E. T. Albert to plan the building of a school for the black community.[47] Blacks lived mostly in Third Ward. However, several lived in isolated pockets that had been former plantations, such as the pocket of blacks who lived on Colonel Nathaniel Terry's plantation, extending from Samuels Avenue to the Trinity River.[48]

When the electric interurban trolley made it convenient for citizens to travel between Fort Worth and Dallas, Stop Six was one of the oldest, serving a predominately black community in Tarrant County. In 1899, the electric trolley made the Sixth Stop from downtown Fort Worth, and the name Stop Six survives until this very day. This community, originally named Cowanville, was a rural-oriented farm center with a hodgepodge of "shotgun" and wooden shacks each with a minimum of one acre devoted to cotton and vegetables such as beans, corn, black-eyed peas, squash, cucumbers, or any other vegetables used for food or sold at the market. Stop Six further developed as a place where blacks resided who worked for employers in the Polytechnic and Meadowbrook areas.

In 1896 Amanda Davis was one of the first black property owners in Stop Six; she bought a one-acre plot and Amanda Street was named in her honor. Her grandson, Reverend Frank Howard, Pastor of St. Paul Reform Church, often related that his grandmother relied on the forces of nature to heal her body and never had a physician to attend her medical or physical needs. Other black entrepreneurs operated small businesses to serve the needs of that community, but few expanded or became large competitive establishments.

Adjacent to Stop Six, Carver Heights emerged in the 1950s when black realtor L. V. Johnson began selling lots for Howard Patterson, President of the Western Management Corporation. This area, bounded by Rosedale Street on the north, Truman Drive on the south, Loop 820 on the east, and Stalcup on the west, became one of the upscale neighborhoods built solely by black homeowners. Its manicured lawns, shrubs, and bushes differentiated Carver Heights from the adjacent Stop Six.

The Bunche-Ellington Club was formed in 1962 in an endeavor to maintain the quality of the neighborhood. When a developer attempted to place some low-quality manufactured homes in the area, Walter B. Barbour and this writer fought this encroachment with the City of Fort Worth and the Housing and Urban Development Commission, and the developer had to desist in his construction. Today this club is still fighting with state and local government to improve East Rosedale in the same manner they're doing on the west side of town.

On the west side of Fort Worth, blacks also lived in areas adjacent to their place of employment, such as in Lake Como. Arlington Heights, Fort Worth's first suburb, was built by financier H. B. Chamberlain in 1889. The next year, Lake Como was developed to provide water to generate electricity for a new, plush gambling pavilion. The inn burned in 1893 and the area became a "ghetto servant quarters" for white employers in Arlington Heights. An elementary school was built in the community but the high school for blacks remained on Baptist Hill.[49]

In 1891 there were 3,478 white and 709 black students in Fort Worth schools. All black pupils were required to attend the Ninth Street Colored School, except the first, second, third, and fourth grade pupils who lived south of the Texas and pacific Railroad, where they attended James E. Guinn Elementary School. I. M. Terrell, a graduate of Straight University in New Orleans, Louisiana, was appointed principal of the Ninth Street School. His academic preparation was in one of the best universities established after the Civil War. Straight University was founded in 1869 and operated by the American Missionary Association of the Congregational Church. This prestigious school had one of the few law schools in the South from 1876 to 1886. On June 6, 1930, it was consolidated with New Orleans University and is now Dillard University.

When I. M. Terrell accepted the position at Ninth Street, he was employed at a salary of $50 per month. The new principal devoted most of his time to the eleven eldest students, three in the seventh grade and eight in the eighth grade.[50] In 1888 there were no Negro pupils beyond the eighth grade.[51]

Other members of the faculty were Clarissa Thompson, fifth and sixth grades; G. B. Sampson, third and fourth grades; M. L. Terrell, third grade; H. G. Butler, second and third grades; A. B. Woodard, first and second grades; and Daisy O. Truly and V. L. Moore, first grade. Eight years later the faculty included three teachers who were graduates of the Ninth Street Schools: Miss L. V. Terry, Miss Alice Williams, and Mr. T. J. Benjamin.[52]

Around 1909 or 1910, a new eighteen-room school for blacks was built. It contained all elementary grades through the eleventh grade. In 1910 Ninth Street School became the high school and was named I. M. Terrell in honor of the outstanding educator. During the war years, 1915 to 1918, Terrell served as principal of Prairie View State Normal and Industrial College and was replaced at the school in Fort Worth by Professor Bundy. Mr. Bundy served as principal from 1916 to 1920. He was an honor graduate from Howard University and a prolific writer. Being a close friend of Bill McDonald, he wrote an autobiography of the Masonic financier.

In 1920 L. M. Johnson was assigned as principal of this all-black school, a position he held until his retirement in 1945. Black students who attended this school were exposed to the finest cadre of teachers Fort Worth had ever known. Discipline was not a serious problem when teachers like Ms. Crawford, who taught homemaking, reigned as the guardian of the lower floor; W. F. Bledsoe, who taught history and composed the I. M. Terrell school song; Clara Willa Jones, who taught civics with enthusiasm and "paddle persuasion"; and above all, excellent English teachers such as Laberta Phillips and Hazel Harvey Peace, who introduced their students to the joys of literature.

Hazel Peace was the educational "Stadtholder" of I. M. Terrell High School. No one escaped the influence of this dynamic personality. If a student got out of hand, he had to reckon with her. Kerven Carter, former principal at Maudrie Walton Elementary School, called Ms. Peace "a brand of fire." She demanded the best performance from her students and yet was sympathetic to their concerns and needs. The educational and social highlight of Fort Worth for many years was the Annual Boys and Girls Debate, directed by Ms. Peace. Students who were selected to participate in the debate had to know both sides of an issue and be prepared to defend either side they were assigned. Ms. Peace also drilled her students in inductive and deductive reasoning. Motivation was the key to Hazel Peace's success. She encouraged teachers "to take the potential of students, unfolding hidden qualities that slip by undiscovered."[53]

Hazel Harvey Peace retired from her legendary domain in 1972, going on to teach at Bishop College, where she continued her struggle to upgrade the learning process and to help young blacks develop leadership roles for first-class citizenship. I. M. Terrell High School was closed in 1973 as a part of the court order implemented by the district court in partial desegregation of the Fort Worth Independent School District. Hazel Peace continues to carry on in the community. She is active in the Southeast Economic Development Corporation, and in December 2000 the Fort Worth Public Library honored her by designating a 33,000-square-foot Hazel Harvey Peace Youth Center in the Central Library. But to top it all, on December 12, 2001, at age 94, my high school teacher was a torch-bearer in the relay ceremony in Fort Worth for the Winter Olympics to be held in Salt Lake City, Utah. Hazel Peace is still carrying the "torch," and her influence goes on and on.

Nostalgic reflections inspire the hearts of alumni and citizens of the Fort Worth community. For many years, baccalaureate and graduation exercises for I. M. Terrell graduates were held at several black churches because these religious entities had always been the center of black educational, social, and religious activities. Thus it is imperative to ascertain the impact some of these institutions had on the city of Fort Worth.

Mount Gilead Baptist Church has an illustrious history. It was a "splinter" of the Old Baptist Church, in which black Baptists had worshipped prior to 1875. Baptist Hill was the name given to the area east of downtown Fort Worth, where the Baptists congregated and worshipped. However, when Old Baptist divided, the newer members moved to 13th and Jones Street and organized Mount Gilead in 1875 under the pastorate of the Reverend C. A. Augustus, who served as pastor for two years. He was followed by the Reverend W. W. Hay, who continued to increase the number of worshippers. Revivals were numerous and sometimes lasted for weeks. On Sunday, July 25, 1880, fourteen candidates were baptized on the riverbank at the brickyard crossing at the foot of east Fifth Street.[54] This was a big event, with five hundred people in attendance. Later, when Reverend C. P. Hughes constructed an indoor baptizing pool, many converts "refused to be baptized in that thing."[55]

Reverend E. H. Smith was called to the pastorate of this dynamic and growing church and then moved the church to a new site. The cornerstone-laying for the new sanctuary was another gala affair. The Texas and Pacific Central Railroads had special reduced fares to Fort Worth for this weekday ceremony. The Fort Worth *Daily Democrat* carried the following account:

> The stone of Mount Gilead Baptist Church of Fort Worth will be laid on Thursday, May 26, by the following ministers: Rev. William Massey, Waco; A. R. Griggs, Dallas; R. Curry, Sherman; A. P. Dupree, Honey Grove; William Jackson, Denison; Z. T. Pardee, Corsicana; John D. Morrow, Waxahachie; J. D. Dunbar, Mexia; W. W. Hay, Corsicana; A. Oliver, Hillsboro; J. H. Brenham, Tyler; C. Augustus, Gainesville; Professor Smothers, Dallas; C. Shaw, Dallas.[56]

Nevertheless, dissension soon developed in Mount Gilead and the church split again. The Reverend A. R. Griggs, President of the National Baptist Convention, assumed the pastorate of Mount Gilead, and the Reverend J. Frances Robinson, the former pastor, organized St. James Baptist Church, which is currently on Harding Street.

In 1909, when the Reverend Prince Jones, Pastor of Mount Gilead, died, the

Reverend Lacey K. Williams was chosen pastor. In Fort Worth, L. K. Williams expanded Mount Gilead into one of the finest sanctuaries in all of north Texas. He was also the voice and exponent of racial harmony and was most vociferous in his denunciation of the liquor traffic, becoming one of the leading prohibitionists in Texas. Fort Worth and Mount Gilead could not contain L. K. Williams; he accepted the pastorate of Olivet Baptist Church in Chicago, Illinois, and left in June 1916. Immediately a phalanx of ministers attempted to fill the void left by Lacey. Reverend A. L. Boone came on the scene, and launched an expansion and remodeling campaign. A new building was bought to be used as a hospital, and new stained glass windows, pews, and a pipe organ were added to the church.[57] Reverend Boone left in 1923 and was succeeded by Reverends C. A. Green, T. S. Boone, R. T. Andrews, and L. P. Mitchell; continued conflict caused more splintering and Reverend Mitchell took some of the dissidents and organized the Greater New Hope Baptist Church.

Then came C. C. Harper, who became the fifteenth pastor of Mount Gilead and for twenty-seven years brought dynamic leadership and stability to Fort Worth's mother church. He had been preaching since he was nine years of age in Arkansas. His training was a phenomenon of the twentieth century. His Doctor of Divinity degree had been conferred upon him May 31, 1927 by Wiley College; Bishop College conferred a special degree upon him, and he was one of the few blacks in the nation who held a Ph.D. from Princeton University. In 1930 Reverend Harper matriculated in an extension course at Howard University, where the outstanding statesman and educator Mordecai Johnson was president.

Reverend Harper was one of the principal leaders and builders of the St. John Institutional Baptist Church on Trinidad and Allen Streets in North Dallas. From 1915 to 1928 he was the dynamic and titular head of this church. Reverend Harper was acclaimed throughout the United States and most of his time was spent conducting revivals in major American cities. From 1926 to 1931 he conducted evangelistic meetings in New York City; Chicago; Macon, George; Birmingham, Alabama, and countless other cities. Public demand for the services of Reverend Harper was so great that dissention arose in St. John over the continued absence of its pastor. In 1928, by a vote of 186 to 183, he was ousted from St. John. Immediately churches from all over the country sought the services of this orator and scholar.

In 1943 Reverend Harper was called to Mount Gilead, where he served with distinction. In July 1970 he journeyed to the Holy Land; shortly after this trip he died. The Harper's Memorial Reading Room in Bishop College's library is a monument to this stalwart leader.

Church splitting has been one way of expanding the number of Christian adherents in Fort Worth and other communities. As has been noted, when Mount Gilead split from the Old Baptist Church, the old reliable members stayed; in 1878, Reverend T. W. Wilburn assumed the leadership of this group, reorganized and renamed the church, Mount Pisgah. He was pastor until 1887; the Reverends J. L. Griffin and P. W. Upshaw shared in the continuous growth of this congregation. In 1882 Mount Pisgah became the epitome of affluence by installing an extraordinary seventy-two-foot bell tower which echoed over the entire city as it tolled the call to worship or indicated the beginning of a funeral service. Members and friends on Baptist Hill came from all directions when they heard the bell, rain or shine. Its minister, Reverend H. W. Jackson, was called to Galveston and was succeeded by Reverend S. R. Prince in 1908. This stern, dignified, and charismatic preacher ushered Mount Pisgah into a new era of spiritual sophistication unparalleled on Baptist Hill. He stressed religious training for specific positions and established the first departmentalized educational buildings among black churches.

For forty-three years S. R. Prince and Mount Pisgah were landmarks among the family of churches in Fort Worth. Prince served as Superintendent of Missions of the General Baptist Convention, Moderator of the North Texas Association, President of the Missionary Baptist Convention of Texas, President of the State Sunday School Congress, and Secretary of the North Baptist B.Y.P.U. Board.

In 1953 Reverend Prince was diagnosed with a terminal illness and resigned as pastor. The Reverend H. R. Bradley of Beaumont, Texas, was chosen for the pastorate of this ecclesiastical entity. Four years later the church's property at 15th and Crump Streets was purchased by the Texas Highway Department for the construction of U.S. Highway I-35. For a short while the Mt. Pisgah membership worshipped with the Antioch Baptist Church on East Rosedale, where the Reverend W. S. Brent was pastor. The membership in turn purchased the old Evans Avenue Baptist Church (white) on the corner of Evans Avenue and Allen Streets, where it is presently located.

Death claimed Reverend Bradley in August 1963 and the Reverend Nehemiah Davis of Cuero, Texas, accepted the leadership of this dynamic membership. His tenure as pastor was exceeded only by that of S. R. Prince, who ushered in a new breed of college-trained ministers, a rarity in Baptist churches in early Fort Worth. Nevertheless, many churches experienced exceptional growth with those who were not so endowed.

The founder of Rising Star Baptist Church is an example of a leader with mediocre educational training becoming the catalytic force which became monumental in its results. The history of this Fort Worth church is replete with evidence of divine providence. The dynamic and personable pastor, Reverend S. Cary, Jr., born September 5, 1899 in Anderson County, was the son of Reverend Smith Cary, Sr. He joined the New Hope Baptist Church in Jacksonville, Texas, and was licensed and ordained by the Reverend Henry Dews. His parents were very poor and his opportunity for formal education limited. Reverend Cary attended Lincoln High School in Palestine, Texas, and later matriculated at Central Texas College, (Butler College) Tyler, Texas, as a part-time student, where he was employed as custodian of buildings to provide financial support for himself.

Cary moved to Fort Worth in 1919 and married Maggie Blanche Alexander. He united with St. James Baptist Church under the tutelage of Reverend J. H. Winn, Pastor, and continued a period of systematic study and training. Subsequently he enrolled in the Fort Worth School of Theology under Reverend Upshaw. In 1919 he was apprenticed by Reverend Winn to a new church near the Trinity River on Fourth and Seaton Streets; this was a missionary unit of the St. James Baptist Church. Its location was a part of the residue of plantations bounded by the Trinity River on the south and the Rock Island Railroad on the north, where Reverend Cary worked at the Purina Mills as a sewer of sacks. Reverend Cary remained the pastor of Trinity Baptist Church for four years. From 1923 to 1938 several ministers served the church until Reverend J. F. Singleton came in late 1938, renaming the church Fourth Street Baptist Church. On October 23, 1955,

Reverend Singleton built a new edifice at 121 Paradise Street; the name was changed once more to Paradise Baptist Church, a name it retains today.

Reverend Cary had a brief sojourn at Mt. Moriah Baptist Church on Church Street in Hillsboro, Texas, and at Jerusalem Baptist Church in Greenville. There he had a membership of two hundred and only one member regularly employed as a domestic housekeeper. Weekly collections were very meager, but often supplemented with vegetables and chickens, the fruits of the Great Depression.

Fort Worth offered more opportunities, so Reverend Cary returned to his former employment at Purina Mills, sewing feed sacks. Simultaneously he answered the call of a few dissident members of the Jerusalem Baptist Church on New Orleans Street. Mrs. Sylvia Scott offered her home on the corner of New Orleans and Morphy Streets to the group for organizational meetings. Jesse and Minnie Byner, Sylvia Scott, Ardelia Garrison, Lucille Ross, Mary Slater, and M. B. Cary made up the charter members. (This author, Reverend Cary's son, was too young to be counted.) Organizational plans were completed on September 21, 1931, to start a church in the Greasy Spoon on the corner of Irma and New Orleans. Whiskey bottles had to be removed so that the Word of God could find nurture. The gamblers, after much resistance, reluctantly moved to another location; occasionally they vented their anger to making threats to these Christian intruders, but this did not deter the group from its mission. The dilapidated gambling shack was thoroughly cleaned and services began.

Four coal oil lamps, a piano, and a table were borrowed from Bishop Gill of the Church of God in Christ, and twelve benches were obtained from Macedonia Baptist Church (Reverend W. L. Brown, Pastor). The community watched the development of "another little old Baptist church." Because he was a church-builder, Reverend Cary repeatedly remodeled the Greasy Spoon. A determined pastor, he walked from Barber's Lumber Company on Magnolia and South Main Streets and carried the lumber of the church's site on Irma Street. At one time Reverend Cary prematurely tore down a house that a Mr. Stone had halfway promised him. When the owner arrived, he uttered some unchristian expletives and said, "Preacher, don't you leave one bit of that lumber."

One new member who joined the new flock was Reverend J. H. Vinson, a carpenter, who became an assistant to Reverend Cary. Vinson devoted his talent and labor to the building of the new edifice, free of charge. Many times it did not meet building code standards, but it served its purpose as the membership continued to grow. Even if Vinson had charged for his labor, he could not have been paid in cash; many Sundays the offerings never exceeded three dollars. Nevertheless, three frame buildings and a brick church building were completed.

Financial problems continued to plague this expanding church as the depression maintained its economic stronghold on the black community. Homer Baughman, Jr., who held the mortgage on the church, threatened foreclosure several times, but each time the members rallied to save their church. Men like Deacons Mal Williams and Eddie Boulden would pawn their clothes and furniture in order that the church doors would remain open; nevertheless, the membership continued to grow.

One of the positive attributes in attracting people to this small church was the excellent singing talent of its pastor. His abilities had been developed as he often accompanied Reverend J. H. Winn on his revival circuits and in his capacity as moderator of the St. John Landmark Association. Singing was a basic component of the worship services, and other persons with similar talent formed a musical nucleus unparalleled in this growing metropolis. The Cora Lynn family, who lived in the neighborhood, joined Rising Star; one daughter, Thelma Jackson, became one of the first choir members and M. B. Cary, the pianist/organist. Thelma and Reverend Cary could be heard blocks away as they lifted their voices in melodious harmony, aided by outside loudspeakers. Parishioners loved to hear Thelma sing "How I Got Over." There was always amazement as how the church continued to grow in a poverty-stricken community.

Divine providence again altered the direction and accelerated the growth of the Rising Star Baptist Church. The planning and construction of U.S. Highway I-35 (North-South Freeway) caused the church to relocate, as it was in the path of the proposed interstate. In 1949 the city of Fort Worth paid $35,000 for the church and allowed the congregation to dismantle and use the material in its new location at 1333 Evans Avenue at Morphy Street.

Racist attitudes attempted to thwart the progress of Rising Star, however. White homeowners became annoyed and threatened to bomb the church if any blacks moved in the neighborhood. This Klan-like technique of violence was put into action. A white man was caught as he attempted to plant a bomb under the house of Robert Macklin, who had purchased a house across the street from the proposed new sanctuary. A blast from the new homeowner's shotgun changed the mind of the culprit. Robert Macklin was the superintendent of the Rising Star Baptist Church Sunday School and currently is pastor of the Rising Star Church of God in Christ in southeast Fort Worth.

Another suspected conspirator to keep blacks out of the community was the owner of the grocery store on Magnolia Street and Evans Avenue. Economic boycott was utilized to retaliate against pending racial violence. Each Sunday, Reverend Cary preached a series of sermons that exhorted blacks not to trade at the store, which depended on the black community for 90 percent of its sales. The boycott was so effective that the owner denied complicity in the scheme and gave a large donation to help the new church move forward. Construction moved at a rapid pace. So did other more significant results which affected the racial, social, and cultural relations of the entire city. Building Rising Star on Morphy Street and Evans Avenue initiated the integration of all of the Morningside community. The arches came down and blacks moved in as whites moved out. Mount Olive Baptist Church moved from Crawford and Hattie Streets to Evans Avenue; Mount Pisgah moved from Baptist Hill to Evans Avenue and Maddox; and Morningside Methodist moved to 2680 Evans Avenue.

On Sunday, December 4, 1949, the formal entry and dedication service was conducted by Dr. W. S. Brent, Pastor of Greater St. James Baptist Church and Moderator of the St. John Landmark Association. The congregation grew so rapidly that a remodeling and expansion program was initiated and completed in a relatively short time. Upon the demise of the assistant pastor, J. H. Vinson, the Reverend Langston Perry assumed the vacated position. He had been a former quartet singer who was called into the ministry.

Rising Star's choir grew so rapidly it had to expand to three different choirs. When blacks were finally permitted to broadcast on the radio, Rising Star became one of the first churches to broadcast on WBAP and KXOL under auspices of the General Ministers

Association. Then KCNC came into the Fort Worth area and Rising Star's choir became a by-word of excellence in religious programming. Hundreds of radio listeners who could not get into the sanctuary at 11 A.M. waited for the radio to transmit "He Delivered Me." This signaled a half-hour of gospel singing from the one hundred-voice choir. Soloists Dave Johnson, Kathryn Eldridge, and Ruth Hood lent their talents in religious syncopation with that of Anthony Tramble, who sang at almost every service.

The prestige of Rising Star's choir was further heightened when a fifteen-year-old high school youngster, Francine (Reese) Morrison from Paris, Texas, joined Rising Star on the Sunday preceding Christmas, 1950, and electrified the congregation and Fort Worth community with the most beautiful voice the city had ever heard.

After finishing I. M. Terrell High School, Francine attended Bakersfield Junior College in California, where she sang as the leading contralto of that school's a cappella choir. The starlet skyrocketed to state and national acclaim as she performed for most of the communications media and at state functions. In 1962 she became the first black person chosen to sing at the Texas Democratic Convention in Austin, and the first to sing at a Texas governor's inauguration, John Connally's, in 1963. Her itinerary included numerous appearances on radio and television, and she recorded several albums.

In March 1968 Mayor DeWitt McKinley proclaimed "Francine Day" during special services at the Rising Star Baptist Church. This event initiated a fund-raising effort to help the singer make a tour of the Holy Land. The venture was successful and Francine realized a dream of a lifetime in "Walking in Jerusalem." Two other members, Evelyn Anders and Ella Crayton, accompanied her on April 21, 1968; they returned to the United States, May 16, 1968.

"Walking in Jerusalem" was a favorite song of a young Christian convert who grew up the Rising Star Baptist Church. Sheldon Bolden's talents burst forth spectacularly as he accompanied Reverend Smith Cary to state and national conventions or wherever the pastor went. The last trip the pair made together was to the Martin Luther King Convention in Indianapolis, where Reverend Cary was one of the principal speakers. Sheldon electrified the convention with his unique renditions of gospels, hymns, and spirituals. Upon their return Reverend Cary pledged Rising Star to assist the young singer by paying for professional voice lessons from a voice teacher associated with Texas Christian University. Later Sheldon enrolled at North Texas State University and completed requirements for a degree in Radio-Television Communication.

Sheldon Bolden performed admirably in concert, on stage, and for radio and television. He was chosen as one of the leading participants in several productions at Casa Manana, including *Annie Get Your Gun*, 1968; *Show Boat*, 1971; *Stairway to the Stars*, 1970; and *Porgy and Bess*, 1972, in which he starred as Mingo. From 1973 to 1976, the young artist was selected to sing in the television series *Spring Street, U.S.A.*

The mantle of divine calling fell on Sheldon and he became a licentiate minister at the Mount Zion Church where the Reverend L. B. George was the pastor. It is interesting to note that under the tutelage of Reverend Cary, some forty-three persons were called to the ministry and ordained.[57] Some of these ministers are: Milford Kelly, Mount Rose Baptist Church; Charles Kelly, Antioch Baptist Church; R. B. Gray, St. Stephen's Baptist Church; W. Ealy, Greater St. Paul Baptist Church; Roy Bivens, Sweet Home Baptist

Church; J. W. Briscoe, Zion Baptist Church; John E. Petty, El Bethel Baptist Church; Frank Turner, Friendship Baptist Church; and Robert Macklin, Rising Star Church of God in Christ. Many have reached the pinnacles of success and have large congregations of their own. The Reverend Robert Boyd Gray was ordained in 1940 and organized the Friendship Baptist Church in west Fort Worth and later pastored the Greater Stephen Baptist Church until his death in 2001. One of the young ministers who grew up under the tutelage of Reverend Smith Cary and the last one ordained by him was Reverend George Polk. When he organized his Humble Chapel Baptist Church in the Stop Six community, the echo was similar to that when Smith Cary started Rising Star: "just another little old Baptist church." Who can ascertain the future?

Shortly after the trip to Indiana, Reverend Cary was hospitalized. While convalescing in the hospital, he had another vision of expanding the church facilities. A plan of action was presented and immediately the officers and congregation responded with positive action. Property north and south of the sanctuary was purchased. The builder was never able to see his dream fulfilled; he died January 6, 1969. The motto he had always lived by came to fruition: "Do all the good you can, while you can, for you'll never pass this way again. The days that know us now will shortly not know us anymore, for we'll soon be resting out there in the shadow of a rock."

Where Reverend Cary planted, others reaped the harvest. In 1969 the Reverend T. H. Davis of Greenville, Texas, was called to the pastorate of the Rising Star Baptist Church to fill the void left by the former organizer and builder. After a division of the membership in October 1971, Reverend Davis initiated plans for a new church edifice at 4216 Avenue M. On October 22, 1972, prayers of dedication were part of the entry services to this monumental new church building. Ultra-modern in its accoutrements, it accommodates 1,325 people on the lower floor. Dynamic pastoral leadership and personal evangelism resulted in the note-burning on December 1, 1978.

The splinter group of Rising Star reorganized and bought a church building from the First Pentecostal Church on Beach and Rosedale Streets. Reverend Ace Outland served as the interim minister and the Reverend Albert E. Chew, Pastor of Shiloh Baptist Church, gave his service by preaching and giving the new church divine direction in its embryonic beginning. He recommended his friend Isadore Edwards, Jr., who had been pastor of Friendship Baptist Church in Fort Myers, Florida, for twelve years and was a religious scholar and pastor extraordinary. He was born in Jacksonville, Florida, a graduate of Florida Memorial College, where he received a Bachelor of Science in Religious Education. Later he was an assistant pastor in the New Bethel Baptist Church in Jacksonville and served as Executive Secretary of the Foreign Mission Board of the National Baptist Convention of America.

Isadore Edwards, Jr. was called to the New Rising Star Missionary Baptist Church as the under-shepherd, December 3, 1972; he initially pursued with fervor the fulfillment of the vision he received for building a new sanctuary. Five acres of land were bought on Berry and Mountcastle Streets, but another vision intervened and the visionary placed his sight on the present building at 5000 Wichita that the members purchased from the Wichita Street Baptist Church in 1987.

In January 1998 a motorcade started on Beach Street and made its way to 5000 Wichita to celebrate the acquisition of the new and remodeled sanctuary. Under Pastor

Edwards' leadership, The New Rising Star Missionary Baptist Church, Inc. has a special Caring Community Program that caters to the needs of the poor. It has a unique Youth Educational Program whose slogan is "Take Time for Kids," which serves the youth in the church and community by helping to equip them with assets they need to succeed in life. This church was one of the first in the City of Fort Worth to receive a special grant from the United Way of Tarrant County to expand the program. Other programs include the Project Hope Committee that is a helping hand for members of the church, and a special Mortgage Depletion Fund to save money in interest on the mortgage. Pastor Edwards is assisted by the Reverend Raymond Spencer who is a graduate and the first black Professor at Southwestern Baptist Theological Seminary in Fort Worth.

The list goes on and on. The black minister remains the community leader in spite of attacks from within and without. Downtown Fort Worth has always been a historical and focal point of black development. In addition to Mount Gilead, Allen Chapel A.M.E. Church a few blocks away at First and Elm Streets has had an enormous cultural impact on Fort Worth. Its historical roots date back to 1787. After America's War for Independence, blacks were not allowed to worship with whites in their church sanctuaries. In Philadelphia on a Sunday morning, while the blacks present knelt in prayer, white ushers forcefully pulled them from their knees and asked them to leave St. George. Richard Allen led the withdrawal of the black congregants and established his first church, Bethel. In 1816 a large number of Negro Methodist congregations from various states formed the African Methodist Episcopal Church. This should not have been a surprise to any of the people in America. This was the same Richard Allen who led a "kneel-in" at the close of the Constitutional Convention because he reasoned that it constitutionalized slavery and fractionized blacks by recognizing them as only three-fifths human.

Allen occupied a unique place in his own time and in ours, but it is equally true that his seemingly impressive title failed to relieve him of the anxieties and tensions that were the common lot of all freemen. He recognized the distinctive religious and theological needs of black people, and in the second category, he applied his theological views to the practical solution of immediate physical and social problems.

The significance of Allen's ministry was not so much that he introduced new concepts to black worship, but rather that he was able to manipulate the winds of social change that whirled about him to achieve a relatively safe and theologically satisfying spiritual home for black people. Allen was convinced that a theology that failed to deal with earthly oppression was not a viable one from their point of view. Thus the A.M.E. groups limited membership to those of African decent and vigorously attacked slavery and the slave trade. A special note must be made at this time. Dr. Vashti Murphy McKenzie was the first woman elected bishop in the 213-year existence of the African Methodist Episcopal Church. This scholarly member of the Delta Sigma Theta sorority was a fashion model and moderator of a Christian radio program before being called to the ministry. Her success as pastor of Payne Memorial A.M.E. Church in Baltimore, Maryland, made her selection possible. She was elected in July 2000 and presides over the A.M.E.'s 18th District in Southeast Africa that includes Botswana, Swaziland, Mozambique, and Lesotho.[58] It was with this African background that Allen Chapel in Fort Worth was started on the corner of First and Elm Streets and today displays a Texas Historical marker presented by Duane Gage, President of Tarrant Historical Commission.

Allen Chapel A.M.E. was organized in 1870; some one hundred names of early pioneers appear engraved in marble in the northern vestibule and on many stained glass windows. In fact, this author's mathematics teacher, Helen Wallis Hannah, was a family member of a leading pioneer in this church. The physical arrangement of this church is different from most churches: one enters the sanctuary near the pulpit, facing the congregation so they don't have to turn their heads to see whose coming in. The Reverend James A. Anderson served as pastor of Allen Chapel from 1909 to 1910. The first private school for blacks in Fort Worth was started at Allen Chapel by Henry H. Butler; tuition was ten cents per day.

Shortly after the organization of Allen Chapel, another group of ex-slaves in northeast Tarrant County, beyond the Euless city limits, founded the St. John Missionary Baptist Church in Mosier Valley. The community had been formed in 1865 when Lucy Lee's parents gave their slaves Robert and Delsie Johnson forty acres as a wedding present; by 1874, a few more blacks acquired property and Mosier Valley came into existence. The church started in a log cabin in a cow pasture in 1874 and was named Oak Grove Baptist Church. The name was changed to St. John in 1911 when the church moved to a nearby location; the present brick structure was completed in 1966.

This small, focused church is still intact, and descendants and friends of some of the original twenty-five members are still carrying on. The dynamic leader, the Reverend L. G. Austin, has been the pastor for over thirty-six years. He is still setting the standards high for the scholastic and educational excellence of the young people who attend that church.

In 1998 the city of Fort Worth extended water and sewer services, but Mosier Valley still lacked sewers and adequate street lighting. Nevertheless, commercial encroachment over the past fifty years has almost annihilated evidence of its existence. Benny Tucker, President of the Mosier Valley Community Council and owner of Earth Haulers, the only black-owned business in Mosier Valley, seeks to preserve the record and history of this historical community. Former city councilman Eugene McCray made the initial efforts to get support for Mosier Valley, and Councilman Frank Moss continued the efforts.

One of the early pioneers was an aggressive and dynamic minister in Fort Worth, Elder Raymond Eugene Ranger, pastor of the Wayside Church of God in Christ on Tresavant Hill in west Fort Worth. This man of the cloth was born in 1899 in Wilson Creek, six miles from Bay City, the county seat of Matagorda County in the Gulf Coast area. He came to Fort Worth in 1930 and made an enormous religious and political impact on this city. He was appointed pastor of the "Little Wooden Church on the Hill," Tresavant Hill Church of God in Christ, in 1945, and under his leadership it was renamed Wayside Church of God in Christ. Reverend Ranger pastored in Fort Worth more than fifty years and the Wayside Church of God in Christ was the first black church featured in a national weekly radio broadcast on WBAP, making him the first black minister to have national radio airtime. Later he broadcast on radio station KNOK and was a black pioneer in live television worship. His wife, Blanche Mae Bailey, was a lead singer of their theme song, "The Old Ship of Zion." His broadcast made him a target of the city officials who felt he was too "uppity." Reverend Ranger had requested a police escort for black church officials attending a meeting and the request was reluctantly granted. In 1953 this minister was arrested at his home in the Wedgwood area because he didn't pay the fine for an $18 traffic ticket; a deacon paid his fine and he was released.

Reverend Ranger was not "uppity." Whites were not accustomed to blacks who were by nature intellectually smart and could think for themselves. His potential and latent talents were manifested in the ways he developed his basic skills. Reverend Ranger developed remarkable intellectual proficiency by taking advantage of the help and resources offered by his employer and mentor, T. N. Smith, a banker and real estate broker who encouraged reading and studying skills and allowed him to use the books in his library.

Raymond Eugene Ranger had spent his school days in the Wilson Creek community and attended classes held at St. Mary's Baptist Church, using Catholic books. At age seventeen, Reverend Ranger preached his first sermon at a Wednesday night prayer meeting; six months later he was ordained by Elder F. C. V. Foard in San Antonio. In April 1920, during a convocation in Temple, Texas, Reverend Ranger was ordained as an Elder in the Church of God in Christ. However, he still maintained his employment as a freight checker with the Southern Pacific Railroad in Houston. Later he quit, persuaded that he was to devote the rest of his life to the promulgation of the Gospel.

In Fort Worth Reverend R. E. Ranger was respected by ministers of all denominations. During Good Friday services, he was the featured speaker for five consecutive years. He was a lifetime member of the NAACP, hosting their meetings for many years and permitting Dr. George D. Flemmings to promote that organization during his weekly radio broadcasts. For many years Reverend Ranger was an active participant in the annual minister's conference held at Prairie View A&M College. He also was politically astute as he encouraged hard-shelled Democrats to vote for a Republican candidate for president, General Dwight Eisenhower. As could be expected, he and his family received many harassing phone calls. These annoyances didn't deter him from his community responsibilities; these were small compared to life-threatening incidents in Atchison, Kansas. As related in a memo from his daughter, Blanche Ranger: "While preaching in that city, a gunman shot at Reverend Ranger, a bullet grazed his head, and he never stopped preaching."

Reverend Ranger served as district superintendent of the Texas Western District Church of God in Christ. He died on January 6, 1992, having fathered eleven children, seven boys and four daughters.

Many black ministers still preach a theology of liberation and promulgation of civil righteousness to minister to the spiritual needs of their parishioners, as well as the physical and political. While many ministers remained aloof from politics, others go beyond the "other-world" religious tenet and help people work within the system on Earth which influences and controls their everyday existence. Such ministers are the Reverend L. B. George, former pastor of Mount Zion Baptist Church; the Reverend Nehemiah Davis, Pastor of Mt. Pisgah Baptist Church and President of the Fort Worth Chapter of the NAACP; the Reverend W. G. Daniels, ex-policeman and pastor of Pilgrim Valley Baptist Church; and the Reverend B. R. Daniels, Pastor of New Bethel Baptist Church.

Black Politics in Fort Worth

Fort Worth and all of Tarrant County went through the same turmoil and violence as that which characterized other parts of Texas after the Civil War. Disfranchisement was by mutual assent of white citizenry to maintain political isolation of black citizens. This nullity of equal rights was very evident as a hidden agenda among the delegates who drafted the Texas Constitution in 1875. Blacks had dominated the state Reconstruction government from 1869 to 1874 under Governor E. J. Davis; a one-dollar poll tax was proposed and adopted to reduce the leverage of black suffrage in this state. Blacks were systematically relegated to nonvoting and second-class citizens and by 1905 the Democrats had completed the political paralysis of former slaves, a paralysis they had formerly experienced during the antebellum period.

When the United States Supreme Court ruled in *United States v. Classic* that the primary was tantamount to election in the general election, this removed the legal rampart which barred blacks from political participation in Texas. Sparks of political emancipation ignited and the emancipated servitors, more aware of their bond of common interest, became viable participants in the Democratic Party. White politicians and black organizers launched poll tax campaigns in the more populous communities to qualify blacks for voting in the gubernatorial contest in 1946.

In Fort Worth, Walter H. Caldwell took advantage of the new opportunities for black voters. He became affiliated with the Democratic leadership and was one of the first blacks to vote in the Democratic primary in Tarrant County and allowed to attend the county and state Democratic conventions. Caldwell was one of the first successful independent car dealers in this city and became the first black elected president of the Tarrant County Independent Automobile Dealers Association in 1976.

Walter Caldwell, a graduate of I. M. Terrell High School, had worked as a Pullman porter on the railroads and received a certificate in law from the LaSalle Extension School. He was a board member of the Metropolitan Black Chamber of Commerce and operated his own car dealership on Berry Street for more than twenty-five years.

Caldwell was not the only Fort Worth citizen to make inroads in the Democratic Party. Martha Byars Singleton had been a political activist for almost forty years in this city. She made two unsuccessful campaigns in District 8 against Councilman James Bagsby in 1981 and 1983. This nursing administrator and wife of the politically sophisticated Reverend J. F. Singleton was a member of the Texas Coalition of Black Democrats and Tarrant County Political Women Caucus. Martha Singleton was the first Afro-American elected to represent District 12 on the State Democratic Executive Committee. What made her election historically more significant was the fact that the first Black Democratic Convention Chairman supervised the voting.

Black voters had turned out in record numbers in 1984 when Jessie Jackson was a presidential candidate. This writer was a coordinator for Jackson's campaign in Fort Worth and helped make the voters aware of the need to return to their polling places and vote in the precinct conventions. For the first time in the history of this city, they did. Consequently, blacks and liberal whites who attended the Tarrant County Democratic Convention at Paschal High School elected the Reverend L. B. George, pastor at that time of the Mt. Zion Baptist Church. He won against a long-standing Democratic leader in District 12, Dr. Ben Proctor of Texas Christian University, who represented the moderate and conservative Democrats in Tarrant County.

Overcoming voter apathy was especially difficult among blacks in Fort Worth. Many felt that their vote was insignificant because "whites were going to do what they wanted to anyway." But there were people like Lenora Rolla, Dr. George D. Flemings, and Sopora Hicks, who had impassioned zeal and belief that change could come by a participating electorate. They were supported in their endeavors by churches, civic groups, and fraternal organizations such as the Alpha Phi Alpha fraternity, whose slogan each year was "A Voteless People Was a Hopeless People." Politics had to be influenced from black grassroots.

The saga and development of Precinct 120 in Lake Como is a classic example of a community uniting to solve its problems. The political matriarch of Como was Sopora Hicks. The native of Clarksville came to Lake Como in 1929 during the early days of the Great Depression. Blacks had few rights and virtually no protection by the governing agencies. Her persistence and fearlessness got her involved in the civic and political life of this community. Mrs. Hicks attempted to get the city council to close a gambling shack a few doors from her residence. The building in question belonged to a white businessman who had exceptional influence over the city council and policemen. One told her that "if we make an arrest it would mean our jobs."[59] So gambling and killing continued each week in the Como community.

Finally, continued publicity and her appeal to the Texas Rangers got temporary results. The place was closed but then reopened within a few days. Mrs. Hicks' life was threatened but she never faltered in her efforts. The businessman finally committed suicide and peace prevailed for a time in this community beyond the lake.

Sopora Hicks was selected precinct chairperson in June 1966 and was the guiding light for that community for almost twelve years. Whichever way Sopora Hicks voted, so did Precinct 120. Her secret, according to her, was that "all of her work is based on religion"[60] and a concern for her fellow man. But what "Lake Como patrons lack is some leverage...they must reach beyond their own locale and broaden their base of action to include other blacks in the city."[61]

At age eighty-seven in the year 2000, Viola Pitts was the viable political matron and Democratic Precinct Chairwoman in Lake Como. This community is isolated between Ridglea on the west and Arlington Heights and its cultural district on the east. For years Como residents were separated from their Ridglea neighbors by a mile-long brick wall. Viola Pitts fought hard and got this wall removed. She made outstanding contributions to all of her community when she was instrumental in getting the Como Community Center Health Clinic staffed with a doctor and two registered nurses. Ms. Pitts has been on the John Peter Smith Board of Management for more than ten years and Precinct Chairwoman for more than eleven years. Precinct 1120 is still the envy of others because of its ability to get out a solid vote and get the attention of any group of politicos. However, even with all its political muscle, it never has elected a black Como resident to public office.

In those early days, when this author lived on Kilpatrick Street in Lake Como, Vickery Boulevard was called the Stone Foundry Road. One could see remnants of the bridge that used to cross Lake Como, and the Bluebird Café was a community attraction. Initially for black patrons only, it didn't take long for white patrons and musicians to frequent this club late at night or early in the morning. One of the main attractions in the late '70s was bluesman Robert Ealey, who was born in Texarkana, Texas, and moved to Fort Worth in 1956. He was famous for his air harmonica, which he vocalized from the cavity of his deep lungs. After being closed, reopened, and remodeled, the Bluebird Café became the New Bluebird, the last of the "juke" joints. Many local guitarists and other musicians received their tutoring from this Godfather of Blues and Blues Magician. Robert Ealey served his country in the United States Army during World War II. His impact on the city of Fort Worth and the main world was so great that on his death a funeral wake was held at the Caravan of Dreams on Sunday, March 11, 2001, in memory of this musical innovator.

The struggle in Fort Worth to elect black public officials who were responsive and understood the concerns and needs of the dispossessed has been a long and frustrating struggle fraught with failures which mirror the helplessness of the Black community. No substantial changes were made in the political governance of blacks in Fort Worth until the advent of the national emergency of 1940s. World War II produced new attitudes among whites and as a result made the political conditions of blacks more tolerable. However, they could not overcome very easily the stigma and past history of white domination and white exclusivity in all political subdivisions of this city.

In 1949 a charismatic, outspoken, and aggressive Navy veteran filed his candidacy for Place 4 of the Fort Worth City Council, Robert (Bob) Thornton, president of the newly organized Fort Worth Business and Distributive Education School. He was also an activist who had organized and effectively staged boycotts of white business establishments that would not hire black employees. Houlihan's Grocery on Hattie and Illinois Streets was the first to feel the sting of an economic boycott. "Stop the cash register and you get the businessman's attention" was the motto of the boycott leader. Several black clerks were hired as a result of Thornton's efforts.

The Coca-Cola bottling company refused to hire black salesmen, and Bob staged another boycott. He had excellent cooperation with many black consumers and businessmen on the Southside and Stop Six communities. Sales dropped off drastically and within two weeks a black driver was hired. Other businesses took heed and hired blacks without being asked.

Bob Thornton then decided to seek a seat on the city council. He immediately met determined resistance from the Committee for a Greater Fort Worth, who dominated the council in this metropolis. State officials were encouraged to investigate Thornton thoroughly. "Crab-like" jealousy leaped from the black community, and slanderous information was given to white officials that "he had become the subject of a state auditor's investigation before he was dismissed as Distributive-Education Field Man for Prairie View A&M College."[62]

A culturally denigrating trait, which is a by-product of racism, is that of "snitching."[63]

Historically black activists have been victims of their own kind. Gabriel Prosser, Denmark Vesey, and Nat Turner were all betrayed by other blacks who sought favor with their masters. Blacks should not be surprised nor expect to be immune from this prevailing paranoia in Fort Worth or in other cities.

Further allegations were made that "Thornton had made false representation concerning degrees which he had never received from California and New York Universities."[64] Pressure came from all sides on this black pioneer who attempted to break the cycle of political exclusion and subordination. On April 3, 1949, Bob Thornton capitulated. He sent a letter to City Council, withdrawing his name from Place 4 on the ballot. He stated later he "had been blasted out by cheap political propaganda...pushed out by the political machinery."[65] Thornton still received 358 votes in Place 4.

A by-product of Thornton's vocal and activist stand was the acceptance of blacks to the police department in 1953. Four were recruited for the first time, including Lonnell Cooper, a graduate of I. M. Terrell High School and a veteran of the Marine Corps during World War II in 1942. He was the first Afro-American from Tarrant County admitted to the United States Marine Corps and served in the Pacific theater. Cooper grew up in Fort Worth and attended Prairie View A&M College for two years. In 1949 he worked as a psychiatric aide at the U.S. Public Health Service in Fort Worth.

In 1953 Cooper became one of four black applicants permitted to serve as officers in the Fort Worth Police Department. Initially black officers could not arrest white violators or criminals without a white officer being present. Later, Cooper worked with the Truancy Detail in the Youth Division, and he served on the newly created Police Community Relations Division.

In 1961 Officer Cooper was dispatched to investigate a reported murder. The killer turned his gun on him and shot Cooper twice, leaving him for dead. Cooper survived and eventually regained the use of his right arm, which had been injured by the assailant. The pioneer police officer served more than twenty-four years and moved from foot patrolman to a constable in Precinct 8 in Tarrant County.

After the Bob Thornton episode, many blacks felt intimidated and it was six years before another one ventured to run for public office. Dr. R. A. Ransom, Jr., a graduate of Meharry Medical College and part owner of Ransom's Clinic, decided to run for Place 1, which was being vacated by Councilman Ellis in April 1955. The entry of Dr. Ransom into the race generated fresh enthusiasm on the part of all voters. Blacks were optimistic and whites were confident yet cautious. The Committee for a Greater Fort Worth had been challenged two years before by the emergence of a new political group, the Fort Worth Voters League, which had garnered more power than had been generally expected. The black vote was siphoned off by Dr. Ransom and resulted in a quasi-coalition of opposites, which appeared to threaten the success of the establishment's committee.

When the election returns were completed, Jimmie Dixon had 811 votes; Dr. Richard McGuire 4,178; Dan T. Murrell 1,987; Joe B. Owens 9,513; and Dr. R. A. Ransom, Jr. 5,031. Owens and the black physician were forced into a run-off election scheduled for April 19, 1955. "The vote for Dr. Ransom was the largest given a Negro candidate seeking municipal office"[66] up to this time. But the white community rose up in a solid phalanx and made sure that Dr. Ransom would not break the color barrier. He received 4,589 votes and Councilman Owens 14,431. As fate would have it, Dr. Ransom's political future was short-circuited by marital problems. The black newspapers made scurrilous headlines out of an extramarital affair, and the physician lost a larger part of his support in the black community.

After two years the black community regrouped and presented new challenges to the political system; persistence was one of its main virtues in any attempt to get a minority elected to a public office. Plans were always made in the interim between elections and in 1957 Almeta Robinson, a personable and brilliant social worker who was executive director of the Fort Worth Urban League, sought election to Place 2 of the City Council. As in past elections, she carried all the black precincts, no whites, and became numbered among other unsuccessful candidates.

The year 1959 saw blacks launch a two-pronged attack on the political system of Fort Worth. Oran McGregor was the first Afro-American to run for a seat, Place 7, for the Fort Worth Board of Education. He was born in Marshall, Texas, a graduate of Bishop College, and did post-graduate work at Prairie View and Texas Southern University. McGregor was a World War II veteran who served in the European field of action. In 1950 he came to Fort Worth, where he quickly rose to the rank of District Manager for Atlanta Life Insurance Company. Oran McGregor felt that it was time for blacks to prioritize their goals and accept the responsibility of bringing them to fruition. He attempted to win a seat on the Fort Worth Independent School District Board. He mustered a little support and lost to Atwood McDonald, who received 8,025 votes to McGregor's 1,480.

The other thrust was the black community's biennial skirmish with the City Council's candidates. A minister whose theology oozed with black liberation threw his hat into the political arena. The Reverend Lucius Caesar Henegan came to Fort Worth in 1954 as the new pastor of the St. John Baptist Church upon the demise of its pastor. This church had had a phenomenal growth under the leadership of the late Reverend W. T. Talley from 1923 to 1953 and provided the newcomer a categorical platform from which to articulate his views. Reverend Henegan was born December 22, 1906 in Lee County, southeastern Texas County, named for Confederate General Robert E. Lee. He attended Conroe Baptist College and came to Fort Worth from Tyler, Texas in 1954. His views were anathema to public officials. Henegan assailed the city council constantly for not being responsive to the black community. He antagonized the police department because it made no progress in the 1955 rape-slaying of Bennie Faye Lennonx, a sixteen-year-old black girl who was beaten to death with a rock on July 27, 1955, near the I. M. Terrell High School grounds. The Reverend Henegan and the St. John Baptist Church posted a $500 reward for the murderer.[67] After seventeen months Fort Worth officials exacted a confession from Richard Harold Thomas, who admitted he committed the crime.

Each Sunday morning, hundreds of worshippers thronged to St. John, and thousands listened to his radio program, through which he continued to cry against the dual system of justice and injustice heaped on blacks in Fort Worth. Henegan's supporters multiplied and included the Taxpayers' Election Coalition, and by the next election he felt he had a good chance of winning. In April 1959 Reverend Henegan was the black candidate for City Council, but his vociferousness had alarmed the white citizenry. When the ballots were counted for Place 8, Ralph McCann had 7,089 votes; Jack Smith 4,146, and

Reverend L. C. Henegan 2,825.

With predictable frequency, whenever a black candidate with credibility in his community seemed to have a chance to enter the forbidden white political realm, disaster and character assassination automatically followed. The accuser became the accused. During the election, Reverend Henegan was arrested for investigation of the statutory rape of a thirteen-year-old black girl who claimed he had had intimate relations with her. The minister was later exonerated but the damage to his character had been done. Undaunted by the loss of the previous election and the recent gyrations, Henegan made another bid for election for Place 2 in 1961, but lost by a larger margin than he had two years ago.

In 1963 thirty-seven candidates vied for seven seats on the City Council; once more, the black community entered its candidate, T. M. Shadowens, a realtor who filed for Place 3. As had other black candidates, he solidly carried the inner city, which proved in capable of victory as a separate entity. Shadowens tallied 4,119 votes; Gilliam 6,070; Middleton 2,507; Charlie Hillard 9,694; and R. M. (Sharkey) Stovall 8,123. A run-off election was necessary, but Shadowens was eliminated.

Fort Worth's first direct election of a mayor by popular vote and the use of voting machines was in 1965. This new innovation in the form of city government gave the black community more leverage because they could very well be the deciding element in a close vote. Too, Edith A. Deen was the third woman to serve on the council, indicating that the populace was softening its attitude about women and minorities holding public office. However, this did not help Dr. A. I. Harris, a black female chiropractor, who unsuccessfully sought to win in the contest for a place on the School Board.

Dr. Edward Guinn, a black physician, campaigned for Place 3 on the City Council and garnered a surprisingly large vote. He received 10,157, while Joe D. Harris and incumbent R. M. (Sharkey) Stovall received 4,205 and 10,535, respectively. Dr. Guinn's vote-getting ability did not go unnoticed. The Good Government League capitalized on the name recognition acquired by the physician in the previous election and selected him as a member of their slate and endorsed him for Place 6. His nomination came from Reverend Leonard Haynes, a black member of the League. Its demographic representation was unique for Fort Worth. It was made up of large and small businessmen, professionals and laborers, black and white, who had "been tapped to serve by fellow citizens."[68] Even the *Star-Telegram* gave its endorsement to the black physician, the first time this had happened in the history of the paper.[69]

Dr. Guinn was another native of Fort Worth who graduated from I. M. Terrell High School. He earned his undergraduate degree at Prairie View A&M College and a medical degree from the University of Texas Medical Branch at Galveston. He served for a short while on the faculty at Prairie View A&M and did post-medical training in several hospitals in Pennsylvania.

A record number of people were attracted to the polls by two of the hottest issues of the day: urban renewal, and independence from the powerful cliques. On Election Day, the results for Place 6 were: T. D. Thompson, 18,977; Edward Guinn, 17,734; and Alfred Lee Crane 2,166. A run-off was slated for April 18, 1967. Many observers felt that the black physician could not win against a white opponent who led in the first election, but the Good Government League remained true to its commitment and pledge T. D.

Thompson received 14,161 votes and Edward Guinn an overwhelming 23,675. History was made on April 25, 1967, when Dr. Edward Guinn became the first black person to be sworn in as a city councilman.

Guinn's election was a paradox to the long and tedious efforts in getting black representation on a government entity. With few exceptions, whenever minority officials are selected and supported by white groups such as the Good Government League, they become dangling puppets. This situation existed because there was no solid economic base in the black community to adequately and independently support the election of a candidate. Consequently, blacks were elated and could boast of their first peer being elected, but they virtually had no representation. Primary concerns of the inner city were subordinated to those of the powerful political cliques.

It was apparent that a white coalition was essential to the success of a black candidate, and the black community must rally to optimum participation. So blacks in Fort Worth were left to their own tangential representative, Dr. Edward Guinn, who was in his second year. The black community seemed to resign itself and acquiesced to the selection of the white-chosen leader. In 1969 Dr. Guinn won reelection without opposition.

During Dr. Guinn's four years of service, "the City Council purchased land for the Dallas/Fort Worth Airport, approved designs for the facility, and hired the first director."[70] In spite of concerted racial opposition to the advancement of blacks, Councilman Edward Guinn and other black leaders made meaningful inroads into the political structure of Tarrant County. In 1967 one of this author's students at Dunbar High School, Cager Mitchell, became the first Afro-American hired by the Fort Worth Fire Department. He graduated from Dunbar High School in 1962, having been an outstanding athlete in football, 1959-61, and a track star, 1959-62. Later he joined the United States Marine Corps.

In 1967 Fire Chief H. A. Owens reluctantly appointed Cager Mitchell as a fireman, and it was not until 1973 that Cager Mitchell became the first minority fire engineer. He later became the first black lieutenant, captain, and battalion chief with the Fort Worth Fire Department. To ensure that he would maintain his qualification for his new positions, Cager Mitchell enrolled in and graduated from Tarrant County Junior College in 1974 and Texas Christian University in 1988. He became the Public Safety Cadet Program Manager, EEO/AA and Chief Recruiter until his retirement, March 31, 2001.

Councilman Edward Guinn also initiated efforts to create the Tarrant County Junior College Countywide Emergency Technical Training program. Dr. Guinn was determined not to become a career politician and didn't run after his second term ended in 1971. Thirty years later he continues to practice medicine in the Stop Six Community.

In 1968 a new venture was made to extricate blacks from their powerlessness dilemma by selecting a black, Charles Gray, to run for Place 3, State Representative, and Dr. Clyde Broadus for Place 1 on the Fort Worth School Board. Dr. A. I. Harris, President of the Precinct Workers Council, endorsed Broadus, Gray, and Don Yarborough for governor. This organization was made up of chairpersons of the predominately black precincts whose goals were to educate their constituents and harness the political strength of the community around one candidate for the mutual benefit of all.

Gray was thirty-seven years of age and an employee of Southwestern Bell Telephone

Company for seventeen years; he was also a member of Local 6201 of the Communications Workers of America. He drew support from the labor unions that had been supportive of the black community and its candidates for sometime. His platform consisted of repeal of the so-called State Right-to-Work laws that proved favorable to union officials. Gray advocated selling liquor by the drink and pari-mutuel betting as proposed economic assets to Texas. Blacks and a considerable number of whites supported Gray in the election of 1968. He carried 89 percent of the black vote (4,290) and obtained 27 percent of the white votes (18,094). His opponent, W. C. (Bud) Sherman, won with a total vote of 48,328.

No political aspirant entered the legislative race in 1970. By default and common consent, the entire community retrogressed to its earlier role of using its votes to influence white politicians who might be considered liberal or sensitive to the needs of black people. In the run-off election in 1970, Don Kennard defeated Joe Shannon by some 6,000 votes for the legislative seat. He attested that "black is beautiful"[71] in that the powerful Precinct 120 in Lake Como gave him a margin of 785 votes to 105; Precinct 127 in Stop Six area mustered 702 votes for Kennard and 105 for his opponent; other predominantly black boxes provided the same margin.

The inner city political strategy changed in 1971. Many observers felt that by entering more than one candidate for the school board, the law of averages or probability would offer them a better chance. Three blacks filed their candidacy: Bert Williams, Place 5; Milton Kirkpatrick, Place 6; and Wilba Alaman, Place 7. Kirkpatrick and Alaman were in the run-off, but both were defeated by the white majority.

The fight for inclusion in the political process never subsided. In every election black electioneering persisted and gained momentum as white liberals and conservatives vacillated in their attitudes about blacks. In 1972 a divisive busing referendum was placed before the voters by the Texas Republicans. This racist barometer was designed to rally and unite the reactionary and conservative groups against a growing black electorate. Sissy Farenthold, a Corpus Christi liberal legislator, gave new hope to the black community as she championed the causes of labor and minority groups. This stance was a basic cause of her defeat.

A real hot race erupted for the State Representative, Place 5, District 32 slot in the Texas legislature. Black businessman Bobby Webber threw his hat into the political fracas. He had consistently articulated the needs of the black community and was a pioneer and participant in the struggle for single-member districts for the state legislature. Bobby Webber enjoyed extensive support from the white community, and funds came from many sources outside his political homestead. He received and spent $7,132.37, and Tom Schieffer spent $5,192.70; a very small percentage of Webber's campaign funds came from the black community.

Sissy Farenthold and Dolph Briscoe were forced into the gubernatorial run-off, as were Webber and Schieffer for the state legislature. Webber had demonstrated his political magnetism by a most impressive vote over the other candidates for Place 5. The final count was tabulated: Tom Schieffer, 41,127; Bobby Webber, 29,232; Tommy Shannon, 14,457; and Tommy R. Beck, 13,669. As expected, Webber lost to his white opponent in the June 3 run-off.

The next year Leonard Briscoe, a realtor and Black Republican, was chosen by the Good Government League to succeed Dr. Edward Guinn on the Fort Worth City Council. He enjoyed the same support as his predecessor. The new council made gigantic strides in race relations as it appointed Vernell Sturns, a black public administrator major, Assistant City Manager.

During Briscoe's second term in 1973, he attempted to articulate the views and needs of the black community. He pushed for equal employment and affirmative action. This new stance alienated him from the city fathers, and in the election of 1975 Briscoe did not carry a single white precinct, resulting in his loss to Woodie Woods, a westside plumber. This was a political setback for the black community. They had to depend on the paternalism and liberalism of a few white councilmen.

Suits for single-member districts for the state legislature and the Fort Worth School Board substantially changed the political environment in this city. Defendants in the legislative redistricting suit maintained that blacks could win in an at-large election. When Reby Cary substituted for Dr. Clyde Broadus, who withdrew his candidacy for the April 1974 election, the stage was set for the first breakthrough in fifty years in the election of a minority to the school board since being chartered in 1925.

Cary filed for Place 1 against the incumbent, Bobby Bruner, owner of several grocery stores, who had held office for six years. The black educator had wide community support that encompassed many ethnic groups. He outflanked the incumbent by receiving the endorsement of the Fort Worth Educators Political Action Committee, the political arm of the Fort Worth Classroom Teachers Association. He overwhelmed Ned Rosario, a candidate of Hispanic extraction who was ignored by the Mexican-American community. Many felt that Rosario had been influenced to enter the race by the Anglo establishment. This technique had always been employed to divide the vote and force a run-off where blacks always lost. Cary was endorsed by various Mexican-American groups, including Fort Worth members of the Mexican-American Committee for Education, Mexican-American Students, and Chicano employees of the school district.

Even the Tarrant County Central Labor Council endorsed Cary over Bruner. Cary had worked cooperatively in many of its educational and apprenticeship endeavors for minorities. However, it was no surprise that a majority of all black groups and organizations supported the black candidate. Quality education was the principal plank in the platform and "busing" was hardly mentioned. Political observers had predicted this would be a hot issue. When the returns were tallied, Cary surprised most Fort Worthians by getting 5,871 votes to Bruner's 4,666. Rosario lost miserably; he received a total of 744 votes, low enough to enable the first black to win this race without a run-off. Bill Eden, a student at the University of Texas at Arlington where Cary was Associate Dean of Students, wrote a personal note to Cary, saying, "Your victory Saturday was not only a victory for Reby Cary but a victory for blacks, a victory for whites and a victory for Fort Worth."[72] The insurmountable barrier of white opposition was overcome and Cary was elected to the School Board for a four-year term, and what a term! It started out with conflict and misunderstanding.

After the run-off election of two other places, which were won by Martha Adams and Green B. Trimble, plans were made for the installation of all board members. Cary was never notified when the ceremony would take place; nevertheless, he found out about it from his secretary at UTA, whose husband worked for a local newspaper. He showed up with his wife, Nadine, and Dr. Wayne Duke, Dean of Student Affairs, University of Texas at Arlington, in spite of obvious disdain and snobbery. From then on, educational and minority concerns dominated the agenda. When the election for School Board President came, Cary's swing vote gave Jim Harris the presidency over Bill Elliott. Cary was nominated for Vice-President but relinquished that position to Green B. Trimble. The black board member was elected Secretary of the Board.

Cary received congratulations from many friends and especially from Dr. Emmit Conrad, black board member of Dallas School Board. He congratulated Cary but told him there would be times he wouldn't get a second to his motion. In June 1976 Cary proposed the development of an affirmative action program by the school district and he didn't get the second. Later he benefited from a newly acquired 4:3 coalition of votes on the board. When Jim Harris requested his help and vote on continuing a contract with Channel 13, Cary was able to get the Rosedale Park Elementary School named for Maudrie Walton. When members of the Rosedale Park Parent Teachers Association and other community leaders submitted a petition to the Board of Education to change the name of the school to Maudrie Walton Elementary School, it was met immediately with opposition from Julius Truelson and Board member Pat Shannon.

Why such opposition? Maudrie Walton had the credentials. She was a graduate of I. M. Terrell High School. Her teaching certificate was earned at Bishop College, Dallas, and she received her master's degree from Columbia University. She also did graduate work at the University of Michigan. Mrs. Walton had been teaching since 1927; she taught at Clinton Avenue on the Northside, twenty-two years at James E. Guinn Elementary School. She was principal of Rosedale Park until her retirement in 1974. However, Mrs. Walton was one of the principals who was very vocal and often challenged Superintendent Truelson and board members when she felt the children in her community were being neglected. Perhaps her aggressive attitude had been shaped when she became one of the first blacks who enlisted in the WAC during World War II and rose to the ranks of lieutenant. Cary had learned a real lesson that when one represents the tie vote and another needs his vote for an equally important decision, swap it out. Cary's 4-3 vote prevailed.

Exhortations for the school district to recommend single-member districts to the state legislature fell on deaf ears. The black advocator received no support on this issue from other board members. In fact Green B. Trimble said he "didn't mind seeing representation, I hate to see Cary's type of representation on the Board."[73] Pleas for voluntary integration of Dunbar High School and the middle school were ignored and rebuttal against the dominant anti-busing constituents was a continuous dialogue and confrontation. The Freedom of Choice plan proposed by Bill Elliott generated more furor than could be imagined. This retrogressive idea would have had the effect of perpetuating segregation and the status quo. Cary retaliated by proposing that if the District Court sustained this plan, then the black community would ask for a separate all-black school district with all the attendant financial resources; i.e., a proportionate share of local, state, and federal funds which accrued to the school district by reason of minority federal legislation. This suggestion was made by Cary's friend Dr. Marion (Jack) Brooks.

Hostile and mixed reactions ensued toward Cary when the popular superintendent, Julius Truelson, suddenly resigned. Because the black board member was most vocal and had constantly challenged the superintendent's administration and recommendations, many whites blamed Cary for his resignation. Nasty letters, obscene telephone calls, threats, and other forms of harassment were directed toward him. Other members of the board became very cool and made another ninety-degree turn to the right. Cary could be guaranteed no support on any issue that concerned blacks or Mexican-Americans.

Just as whites united, blacks demonstrated unparalleled unanimity in opposing a $7 million board issue scheduled for voters approval on March 8, 1977. Cary led the campaign against the proposal because of inequities and the continued perpetuation of segregated schools. The bond package included a new school for Handley area and no new Dunbar Middle School in the Stop Six area. Most black leaders supported the boycott and negative vote. Even Como residents joined in opposition and felt that the fight for a new Dunbar Middle School had serious implications that superceded geographical boundaries. Many had been disappointed in the previous 1964 Bond Issue that Precinct 120 had overwhelmingly supported. Wilba Alaman and Wilma Philpott contended that all they got for their efforts was the closing of Como High School; two other black high schools, I. M. Terrell and Kirkpatrick, had also been closed. For once whites couldn't find any black defectors except for a newspaper reporter who had to carry out the wishes of his chiefs and urged the black community to accept repairs to an old building instead of pushing for a new one. The black community ignored this establishment dissenter and stayed with their plan. This apparent unity served to alarm and brought out a white vote that overwhelmingly passed the bond election by a 3:1 margin. One lesson was evident for all political subdivisions in this city: blacks would no longer be excluded from the decision-making process, and a strong, solid black vote was omnipresent to mandate inclusion.

This new-found unanimity in the black community carried on for a short while longer, but with more tension between it and the school board. In 1979 the board refused to allow Howard Caver to speak because he wanted to talk about Attorney Cecil Morgan, hired by the School Board in 1959 to handle the integration suit and who created three new high schools to circumvent the court order. Howard Caver threatened to bring disruption to future board meetings and accused the trustees of "Gestapo tactics," then scattered cardboard signs over the floor of the boardroom.

Howard Caver, Chairman of the Legal Defense for Quality Education and the Southeast Community Action Group, opposed the NAACP's court settlement because it maintained a segregated Dunbar Schools complex. Another member, Tyree Franklin, contended that the proposal to create a magnet school as only a tool for perpetuating more one-race schools. Further, the black community was incensed at racial and derogatory remarks made by Attorney Cecil Morgan that he would not want his picture taken with Attorney Clifford Davis of the NAACP.

Reby Cary, who was now a member of the Texas Legislature, criticized the compromise reached by the school board and the NAACP after thirteen months of negotiations and testified in Judge Mahon's court that the magnet system would not work based on records in other states and the opposition of whites in Tarrant County. He further disagreed with the decision to hire black administrators until a 30 percent threshold was reached; instead, Mahon should require the school board to hire one black administrator or teacher for each white hired in these fields for the next three years. This proposal was rejected. As a result of the agreement and decision by Judge Mahon, magnet schools were created and a new Dunbar Middle School was built on the corner of Stalcup and Ramey Streets. Blacks were finally included in a bond issue.

Inclusion at all levels of government became the byword in Tarrant County. In 1977 Mattie Nell Compton was selected as the first African-American assistant city attorney by Mayor Hugh Parmer. Compton grew up in Fort Worth and graduated in 1968 from Dunbar High School where her mother, Mae Cora Peterson, served as the Dean of Girls. Upon graduation, Mattie Peterson Compton matriculated at Smith College and obtained her law degree in 1976 from the University of Michigan Law School.

In 1980 Mattie Compton achieved another first by an African-American woman, becoming the first African-American law clerk to the Honorable David O. Belew, United States District Judge in the Northern District of Texas. This was a political phenomenon at the federal level. Judge Belew, a federal judge newly appointed by President Jimmy Carter, made derogatory and racial remarks at a closed meeting by referring to blacks as "niggers." This raised the ire of the local NAACP and several leaders who demanded a meeting with the judge. However, my favorite editorialist and free-lance columnist, Bob Ray Sanders, defended Judge Belew and said that "the use of the word 'nigger' was a weak cause for the NAACP to fight and they should push for more important issues such as school integration and voting against the ineffective and politically manipulated State judges." He further condemned the newspaper as a wrong-doer for even publishing such trivia.

The community group who confronted Judge Belew included Reverend L. B. George; Attorney Louis Sturns; Jonathan Wilders of the Human Relations Commission; former City Councilwoman Walter B. Barbour; Assistant City Manager Vernell Sturns; and City Councilman James Bagsby. The group pushed for equitable representation of blacks in the judicial process. Judge Belew apologized for his remarks and later appointed Mattie Compton. In 1982 she became the first woman to serve as Assistant United States Attorney for the Northern District of Texas; at the time of this writing, she is the Deputy Chief of the Civil Division. In 1994 Attorney Compton was awarded the Director's Award for Superior Performance in her office by Attorney-General Janet Reno. She also served as president of the Fort Worth Black Bar and is very active in the Fort Worth Chapter of the Links, Inc.

Leonard Briscoe brought new hope to Fort Worth's black community in 1976. He ran for the Texas State Legislature and in 1977 became the first black elected to the 65th session from Tarrant County. His campaign created political havoc in the black community. Briscoe was opposed by Laurene Sharp, Reverend A. H. Forbes, Charles Grays, and Bobby Webber. When the AFL-CIO endorsed Bobby Webber, the ministers and other black organizations resented the apparent intrusion in Legislative District 32H; Briscoe won and immediately became a champion of the black community.

The old at-large school board election had been challenged in court, and the legislature was urged to come up with an acceptable single-member district plan. Immediately Briscoe and Representative Doyle Willis sponsored the bill in the House and Senator Bill Mier in the State for the Fort Worth School Board.

Initially, the proposed seven-member plan almost guaranteed two black districts and possibly one for the Mexican-Americans. This apparently gave too much power to the minority communities, and subsequently the number on the board was increased to nine to ensure that the minority vote would not have the clout that had been anticipated. With opposition to the changes from Cary, James Bagsby, T. A. Sims, and Maudrie Walton, the changes were made which had the president and vice-president elected at-large; to this very day, not one minority has been elected to those at-large positions on the Fort Worth School Board.

When Cary filed to run for the state legislature in February 1978, it created a problem for the Fort Worth School Board; he had to submit his letter of resignation and the board had to make a decision to fill it immediately or wait until the April 1978 election. Bill Elliott, President of the Board, recommended that the place be filled immediately by another Afro-American to show good faith to Cary's constituents. However, a bill creating single-member districts for Fort Worth was still being challenged in the federal courts and some members wanted to wait for two more months for the April election.

Upon Cary's recommendation and strong community support, Maudrie Walton became the first black female board member elected from the new single-member District 3 in 1978. Dr. Clifton Tinsley Sparks summarized the feeling of many citizens about Maudrie Walton as she wrote about the "Gardener With A Black Thumb."

> Her human garden has produced many strong, talented, humane, and contributing Americans. The school where she carefully planted seeds, watered, fertilized, and placed sticks in strategic places, was renamed for her. This garden of living gifts is too alive and dynamic to be captured and placed on canvas by even the most brilliant artist.[74]

Subsequently Reby Cary, who had been persuaded by Ben Morrison, Deralyn Davis, and a large group of minorities to challenge Leonard Briscoe in Legislative District 32H, had to refile for the new District 95 because in 1976 the federal courts agreed with Attorney Don Gladden and created Legislative District 90, which Bobby Webber won. Cary won in a run-off election in 1978 by beating incumbent Brisco 1,978 to 1,325 votes. Bob McFarland also won as a Republican from Tarrant County.

Single-member districts and redistricting came simultaneously to the Fort Worth City Council. Because Cary was an associate dean of student affairs and an assistant professor of history at the University of Texas at Arlington, he and Attorney Clifford Davis were able to get support from Dr. Paul Geisel and an Urban Studies graduate class to help set the plan and furnish population statistics for redistricting in the school district. This data was shared with the Fort Worth City Council so they could draw their lines for council districts.

Nevertheless, in 1977 Walter Barbour and James Bagsby were the first Afro-Americans elected from single-member districts to the Fort Worth City Council. After a heated and contested race involving Doug Wright, a former policeman, and Ben Morrison, a realtor, Walter B. (Campbell) Barbour won. Barbour was the first black female elected to the council. She had outstanding educational credentials, a Bachelor of Arts degree from Prairie View A&M College, a Master of Arts degree from Atlanta University, and years of experience as an outstanding teacher and Guidance Counselor at Eastern Hills High School in Fort Worth. She, too, had the distinction of being an assistant secretary to black millionaire Bill McDonald. Walter B. was employed at Ure's Drug Store by Zadilee Payne, Gooseneck Bill's secretary, and when Payne was busy, Walter Barbour would substitute for her at Fraternal Bank and Trust.

Ms. Barbour served as Chairwoman of the Fort Worth Human Relations Commission, which was established in July 1967 to promote interracial harmony. She brought many improvements in streets and other services to her community; more than $6 million in street improvements were allocated to District 5 because of her influence. Even though she decided not to seek reelection in 1979, she continued her interests in the affairs of District 5. Ms. Barbour challenged City Council's decision to spend $5,000 for an orangutan and two chimpanzees when the black community did not have adequate recreational facilities and street improvements. She felt the Park and Recreation Department should be "people-centered, rather than concerned with ape houses."[75] Later she was employed as an administrator with Texas Electric Service Company. Ms. Barbour also tried to expand the Community Trailblazers of her church, Saint Peter Presbyterian Church, to compete with the Minority Leaders and Citizens Council that met on Wednesday of each week, but it did not survive.

Simultaneously, James (Jim) Bagsby was elected to City Council. Bagsby had worked with Ms. Barbour on many projects that affected the black community. Bagsby, a pharmacist, born in 1932 in McNeil, Arkansas, spent his early childhood in Texarkana, Texas, married Dionne Phillips in 1961, and came to Fort Worth from Pine Bluff, Arkansas. He was an experienced community activist who had been involved for years in the civil rights movement. In Pine Bluff he engaged in many sit-ins and constantly challenged the local political entities on rights denied black citizens in Arkansas.

After his election to the Fort Worth City Council, Bagsby became a vocal and politically shrewd councilman. He served from 1977 to 1987, working with his cohort Walter Barbour and her successor, Bert C. Williams. Jim became the lighting rod on the city council, and the difference from other councilmen was that most of his opposition came from his own Precinct 8 and other black factions in the city. In 1980 Bagsby filed a protest with the Federal Aviation Administration because there were no blacks serving on the regional airport board. He opposed the proposed reappointment of Jim Fuller and Henry Meadows, which brought consternation to other council members. However, on Tuesday, October 29, 1980, the city of Fort Worth achieved two firsts with one appointment to the powerful Airport Board. Erma Chansler Johnson, Personnel Director for Tarrant County Junior College and a member of the Fort Worth Public Transportation Advisory Committee, became the first black, as well as the first female, to be named to the board.[76] Later she became the first black and first woman in a Vice Chancellor's position at Tarrant County Junior College.

This promotion was a giant leap for a young lady from Leggett, Texas, in the lumber center of Polk County. Erma received her Bachelor of Arts degree from Prairie View A&M College in 1959, and then taught at Carthage High School in Carthage, Texas. She received a full-time graduate fellowship and earned a Master's degree in business from

Bowling Green State University in Ohio in 1968. She came to Tarrant County Junior College as an instructor in the business department. Councilman Bagsby knew that the city council couldn't claim this appointment was not a qualified choice.

Bagsby's political shrewdness really came to light in November 1980 when he unveiled a proposal for changes in redistricting to possibly get a black congressman in Tarrant County. This county had violated a nondilution rule of federal statutes by dividing the black community between Congressional Districts 12 and 24 and linking to District 5 in Dallas. His charges were ignored and his proposal to keep the minority communities together failed.

Many leaders and voters still don't realize how the splitting of District 12 made blacks lose what little political clout they had. When District 12 was together, blacks in Stop Six, east Fort Worth, Forest Hills, Southside, Riverside, and Lake Como were together and had the potential of definitely influencing legislation and possibly electing a black or Mexican-American legislator. Now District 24 has Stop Six, east Fort Worth, and Forest Hills connected to Arlington, Dallas, Mansfield, Ennis, and Corsicana. That's why blacks can't see their congressman until election time and their interests are subordinated to the majority white community.

In 1982 Democrats extended the dilution of the black vote to Oak Cliff in Dallas. Old partners, NAACP and Republicans challenged the dilution in court, but to no avail. Democrats want black support, but seldom will they support black priorities.

Political sparks and fireworks picked up momentum in 1983 and continued throughout Bagsby's political career. In 1983 he was opposed for reelection by Alexander Davis and Martha Singleton. Bagsby received 1,155 votes, Davis 691, and Martha Singleton 188. Davis considered filing a suit contesting the election because of voting irregularities, but when the votes were canvassed, no irregularities were found. It was common knowledge that the Precinct Workers Council members who conducted the elections had a way of illegally influencing voting results for the candidates they supported.

In October 1984 Bagsby had the distinction of being the only elected city official to be found guilty of theft in Fort Worth's one-hundred-two-year history. He had been charged on a hot payroll check violation. Many supporters claimed the charges were politically motivated and that certain groups were out to tarnish his reputation and remove him from office. This situation didn't help the black community in promotions of some of its highly qualified citizens.

In 1985 a black professional could be an assistant city manager, but not the city manager. Robert Herchert resigned as city manager in Fort Worth to become a senior vice-president and director of human services for Texas American Bank, and the council had a racial decision to make. Vernell Sturns, born in Texas, a 1961 graduate from Prairie View A&M College and with a Master's degree in Public Administration from the University of Kansas, had served very well as an assistant city manager, and many blacks felt he would be promoted to city manager. He received the votes of the minority councilmen, Jim Bagsby, Bert Williams, and Louis Zapata, plus Dwaine Johnson, but lost to the votes of Bob Bolen, Herman Stute, Richard Newkirk, Russell Lancaster, and Kathy Wetherly, who voted for Douglas Harman from Alexandria, Virginia. Vernell Sturns remained as assistant city manager until he was appointed to the Dallas/Fort Worth Airport Board. He served as deputy executive director of the airport from May 1986 until he was appointed Executive Director. Fort Worth took exceptional pride in Vernell because he was responsible for the day-to-day administration of the world's second largest and second busiest airport in America. Jim Bagsby expressed continuous displeasure at the outcome of Vernell Sturns not being chosen city manager and created disharmony in the entire community.

Subsequently, in 1985, the councilman drew three opponents: Roger Williams, a white candidate, who withdrew after two other candidates filed; Emmett Allen, a young realtor who circulated a petition and received 572 signatures of support against Bagsby because he had not helped the Morningside residents restore some ornamental street lights the city had turned off; and Nell Webber, a mortician. On Election Day, Webber received 1,228 votes, Bagsby 1,102, and Emmett Allen 230.

In the April 20, 1985 Run-off Election, Webber lost to Bagsby and claimed that the same voting irregularities which took place in 1983 were still present in this race. Webber said she "should have been declared the winner on April 6 without having to face a run-off with Bagsby."[77] She appealed and lost.

Having two black councilmen gave the black community reenforced balance, and support on their agenda and mutual problems. During the election in 1979, changes took place on the council in District 5. Walter Barbour chose not to seek reelection, and Bert C. Williams, Barbour's campaign manager, became a candidate and was elected. Williams was a graduate of Bishop College and received a Master's degree in business education from North Texas University. He taught several years and helped make Kirkpatrick High School's football team state contenders.

Bert Williams has been an outstanding and meritorious underwriter for Equitable Life Insurance Company. In 1985 Bert was elected Mayor Pro-Tem of the Fort Worth City Council. This achievement put him in a unique position, and he was immediately challenged by members of the minority community. In 1986 Jim Bagsby and Bert Williams both drew fire from young black activities Charles Brown, Anthony Lyons, and Rick Broadus, who condemned them for opposing economic sanctions against South Africa. Williams contended that "economic sanctions are ineffective and would hurt South Africa's oppressed blacks rather than help them"; Bagsby said he "needed further information on the matter before taking a position."[78]

Bert Williams was always the cautious watchdog for the interest of the black community. In February 1988 a proposal was made to reduce the power and independence of the Fort Worth Human Relations Commission. Its chairman, Jeff Bland, proposed changing the city ordinance to place the hiring of the director under the city manager instead of the commission. "Mayor Pro-Tem Bert Williams has said that to change the ordinance will weaken the commission by playing down what it does and making it less autonomous," he said.[79] The commission maintained its autonomy and State Representative Reby Cary, District 95, used the commission in Fort Worth as a model for the Texas State Commission, which became law in 1984.

One of the first bills Cary filed was for the creation of a State Human Relations Commission, a bill which was cosigned by State Representative Bobby Webber, District 90, also from Fort Worth. Representative Paul Ragsdale of Dallas had tried such legislation earlier, but could not get the committee hearing required to present to the House of Representatives for a vote; Ragsdale, Representative Wilhemania Delco, and Texas Attorney John Hill supported the bill. House Bill 1052 was approved on the second reading without debate by a vote of 89:41, but there was no sponsorship in the Senate. State Senator Betty Andjuar, Fort Worth, said later if she had known, she would have sponsored it in the Upper Chamber.

In the next session, Cary, equipped with legislative savvy, asked Senator Ray Farabee to introduce House Bill 61 to the Senate; few senators would challenge this experienced legislator. HB61 passed again in the House, but it could not get a House vote because the Calendar Committee would not place it on the voting agenda, and the Speaker of the House has control over the calendar. When the Texas Employment Commission's Sunset Bill went to the Senate, Senator Lloyd Doggett added Cary's bill as an amendment, creating a Human Rights Division in the Texas Employment Commission; both legislators threatened to temporarily kill the legislation continuing the commission if a conference committee did not create the State Human Rights Commission.

Governor Mark White said he would call a special session if the legislature did not concur before the regular session ended. He was unhappy with Democrat Reby Cary for leading the campaign for blacks over Texas in support of Bill Clements. Cary maintained that Governor White had stood in opposition to the Federal Voting Rights Act, which guaranteed minorities participation in the political process, and he was certainly lukewarm about a human rights bill because it might offend too many of his Democratic supporters.

But Cary's primary opposition to Mark White was because the former attorney general had defied the Black Caucus and State Representative Wilhemania Delco, Chairwoman of the House Committee on Higher Education, on funding Prairie View A&M College and Texas Southern University. For four years Representative Delco requested an attorney general's opinion as to the constitutional designation of Prairie View (A&M College) in the Texas Constitution of 1876 as "a school for colored"—it certainly wasn't Texas A&M. A favorable opinion would give the school access to the $1.8 billion in the state's Permanent University Fund. Mark White continued to ignore this request; Governor Bill Clements pushed for Prairie View to get a special grant of $10 million each year for ten years for the enhancement of its curriculum.

A special session was called while Cary was in Baden-Baden, Germany, on an educational tour with Dallas School Superintendent Linus Wright. Representative Ron Wilson took the Human Rights Bill and it passed. At the signing, no mention was made of Cary's efforts in getting the bill passed. Even Bill Hale, the executive director who helped in its passage, remained silent about Cary's involvement. Nevertheless, Mayor Woodie Woods of Fort Worth gave Cary a plaque in recognition of his efforts in establishing the State Human Relations Commission.

In 1979 redistricting was the foremost agenda item of local and national elected officials. Reby Cary was appointed a member and finally Chairman of the Budget of House Committee on Regions, Compacts, and Districts. Immediately he challenged the state and national Democratic leadership and led the fight for District 5 in Dallas to have its first U.S. Congressman of color. Governor Bill Clements vetoed the redistricting bill because the Democratic leadership would not include this proposed black district.

Cary attempted to show the minority voters in Dallas and Fort Worth an obvious fact, that the Democrats would not support them in their priorities of representation and the Republicans did. The Representative of District 95 became the first black Democrat to actively and publicly support a Republican candidate, Bill Clements. Then he added insult to injury by challenging Tarrant County Democrats who tried, and were successful, in taking Bobby Webber's seat for the benefit of Representative Doyle Willis. Democrats in Tarrant County maintained their togetherness in asserting that the black community did not deserve two representatives.

This assault on black representation by Democrats was continued in the year 2001. State Representative Ron Wilson, a black Democrat from Houston, was quoted by Sam Attlesey in the *Dallas Morning News*, September 30, 2001, as favoring a Republican redistricting map over one drawn by his own party designed to protect Democratic incumbents at the expense of creating a black district in Harris County. "You're using us as cannon fodder for Anglo Democrats to get elected," he said. That's basically the same fact that led Reby Cary to change parties.

Many of Cary's supporters deserted him at the urging of Democrats and labor union members who resented his urging black voters to "split your ticket." When the legislator planned a monthly forum for District 95 on October 9, 1982, Vernell Sturns, Assistant City Manager, and Councilman Jim Bagsby told Cary not to mention any names of candidates; if he did, he could not hold the meeting at the Southside Multipurpose Center. Cary refused to give into the unprecedented censorship and harassment from opponents of Governor Bill Clements. Ironically, noted *LaVida News*, "Senator Lloyd Bentsen was to be allowed use of the Center the following Friday night without any such restraint."[80]

The group assembled and marched out en masse and held the meeting on the steps of Mount Zion Baptist Church, which was one-half block away. They were still told to "split your ticket." The Democratic Coalition for Clements aroused the ire of other black Democratic loyalists. State Representative Craig Washington of Houston criticized Bobby Webber and Reby Cary and called them "handkerchief-headed niggers"[81] for daring to leave the Democratic plantation. Cary responded that Craig Washington was also a "house Negrito," one who lived in the big house with his master and sold blacks down the river to keep in favor. Many of Cary's supporters deserted him, and Garfield Thompson defeated him in the election of 1984.

Thompson had been an ardent Democratic Party supporter and a leader in the labor unions of Tarrant County. He too was a graduate of I. M. Terrell High School and worked hard for the advancement of his community. He had enormous political clout as chairman of the Precinct Workers Council that was instrumental in garnering votes in the black community for Democratic candidates. That group targeted senior citizens and nursing homes to get large numbers of absentee votes. Nevertheless, during the city council elections in 1984-85, this organization came under fire for voting irregularities and possible violation of state law. Alexander Davis, a young businessman who challenged Jim Bagsby and lost, and Nell Webber, a mortician, filed complaints about known voting tactics of the Precinct Workers Council and conflict of interest. For years, in spite of the oath they took as county employees, these election judges accepted money from Democratic candidates for their endorsement and support in any election. In its editorial, a local newspaper chided the organization for its posture of "Votes for sale!" Garfield Thompson threatened nonsupport of those candidates who didn't pay them $650. The court withheld its decision of the irregularities until after the election and charges remained moot.

Garfield Thompson still had the support of the Democrats and they wanted him to defeat this author because Cary had been urging black voters to "split your ticket" and support a Republican candidate; they wanted to be assured they could retain their racially predetermined bloc vote. Thompson won the legislative seat for District 95 in 1984 and sent Reby Cary into retirement. Thompson served two years; however, in the 1986 election, Thompson and the ballot manipulations of the Precinct Workers Council were challenged by another District 95 candidate, Donna Evans. She was an ardent political worker in Forest Hill and a former employee of the Tarrant County Planning Department. Donna Evans understood the illegal voting procedures carried on in many of the black precincts. She asked the Secretary of State to monitor the precincts for voting irregularities and payoffs. It didn't work; Thompson won the election over Ms. Evans and candidate Glen Lewis. In 1990 he was replaced by Attorney Glen Lewis, who is still the only black state legislator representing Tarrant County.

A valuable lesson was learned that when one takes a stand for what he or she believes to be in the best interest of the whole community, and black and Hispanic voters divide their party allegiance and split their tickets, unexpected benefits accrue. When Bill Clements called Reby Cary to his office to thank him for assisting with his election, he asked what he could do to show his gratitude. Cary's response was that blacks in Tarrant County had never had a black judge in a county or district court. Many black citizens had been petitioning the Commissioners Court for years trying to get them to consider Maryellen Hicks, but to no avail. Shortly after meeting with Governor Bill Clements, and on Cary's recommendation of Louis Sturns in 1983, he appointed Attorney Sturns as the first black state judge to Tarrant County Criminal District Court No. 2. Sturns was sworn in Monday, January 17, 1983.

Louis Sturns was well qualified for this position. The scholarly Afro-American from east Texas was a 1973 graduate of the University of Kansas Law School with a Juris Doctor's degree. He was commissioned in 1970 as a 2nd Lieutenant after four years of U.S. Army ROTC; he received his Bachelor of Arts in political science from Wichita State University in the same year. From 1976 to 1983, Louis Sturns practiced domestic and criminal law in Fort Worth until his appointment by Governor Clements. His appointment brewed a hot confirmation battle in the Texas Senate. Senator Hugh Parmer would not confirm Sturns' appointment because he had been promoting one of his white counterparts, and Parmer joined other Democrats in blocking Governor Clements lame-duck appointments.

In the meantime, with the help of former Texas attorney Waggoner Carr, Judge Sturns filed a suit restraining Governor Mark White and the Texas Senate from replacing him with another nominee. Many supporters of Senator Parmer were outraged at his action and arrogant attitude toward the delegation that went to Austin to express their concerns about Sturns' confirmation. The leader of this delegation was the well-respected Reverend L. B. George, pastor of the Mount Zion Baptist Church in Fort Worth, who had been an active leader in challenging problems his members and community faced. In the 1960s Reverend

George fought against segregation in Amarillo, Texas. His eldest daughter was the first to attend an integrated public school in that city and was one of the first to matriculate at West Texas State University.

Reverend George came to Fort Worth in 1966 as pastor of the Mount Zion Baptist Church, and two years later was elected president of the Fort Worth Interdenominational Alliance, where he served for 16 years; he also served on the Board of Directors at the Eastside Bank on Berry Street. His ministry was characterized by his "Four Ps": PREACHING, PRAYING, PROTESTING, AND POLITICS. Reverend George was an essential contact person for any politician seeking office, but he remained an independent supporter who stood fast on his belief for the good of the community. After much pressure from Reverend George, Dee Jennings, and other groups, Parmer set aside his personal choice and recommended Attorneys Clifford Davis and Maryellen Hicks. When Hugh Parmer was mayor of Fort Worth in 1978, he appointed Maryellen Hicks the first municipal judge in Tarrant County, where she served for five years. She was a graduate of Texas Tech School of Law and a member of the State Bar of Texas and American Bar Association. Ms. Hicks ran for judge of Criminal Court No. 1, but white Democrats classified her as a militant and would not support her; Frank Coffey, a Democrat won. So, when Parmer appointed Maryellen Hicks to the 231st District Family Law Civil Courts, the Reverend L. B. George quipped that since Parmer owed blacks a debt, "we decided we wanted another pair of shoes—we got two black judges." Judge Hicks is remembered for her rousing commentaries on her weekly talk show and being one of the leaders of Delta Sigma Theta sorority's drive to name the Poly Freeway in honor of Dr. Martin Luther King, Jr.

Maybe, because of Hugh Parmer's negative actions, three black judges were given an opportunity for service in Tarrant County and, at this writing, Judge Wayne Salvant, a Republican, is the only Afro-American judge in a state court in Tarrant County. He was born in New Orleans in 1946 and attended high school in that city. He attended Southern University in Baton Rouge from 1964 to 1968 and graduated with a degree in business administration. From 1968 to 1971 he served as a United States Marine Corps officer with a tour of duty that included combat in Vietnam. At the end of his term of enlistment, he pursued further academic training at the Southern University School of Law from 1971 to 1974.

In the summer of 1972, before moving to Fort Worth, Judge Wayne Salvant worked as a legal assistant in the Baton Rouge Bail Bond Program; his duty was to interview indigent misdemeanor offenders to determine their eligibility for pre-trial release. Then, in 1974, he was employed as an attorney for the United States Securities and Exchange Commission, a position he held for three years. In 1977 he opened his own law office, where he represented clients in state and federal courts. At the same time, he was an adjunct professor in business law at undergraduate and graduate levels at the University of Texas at Arlington.

Wayne Salvant has always been community-oriented. He served on the boards of the Lena Pope Home and the Sickle Cell Anemia Association. When the Frederick Douglass Republicans of Tarrant County organized in 1985, he drew up the constitution and by-laws so that group could meet the requirements for certification by the state of Texas. In the 1986 primary election, Attorney Wayne Salvant filed as a Republican candidate for

Criminal District Judge, Place 4, against Judge Joe Drago, a Democrat. Wayne Salvant sailed freely through the primary but lost to the incumbent in the general election. Joe Drago won 52.3 percent of the votes (109,236) and Attorney Wayne Salvant 47 percent (99,613).

Parts of the black community started waking up to Hugh Parmer's ignoring many black leaders. Doug Harlan, San Antonio columnist, wrote, "what is at work here is a simple case of vindictive politics...simply because Clements is a Republican."[82] Carl Freund, *Dallas Morning News*, printed a quote from some Democrats that they

> plan to trim the sails of State Representative Reby Cary, the only black member of the Tarrant County Legislative delegation, because he urged blacks to support Bill Clements when the Republican governor ran unsuccessfully for reelection in the November 2 General Election. Cary could face problems in getting his proposals approved in Austin.[83]

Other leaders in Fort Worth seemed suddenly to wake up to the value of redistricting in assuring minorities fair representation at all levels of government. Spearheaded by the Minority Leaders and Citizens Council in 1979, Attorneys Don Gladden and Louis Sturns filed a suit in Judge Eldon Mahon's Federal Court against the Tarrant County Commissioners Court. The plaintiffs were City Councilman James Bagsby, State Representatives Reby Cary and Bobby Webber, Attorney Pamela (Dunlop) Gates, Roy Charles Brooks, Timothy Stewart, Spencer Griggs, and F. L. Riley. They alleged that the black community's vote was broken into three illogical parts so as to dilute the black vote in commissioners' precinct elections. Those lines had been drawn in a pie-shaped configuration with minorities in the center, which meant that their votes made minimal impact in all districts.

The group really became infuriated over the threat made by District Tim Curry that he would seek financial restitution and make the plaintiffs pay for bringing a groundless suit. It got so contentious that the whole effort seemed headed for the U.S. Supreme Court. One of the main points of disagreement was the establishment of a sub-courthouse in the minority community. County Judge Mike Moncrief, Commissioner Lynn Gregory, Jerry Mebus, and Attorneys Gladden and Sturns made a compromise. The court hearing was postponed with the condition that the attorney fees would be waived, Commissioners Court and Justice of the Peace lines redrawn, and a sub-courthouse built in the minority community that today is named after its first black Justice of the Peace in Tarrant County, Charles Griffin.

Born in Corsicana, Texas, Charles Griffin lived in Oklahoma City and Dallas, served four years in the United States Army, moved to Fort Worth, and was employed by the General Services Administration in 1952. Because of his successful efforts in bringing needed changes to Fort Worth and the Stop Six community, he was called "the Bronze Mayor of Carver Heights," an area adjacent to Stop Six. He was one of the first homeowners in this new addition to Fort Worth where blacks did not move in when whites moved out, but the area was developed initially by black homeowners. This was a middle-class community where the majority of the black elected officials resided: city councilpersons Walter B. Barbour, Bert Williams, Eugene McCray, Reverend McKinley Jackson, and Frank Moss; school board members Maudrie Walton, Christene Moss, and Reby Cary, who was also a state representative for District 95; and Tarrant County Junior College Board members Harold Odom and Gwen Morrison. Judge Clifford Davis is also a resident of the Carver Heights community.

Justice of the Peace Griffin was a member of the Mayor's Human Relations Committee and Chairman of the President's Committee on Equal Opportunities; he was also instrumental in establishing the Texas Sickle-Cell Anemia Association and served twelve years with that organization. In 1981 Charles Griffin was appointed Justice of the Peace, Precinct 8, and was reelected twice to the position until his death in 1987.

Roy Lee Richards was appointed by Dick Anderson, a county commissioner, to succeed Griffin and serve out his term, which would end in 1990. He had good qualifications as a graduate of Texas Christian University in 1976 with a degree in journalism, and a law degree from Howard University Law School in 1981. Richards had also served as community liaison for Precinct 1 County Commissioner Dick Anderson. In 1998 Roy Lee Richards defeated four challengers to serve out the remainder of Judge Griffin's term. But a major blot came on his tenure in office. In November 1989 an arrest warrant was issued against Richards for possession of a controlled substance he claimed he was involved in a Federal Bureau Investigation, but the evidence proved different. He was convicted, and County Commissioner Dionne Bagsby had to make an appointment in Richards' place. She appointed a recognized leader in Fort Worth, Walter B. Barbour, as an interim replacement until Sidney Thompson was elected Judge of Precinct 8 in Tarrant County by defeating Alfred Nelms, a Tarrant County Frederick Douglass Republican.

Sidney Thompson was a 1965 graduate of Dunbar High School, Fort Worth, Texas, and attended Texas Wesleyan University in the same city. He was a veteran of the Vietnam War and served in the United States Navy. After the war, Judge Thompson, an active Democrat, was elected Precinct Chairman in the Eastwood Addition and often a delegate to the Democratic State Conventions. He has been elected Justice of the Peace in District 8 in six consecutive elections. The Judge is a member of the Texas Justice of the Peace and Constables Association.

When the 1984 Commissioners Court election came, blacks still had not produced a candidate. Dick Andersen, the Commissioner in Precinct 1, had no Democratic opponent. In 1989 Dionne Bagsby became the first black elected to the Commissioners Court in Tarrant County. She was the wife of Councilman Bagsby, but they were divorced in 1987. Commissioner Dionne Bagsby was a graduate of Illinois Wesleyan University with a Bachelor's degree in Communications and a Master's from Texas Christian University. She was employed as a reading specialist by the Fort Worth Independent School District.

Dionne Bagsby had been a part-time legislative aide to Representative Cary in 1979, and was encouraged to run by Attorney Jessie Gaines, her campaign manager. Routine and expected opposition came from the Coalition of Black Democrats and the Precinct Workers Council, who supported Dick Andersen, the white incumbent.[84] Nevertheless, she won even though the minority population was only 30 percent in District 1.

When the minority community pushed the Commissioners Court in 1990 to expand the board of directors for the county's new Crime Control and Prevention District,

Commissioner Bagsby proposed increasing the board from seven to eleven members. Cary, initially opposed the Crime District as being unnecessary, contended that if the sales tax was approved, more minorities should be placed on the permanent board as Commissioner Bagsby had proposed. She also wrote the Affirmative Action Program and the companion Disadvantaged Business Program, which enhanced the number of minority vendors doing business with the county.

Triggered by the 1990 census, redistricting came back to the forefront in 1991. Viola Pitts objected to the placement of her Precinct 4120 in Lake Como to Commissioner Bagsby's District 1. She was content for her constituents to be 5 percent tokens in J. D. Johnson's Precinct 4. Commissioner Bagsby said it was apparent that "the redistricting had more to do with protecting incumbents rather than dealing with minority interests."[85]

But this commissioner's incumbency was protected because of her expertise and tenacity in protecting the rights of her constituents. She led the fight and forced the John Peter Smith Pharmacy to assess its failures and reorganize to more effectively serve citizens in Tarrant County. Needless to say, Commissioner Bagsby was reelected in the November 8, 2000 election by garnering 57 percent of the votes against her opponent, Carlos Puentes (GOP).

Bagsby's reelection meant that she would continue to be the only Democrat on the five-member board, which she wanted to remain diverse. "I'm a minority in two senses, by race and gender, and by political affiliation," she said. "It's important to have an independent voice, and that's what I am."[86] An independent voice is good when you can generate support in a small political subdivision, but it is something else when that is tried statewide. Louis Sturns proclaimed himself an independent, but had to be supported by a Republican governor. When Governor Clements was elected to a second term, 1987 to 1991, once more he made history by helping blacks in Texas attain higher positions in government.

In 1986 Louis Sturns won the judgeship of Criminal District Court #1 by defeating incumbent Tony Goldsmith. Once more, when Governor Bill Clements won his second term, 1986-1990, he attempted to break the color barrier and simultaneously thwart the political strategies of the Democrats, who were pushing the candidacy of Judge Morris Overstreet of Potter County Court at Law in Amarillo, Texas. Clements appointed Louis Sturns to the Texas Court of Criminal Appeals. Sturns had served four years in Criminal District Court #1 and possibly would have no problem winning reelection. If he accepted the appointment, state law required him to run again in November. On March 16, 1990, Louis Sturns accepted the Appellate Court appointment.

Once again Judge Sturns faced the same black opposition that had confronted him during his first appointment by Governor Clements. This opposition is always generated by the Democratic Party leadership solely for their benefit. Unfortunately, many blacks are "Democrats" first and their ethnicity and priorities are secondary, as exemplified by the coalitions of Black Democrats. Judge Overstreet challenged Judge Sturns and won 51 percent to 49 percent of the votes cast. Judge Overstreet served very well, but when time came for his reelection, the leadership deserted him in favor of Jim Mattox. Mission accomplished.

Availability of adequate medical facilities and services has long been a problem for blacks in Fort Worth. Before the 1950s, white hospitals either denied or had "basement and backdoor services" for black patients. To meet the medical needs of blacks in Fort Worth, Dr. R. A. Ransom operated a clinic (hospital) on Nichols and Second Streets. Later, in 1947, Dr. Eddie A. Dorsey, born in Calvert, Texas, a graduate of Bishop College in Marshall, and with a medical degree from Meharry Medical College in Tennessee, came from Iberia, Louisiana, and built a twenty-bed hospital next to his residence on Sixth and Jones Streets in downtown Fort Worth. He had a landscaped courtyard that separated his residence and the two-story clinic-hospital, and operated that facility for more than thirty years. Later he organized the New Chance Foundation, a drug and alcohol prevention and treatment program, and sponsored Fort Worth's first long-care nursing centers for Afro-Americans.

One of the memorable highlights of Cary's tenure in the Texas State Legislature that had a substantial impact on blacks in Fort Worth was his challenge of racial discrimination against black physicians who were denied the opportunity to serve their patients in the major hospitals. After attending a meeting called by Dr. Michael Byrd at his father's residence and listening to the complaints of some twelve black physicians, Cary concluded that there was a conspiracy among the hospitals to keep black doctors out, resulting in black patients not having access to the same quality care available to whites. Dr. Byrd was the leading advocator of the black doctors and asserted that undue pressure had been placed on him because of his protest. He was an obstetrician-gynecologist in Fort Worth and had served as a city health officer for Forest Hill, Texas, for over eight years, and as a health consultant for the National NAACP. Dr. Byrd later gave expert testimony before the Civil Rights Subcommittee of the House Judiciary Committee as they considered HB-5540 Health Care Quality Improvement Act of 1986.

This bill set the clock further back for black physicians because it drastically increased the punitive power of peer review to eliminate unwanted physicians and their patients. None of the hospitals in Fort Worth had substantial black representation in the administrative or disciplinary sections. Many patients of these black doctors were puzzled as to why they had to be served in the suburban hospitals, where an increasing number of black physicians were being relegated.

A more serious perception was that there was an invidious effort to reduce the number of blacks and poor in Harris Methodist Hospital, All Saints Episcopal, and St. Joseph Catholic hospitals by denying black physicians hospital privileges. This perception as reenforced when it was noted that in the previous three years, serious hospital staff disciplinary actions had been taken against 50 to 60 percent of the actively practicing physicians in Tarrant County. Three physicians had been taken off all major hospital staffs, and five others had had drastic reprimands and actions against them. This type of action was not applied equally to the majority of the white physicians, plus there was no affirmative action program in existence at any hospital in Tarrant County to monitor racial fairness.

These concerns were expressed in a meeting arranged on October 10, 1983, at the Fort Worth Medical Association Building with the Board of Directors of Harris Methodist Hospital, John Peter Smith Hospital, and Medical Plaza. Dr. Marion J. Brooks was invited by Representative Cary to verify and substantiate the accuracies of the charges being made. Overall, St. Joseph Hospital had 621 doctors and 14 black doctors allowed to practice; of the 319 doctors at John Peter Smith, only 4 were blacks, and of its 88 interns, none were black.

Once the threat of a class-action suit surfaced, it became apparent that this problem with black doctors was not limited to Fort Worth. Doctors in Dallas, Houston, and other cities expressed similar problems. A state meeting of the Lone Star State Medical Association convened at the Am Fac Hotel at DFW Airport and pledged to join in the lawsuit if it became necessary. Lawsuits weren't filed; Harris Hospital took the lead to address the concerns. Dr. Marion Brooks reported that he had been recommended to serve on a committee and other changes were in the making. Why Dr. Marion Brooks? "Jack" Brooks was highly respected and well known for his activist profile in championing the causes of the black community. During the obstreperous 1960s civil rights movement, he was often spoken of as the "dignified and professional black activist and separatist."

This physician grew up in Fort Worth, graduated from I. M. Terrell High School in 1936, and received his Bachelor of Science degree from Prairie View University in 1940. World War II intervened and Dr. Brooks served in the United States Army, 1942-1946. He attended Howard University Medical School, where he received his M.D. in 1951 and was elected to the position of Fellow of American Academy of Family Physicians in 1990.

Always involved in community affairs, Dr. Brooks was appointed to the Fort Worth City Park and Recreation Board and was associated with the Neighborhood Action, Inc. He also was a quiet sponsor of a militant black group called the United Front. He maintained that blacks were not going to continue tolerating second-class citizenship. They must integrate from a position of strength and not lose their identities through integration; they must nourish and maintain their Afro-American heritage. Dr. Brooks was one of fifty blacks invited to the breakfast at the Texas Hotel in honor of President Kennedy hours before he was assassinated in Dallas.

Dr. Marion J. Brooks was the founder of Brooks Clinic, which included his son, Dr. Clarence Brooks, and his brother, Dr. Donald Brooks. It is currently known as the Evans Avenue Medical Service. In 1970 Dr. Marion Brooks and Ms. Harriet Dawson organized the Sickle Cell Association of Texas. Sickle cell anemia, an inherited disorder, afflicts 8 to 10 percent of the black population in the United States; it also affects other races, including some Caucasians. One of the primary goals of the Sickle Cell Anemia Association has been to establish massive screening programs to identify people with the disease. Ms. Dawson was the executive director until her health failed; her daughter, Fontainette W. Davis, a registered nurse, accepted that position with the Fort Worth Chapter of the Sickle Cell Association. She attended James E. Guinn and graduated from I. M. Terrell High School. She was a graduate of St. Joseph School of Nursing and did graduate work in Health Administration at East Texas State University in Commerce, Texas.

Fontainette Davis worked as Health Coordinator for Head Start and a liaison contact between the Day Care Association and other agencies. She served as an executive consultant with the Home Health Care Management Solution. Fontainette Davis was a member of Eta Phi Beta sorority and very active as a precinct chairman in Precinct 108.

But the work of the Sickle Cell Anemia organization would not lose its momentum in Fort Worth. Visitors to the New Rising Star Baptist Church are always amazed at the eloquence and warmth of the "Welcome" extended to them on Sunday mornings and at other special occasions by Pearl Jones, the new executive of the Sickle Cell Association. The entire audience demonstrates collective appreciation to the welcome as it does what is intended—producing a feeling of togetherness. One should not be surprised because of the scholarly training and background of this member. Pearl Jones was a 1965 high school graduate from M. D. North High School, Orange, Texas, in the southeastern part of Texas. She received several degrees: a Bachelor's in Speech Education from Texas Christian University; a BFA in Speech and Hearing Pathology; and a Master's in Marketing, Northwestern University. This multi-talented church member sings in the New Rising Star Baptist Church choir and serves as an auxiliary organist.

Governor Rick Perry appointed Ms. Jones to the TEXGENE Advisory Committee that does research in genetic science and health issues. In January 2000 Ms. Jones was elected State President of the Texas Sickle Cell Association.

Black Economic Activities in Fort Worth

Racial separation was the main agent which generated separate business activity. In some ways this was an unintended benefit. Since local and state laws mandated separate public facilities for blacks and denied them access to white business facilities, it was necessary for blacks to develop their own businesses. Barber shops, beauty shops, funeral homes, restaurant, and all personal-oriented businesses flourished.

THE FRETWELLS. The *Fort Worth Star-Telegram* reported, "N. Q. Fretwell owned and operated the first and only black-owned soft drink bottling company in Tarrant County, which produced Arkola Cola."[87] The Trinity Cemetery on NE 28th Street was established by his family in memory of his father, Gene Fretwell. His family had lived in Spears Grove between Watauga and Keller in 1878. From 1918 to 1950, N. Q. Fretwell (Nunq) worked for the Katy Railroad; he lived to be one hundred years old. The operation of black-owned business in the family was carried on by two of his heirs, D. M. Fretwell and Carl Q. Fretwell, at 3320 NE 28th Street as Fretwell Building Contractors and Fretwell Welding Company.

LUCILLE B. SMITH moved to Fort Worth in 1912 from Crockett, Texas. She often quipped that she "discovered America in 1892." She was an excellent culinary expert who practiced her expertise for seventy years. She invented the first hot roll mix in the United States and later her "chili biscuits." Her biscuits were served at the White House and on American Airline flights. Many supermarkets carried her bread until investors took her formula in production of their own.

Subsequently Lucille Smith headed the first Commercial Foods and Technology Department at Prairie View University, where she perfected her famous *Lucille's Cookbook*. Her childhood training came to fruition when, she said, her mother told her "find a good home, a good church, and a good bank." She moved to Fort Worth and was a faithful member of the St. Andrews Methodist Church. In 1936 Smith's Catering Service was established and managed by her son, A. B. Smith.

Lucille Smith served on the Gift Lift Committee of the Fort Worth Chamber of Commerce, where she baked and sent 330 fruit cakes to Vietnam soldiers from Tarrant County. She was the first life member in the Women's Division of the Fort Worth Chamber of Commerce. She and her husband, Ulysses Smith, had always believed in helping others. Governor Preston Smith proclaimed Lucille B. Smith a member of his Commission on the Status of Women in January 1970. In 1976 she was honored as the Texas Mother of the Year.

WILLIAMS BARBER COLLEGE. Lewis Williams, Jr., was born in Marshall, Texas, in 1900 and moved to Shreveport, where he began his career as a barber. In the 1920s he came to Fort Worth and was employed as a porter for the Texas and Pacific Railroad. In

1953 Lewis Williams, Jr., married Thelma Johnson and the two had six children. He had very good musical talent so he formed a family orchestra and taught each of his children to play with proficiency. In the meanwhile, Lewis Williams, Jr., decided to put his vocation and avocation to work and resumed his tonsorial business.

In 1940 the Williams' purchased a building at 1063 Evans Avenue. Four years later they changed their modus operandi and opened a barber college at 1251 Evans Avenue, where it remains today. In 1952 his sons, Cecil and Charles, decided to get involved in the barbering business with their father. They too recognized the need for training because black men and women found it difficult to get formal and accredited training at the white barber schools. In cooperation with A. B. Heath, the Williams Barber College was approved by the State Board of Barber Examiners on April 30, 1956.

The school trains hundreds of young black barbers in hair styling, coloring, and skin care; the instruction also includes personal hygiene, professional ethics, and shop management. Lewis Williams, Jr., died in 1991, but his sons still carry on the operation of this legendary institution. Cecil Williams is a member of the Fort Worth Metropolitan Black Chamber of Commerce. The Texas Association of Barber Schools, National Association of Tonsorial Artists, and the Frederick Douglass Republicans of Tarrant County. In 1996 Cecil Williams was honored in the annual awards luncheon by the Quest for Success.

FUNERAL HOMES. The Baker name is well known among Fort Worthians. The Baker family is one of the oldest families in the city and is certainly one of the oldest mortician establishments in Fort Worth. In fact, at the time of this writing, Jimmie Baker and his mother, Paula Baker, are still carrying on the family tradition. James Nathan Baker started his funeral business in Cleburne, Texas, in 1919. The family moved to Fort Worth to its present location, 301 East Rosedale, in 1926. Reverend Henry Baker, founder of Baker Chapel African Methodist Episcopal Church and father of James Nathan Baker, had a shoe shop, and his son moved in with him. Prior to becoming a mortician, James Baker was a Pullman porter working out of Cleburne, Texas.

At one time the Baker family owned the Diamond Mutual Burial Association, which was taken over for reinsurance purposes in 1968 by Joe Terrell, who owned the Texas Capitol Insurance Company. After his death, the insurance company was purchased by the Bankers and Farmers Life Insurance Company of Waco. Herbert and his wife, Ruth Baker, carried on the family business with the same efficiency in service as their predecessors. In June of 1973 Herbert Baker was elected Chairman of the Fort Worth Park and Recreation Board. He became the first black to head one of the city's semi-autonomous boards. During his second year, opposition to his chairmanship came to the forefront, and in a secret vote, Herbert received four of the six votes cast. He resigned from the board in 1975. The board was then revised by the city to serve as an advisory board to the city council.

While Baker's Funeral Home was well known and conservative in its services, Brown and Hardee Funeral Home emerged with an added flash. They rebuilt their mortuary on Baptist Hill and used some new Cadillacs for hearses, attracting many families of departed ones to use these pretentious vehicles. Also, Hardee wore full-dressed (tails) suits during funeral services, which many mourners appreciated. Before there were motorcycle escorts, Hardee could be seen stopping traffic at various intersections on his way to the cemetery and often could be heard proclaiming expletives to uncooperative motorists.

Today Gregory Spencer is the epitome of all past and future morticians; he is a multi-talented person. He is an outstanding tenor vocalist, music composer, pianist, and organist, and writes beautiful poetry, which he encompasses in the printed programs. Recently, in response to the Wedgewood Church shootings in Tarrant County, Gregory Spencer wrote and produced an album, *Healing the Land*, and a CD entitled *G-Sharp*. He is also an ordained minister who pastors The Church at Philadelphia. If a choir is not present at a funeral service, Gregory Spencer can do it all.

Spencer's early childhood was spent in Lake Como, where he worshipped regularly at the Zion Missionary Baptist Church (Reverend G. W. Burton, Pastor). He attended Crossier Day Care Nursery and Como Elementary School. In 1974 he enrolled and graduated in 1975 from Green B. Trimble Technical High School. Gregory pursued an early life goal of becoming a mortician and became a graduate of the Dallas Institute of Mortuary Science with a certification in Funeral Directing and Embalming. He had worked as an apprentice and was employed for ten years under the leadership of Herbert Baker of Baker's Funeral Home.

On October 1, 1980, Gregory Spencer opened Love and Care Funeral Home at 5805 Curzon in Lake Como. In 1984 the landlord of the funeral home lost the property by foreclosure and Gregory Spencer had to share a facility with Foster Family Circle Funeral Home. His crowning glory came to fruition on April 9, 1985, when he moved into the modern facilities now located on Miller Street. Today Gregory Spencer conducts over six hundred funeral services a year in Tarrant County and a large number in other parts of the United States. Besides his large fleet of stretch limos, he has his own floral shop and printing service and intrigues the new generation with the military-like procession his staff engages in when carrying the casket. He continually strives to be "the premier funeral home of choice."

Other black-owned funeral homes which play an important and historical role in Fort Worth are Williams Funeral Home, Morris-Bates Funeral Home, Russell's Funeral Home, and Reverend's Parlor.

THE BLACK CHAMBER OF COMMERCE. It is a peculiar thing, yet one of the Negro citizenry in Fort Worth, that a mere fishing trip could result in the reestablishment of one of the most potential and needed organizations in this city. And yet it is out of such an incident that a rebirth of this organization was visualized. Thus, one evening on the brink of a lake as Elmer Williams and Harold Odom cast for fish, the idea of a Negro Chamber of Commerce was reborn.

As a formal step in the organization of a chamber of commerce, it was felt that in order for this proposed body to become effective, it would be necessary to have the endorsement and cooperation of the white chamber of commerce in this city. Subsequently Mr. Foster, Industrial Director of the Fort Worth Chamber, was chosen as the main speaker for the night of May 13, 1946. But seemingly, as other nights in the week, Monday was a bad one: it was the opening night of the Fort Worth Cats baseball season. At the designated time, only Mr. Foster, Reby Cary, and Harold Odom were present. Harold Odom was one of the top directors in the Fort Worth Housing and Urban Development Department and he and his wife, Lonnie Odom, owned Odom's Floral Shop. Imagine the embarrassment and disappointment at the lack of interest on the part of the black citizens. But for men who were determined that a Negro Chamber of Commerce would be established, this was only a stepping stone.

Consequently, on Thursday morning May 30, 1946, at 10:30 A.M. in the office of Mr. T. J. Updyck, T. G. Thomas, Elmer Williams, Harold Odom, and Reby Cary assembled, and after discussing the need and feasibility of organizing a chamber of commerce, it was decided to proceed with organization. However, it was suggested that a more detailed study should be made of other chambers of commerce in Texas, and the next meeting was postponed pending receipt of literature from these chambers.

The week preceding July 19, letters were mailed to approximately one hundred business owners and interested citizens encouraging them to attend the meeting of the proposed organization. Seven people were present. The discussion then arose relative to the election of permanent officers, but it was motioned to postpone the election until July 25, when a more representative number would be present. Sure enough, on July 25 more members were present—twelve. But the election was carried on and the following roster of officers was elected: President, Elmer Williams; Secretary, Reby Cary; Treasurer, E. C. Chase. Calvin Littlejohn, local photographer, took a picture of the group for news releases and the publicity campaign was underway.

On August 29, 1946, Harold Odom, Harold Baker, Jr., and E. C. Diamond presented to the Negro Chamber of Commerce a proposal of the revised constitution and bylaws, which was unanimously adopted, and an application for a charter was made to the State Department by Attorney Holton and later granted by that agency. A month later the Fort Worth Negro Chamber of Commerce, unable to function as a mobile unit, made arrangements with the Fort Worth Urban League to use one of its offices as a temporary headquarters.

The month of October may be looked upon as the crowning month for all the hardships and discouraging setbacks its organizers faced during the chamber's infancy. The black grocers organized under the leadership of E. J. Bazy, owner of a grocery store on Hattie Street and famous as a candymaker. These businesses were able to combine their money and buy groceries wholesale so as to be competitive with the larger stores. This helped stabilize the continued growth of these small businesses. But the crowning glory was when the establishment of a vocational school for black veterans, who were not allowed training at other schools of this type.

Elmer Williams, Mr. and Mrs. Charles H. Robinson, Professor G. W. Williams, the Reverend J. W. Washington, Reby Cary, and other members of the Chamber of Commerce spearheaded the drive for the establishment of the only institution of its magnitude and kind in the southwest, The Southwestern College of Industrial Arts. Segregation and racial discrimination continued in the post-World War II period. Vocational training was provided for white veterans only, and the labor unions continued their policy of discrimination by not allowing black workers to have access to their apprenticeship programs. The Southwestern College of Industrial Arts' board leased the basement space under the Masonic Temple building on East Fourth Street, remodeled it, and offered classes in radio, auto mechanics, tailoring, business administration, carpentry, and upholstering. More than eight hundred veterans were able to matriculate and learn a valuable trade.

The Fort Worth Black Chamber of Commerce went through its usual functioning and nonfunctioning activities. One person who attempted to keep the Chamber relevant to the needs of this community was Ben Morrison. He was one of the first conservative black Republicans since 1945 and an upcoming businessman who was both a building contractor and insurance underwriter. He became President of the Black Chamber of Commerce in 1977. He expressed a need for a new image among black businesses. The lack of capital forced black entrepreneurs to accept gradualism as its method of economic development. They also had to overcome the impact of racial inferiority, which dictated an erroneous concept that "white-owned ice is colder than that sold by blacks." In October 1978 Ben Morrison endorsed Fort Worth's twenty-three-Point Anti-Discrimination Plan, which provided for the promotion of blacks to administrative position in the police department. He also set as a goal for the Black Chamber of Commerce the protection of consumers by establishing standards of quality for black business owners. This goal was not reached, but Ben Morrison continued to serve in the black community and his zeal was passed on to other leaders in Fort Worth.

The black phoenix once more rose up from the ashes of the past and came forth with new vigor and determination. In 1979 another group of black business-oriented citizens met to restructure the chamber so it could be helpful and more responsive to the needs of black entrepreneurs. It also could provide information to businesses with a desire to relocate in Fort Worth. A group of citizens redrafted the chamber's constitution and changed its name to Fort Worth Metropolitan Black Chamber of commerce, which was rechartered on October 11, 1979, by the state of Texas.

A few of the Black Chamber members followed the impact cable television was having on America. A great deal of economic rumbling was heard in Tarrant County when the television industry targeted Tarrant County. Black entrepreneurs were determined to be part of this historic endeavor. Reby Cary, Attorney Louis Sturns, William Ford, and Maurice Barksdale incorporated the Metro Community Vision Cable Company on July 17, 1979, in an effort to obtain a cable franchise in Forest Hill, Texas. Sammons Cable System had agreed to furnish the technology, but Metro Vision could not get a majority of the council to support them.

When Sammons Cable began negotiations with the Fort Worth City Council in 1981, the three minority council members, Jim Bagsby, Louis Zapata, and Bert Williams, made minority inclusion as part of the city's requirement. Metro Vision Cable Company joined the Panther City Cable Television and formed the Metroplex Cable Television, which was incorporated into Sammons of Fort Worth. The minority members were Reby Cary, Reverend L. B. George, Bobby Webber, Eugene McCray, William Ford, and Eddie Stamps; the others were Bill Elliott, Edwin B. Conley, Taylor Gandy, Lee Goodman, Dennis Hopkins, John McMillan, Clifton Overcash, and Charles W. Tindall, Jr. This was the first time in the history of Fort Worth that blacks were investors and owners of a major industrial component in the metropolis.

However, this proved to be an ephemeral operation, as had been predicted. In less than two years, the black investors and Metroplex Cable were forced to sell and Sammons "swallowed up" their 10,000 shares. Sammons later sold its interest to Charter Communications.

Devoyd (Dee) Jennings, an organizational stalwart and continual backbone of the Fort Worth Black Metropolitan Black Chamber of Commerce, reminded his colleagues that in earlier times they did not have a fiscal budget or an office staff. They only had a few concerned citizens who knew the importance of economics to any municipality or group of people. "Dee," as everyone called him, grew up in the Butler Housing Project pushed by a protective mother, Margaret Jennings, who insisted, "Education is the key." He was a lettered basketball player at I. M. Terrell High School in 1966, and at Texas Wesleyan University, 1969-70. Dee attended Tarrant County and Navarro Junior Colleges and graduated from Texas Wesleyan University. He later was elected to the Board of Directors at that institution.

Devoyd Jennings is a community fixture in most organizations in Tarrant County and the state of Texas. He has been a board member of the Texas Society to Prevent Blindness, Sickle Cell Anemia Association, Community Development Fund, and the Fort Worth Metropolitan Chamber of Commerce. In 1997 the Small Business Administration honored Devoyd Jennings as the Dallas/Fort Worth Minority Small Business Advocate of the Year. Dee has been an employee of Texas Electric Company for the past twenty-seven years. One of the major contributions the utility company makes to Tarrant County is allowing Dee to work as an "employee on loan" to the United Way, Black Chamber of Commerce, or wherever there is a need. From 1986 to the present, Dee and other leaders have continued the work of attempting to meet the economic needs of black entrepreneurs. His monthly "E-Lunch" epitomizes the ingredients the Black Chamber has for sharpening the professional skills needed to run a successful business: "Education, Empowerment, Enhancement, and the Entrepreneur in you."

The focus and concerns of women and children could not be ignored because of the concerns and persistence of Devoyd Jenning's wife, Gwen Barbee. She has been president of the Women's Auxiliary of the Metropolitan Black Chamber of Commerce. In 1992 the auxiliary established an Annual Scholarship Banquet for residents of the Butler Housing community; they also sponsored the Miss Black Teen-Age Fort Worth Pageant.

Gwen Barbee's extensive background in merchandising prepared her for the requirements of the business industry. She grew up in Dallas, pursued training at El Centro College, University of Texas at Arlington, and modeling courses at John Robert Powers. Not only was she a model, she was fashion coordinator at Lou Lattimore, Sanger Harris, Montgomery Ward, and Neiman Marcus. Gwen is such a strong believer in the free enterprise system that she formed her own company, Color Me Beautiful. She also works with Promofacet, a promotion firm of cosmetics and perfumes.

In 1989, with Devoyd Jennings, Chairman of the Board, and Ralph Mason, President, the Fort Worth Metropolitan Black Chamber of Commerce established the Fort Worth Metropolitan Industrial Development Corporation, designed to utilize the Community Reinvestment Act and the City of Fort Worth's Enterprise Zones to rebuild the economic base of the African-American community. William Mann, Don Hubbard, and Reby Cary initiated a study and filed complaints against the local banks for violating the Federal Reinvestment Act by discrimination in the granting of loans to minorities. Banks could not merge or sell their banks without rectifying such discriminatory violations. They fashioned an agreement with Texas American Bank to earmark $2.3 million for development in the affected areas. The William Mann Fund was established after the death of William Mann in recognition of his outstanding economic expertise and achievements in helping those in economic distress.

William Mann received his Bachelor of Science degree in architecture from Hampton University in Virginia and additional training in structural engineering from Drexel University and urban planning from George Washington University. He served as a consular officer in the Foreign Service in many countries. William Mann served as a consultant in architectural designing and environmental impact in Ghana, Sierra Leone, Nicaragua, Panama, Chile, and Paraguay; he spoke Spanish fluently.

In Tarrant County, Mann was the Black Chamber's financing expert for businesses and consumers. Financial institutions knew that the creation of such a fund is one of the main ingredients in helping to foster and develop businesses in the black and Hispanic communities and help lift them out of poverty.

The William Mann, Jr., Community Development Corporation is a consortium of local banks in Fort Worth. Its mission is to assist economic development initiatives in targeted areas in southeast Fort Worth. It provides debt and equity financing in conjunction with investor banks. Since its inception in September 1994, it has made fifty-five loans totaling $2.5 million; an estimated 405 jobs have been created or retained. It is one-step assistance for minorities who need help in establishing or maintaining a successful business.

Economic development in the new millennium is still a number one goal; Glenn Forbes, Chairman of the Fort Worth Metropolitan Black Chamber of Commerce, and Jimmy A. Madison, President/CEO, maintained that "the Chamber is one of the stalwart organizations dedicated to the specific economic interest of African-American entrepreneurs and to the community in general."[88] Glenn Forbes was named the President and Chief Executive Officer of the Southeast Fort Worth, Inc.; his function is to coordinate and help determine the best way to revitalize this area and to maximize the labor-business potential in a mixed-use economic development program. Forbes has excellent business connections since he was a former executive officer at Comerica Bank, Bank One, and the Intel Corporation.

NORMA ROBY. In 1986 when the Metropolitan Black Chamber of Commerce needed funding beyond that provided by its roster of members, an astute board member provided the financial thrust the chamber needed to survive. Norma Roby, a member of the Fort Worth Convention and Visitors Bureau, was selected as the liaison to the Black Chamber of Commerce. She had a strong interpersonal involvement with business, political, and community leaders. Norma Roby grew up in Fort Worth and graduated from I. M. Terrell High School. She received a Bachelor of Science in Zoology from Howard University and is a member of the Mount Pisgah Baptist Church and the Fort Worth Chapter of the Links, Inc.

This dynamic local entrepreneur had always had a business connection which involved the culinary experience of her father, Maurice Moore, and her mother, who developed Moore's Memorable Occasions, a pioneer food catering service in Fort Worth. With this family background, Norma leaped into prominence in the business world. She proved her adeptness in collaborating and pooling resources in accomplishing her desired goals and objectives.

Norma Roby had one of the first black-owned retailing businesses at the Dallas/Fort Worth International Airport. It was Classic Concessions, dba, The Classic Yellow Rose of

Texas. During the seven years she operated that gift and souvenir facility, she developed a lucrative import and export business that required regular travel to Europe and Africa. But her crowning achievement is her ascendancy to President of American Raceway Concessions, one of the first black-owned concessions at Texas Motor Speedway at the Alliance Airport Complex.

An economic and social activist, Norma Roby has been associated with numerous prestigious boards and committees: the Metropolitan Black Chamber of Commerce, the Fort Worth Chamber of Commerce (East Area Board), the Airport Minority Advisory Council, the Fort Worth Economic Development Council, Telethon Chairman, the United Negro College Fund, and the White House Conference, NAFTA delegate. In 1990 Norma Roby was a recipient of the Quest for Success Business Award, Dallas, and the Texas Legislative Black Caucus Outstanding Business Award.

THE BLACK BOOKWORM BOOKSTORE. Many black youths should pattern after Sonia Williams-Babers by making a vocational choice in their early years and systematically take steps to reach that goal. At the precocious age of four she dreamed of owning a bookstore, and this dream stayed with her until she married. In June 1992 she and her husband started a mail-order service for books out of their home. They had very little investment money and she continued to work in passenger sales at American Airlines. In 1993 the Black Bookworm Bookstore moved to a new location on I-30 and Berry Street and her parents operated the new venture while she was at work. In 1994 Sonia Babers resigned her job with American Airlines so she could devote herself full-time to the operation of her business.

The bookstore's main focus on black authors is a cultural asset to the preservation of the history of Afro-Americans and the education of new generations of young blacks. The bookstore also promotes African American greeting cards and educational games. It is also a place where black authors meet the public and autograph their publications.

RENAISSANCE CULTURAL CENTER. When Safeway Grocery Store closed on Evans Avenue and Baltimore Streets, it left an economic void on the south side of Fort Worth. At the same time, that closing made possible a larger educational and cultural possibility for all of this city. Jim Austin and Timothy Grace decided to revitalize the south side with the establishment of the Renaissance Cultural Center. It was incorporated as a 501(c)(3) nonprofit organization in the southeast community of Fort Worth. They began, after much renovation, by dedicating a special room to a pioneer legend, Dr. Marion Brooks.

Each year a group of selected "legends" are recognized for their work in the community. However, the main focus is the awarding of $1,000 scholarships to a large number of academically outstanding students in the high schools in Tarrant County. During the period from 1995 to 2000, the Renaissance Cultural Center awarded over $120,000 in scholarships. It has successfully coordinated contributions from many of the larger corporations and contributors and funds generated from classical performances at the Bass Center. The Renaissance Cultural Center provides special help for students by offering youth enrichment programs and job preparedness training.

Jim Austin is the titular head of this organization. He is a graduate of Howard University and has excellent support in planning and production from his wife, Gloria Austin. This dynamic duo continues to provide a diversified mix of cultural activities and community services to educate, stimulate pride, and enhance economic development. Jim Austin is a connoisseur of economic development. He has been an outstanding commercial and residential realtor for many years. In 1999 Tarrant County blacks were proud and honored when Governor George W. Bush appointed Jim Austin to the Texas Board of Realtors and the Board of Directors elected him secretary of the commission. He replaced Realtor Hazel Lewis of Arlington, Texas.

RICHARD BURNETT. In 1987 a native of Indianapolis, Richard Burnett, came to Fort Worth as an area director for nine stores of Church's Chicken. He soon decided that since he had been successful with a major chicken firm, he could own and operate one for his own benefit. Richard Burnett had an associate degree in business from Southwest Christian College and a BBA degree from Dallas Baptist Union. The culinary artist had the unique ability to train and motivate employees to get the maximum results for the business establishment.

Richard Burnett began working in 1990 as a franchisee with the renowned Hiawatha Williams in Dallas, who had already established himself as the "King of Fried Chicken." Richard Burnett is now President of the Williams Franchise Association and has established six stores in Tarrant County. He is very active in the Fort Worth community and serves as chairman of the nominating committee on the board of the Salvation Army, a member of the Sickle Cell Anemia Association, and member of the Metropolitan Black Chamber of Commerce. Richard Burnett was a recipient of an award for business from the Quest for Success in 1996.

A BIBLIOGRAPHICAL APPENDIX OF BLACKS IN FORT WORTH

Israel P. Anderson, a resident of Lake Como and the mainstay behind the financial reservoir and success of Gooseneck Bill McDonald. I. P. Anderson was a graduate of Paul Quinn College, Waco, and began work as a bookkeeper for the Farmer's Improvement Bank of that city. He became a cashier and held that position until the Depression in the 1930s forced the bank to close. I. P. Anderson came to Fort Worth as a cashier and director of the Fraternal Bank and Trust on 9th Street that Bill McDonald owned. This bank was the depository for the 22,224 blacks in Fort Worth and the large number of Masons in Texas who used the bank as a favor to Bill McDonald, the state secretary of that group. When Bill McDonald passed in 1950, I. P. Anderson attempted to keep the bank operating but couldn't get the support of local citizens and the Masons.

Dr. G. D. Flemmings. In the early history of Fort Worth, when the black community seemed quiet and nonaggressive, Dr. G. D. Flemmings broke that silence. He had grown up in Marshall, Texas, attended school there, and became a graduate of Meharry Medical School of Dentistry in Nashville, Tennessee.

Dr. Flemmings moved to Fort Worth and served as head of the Fort Worth NAACP for more than thirty-eight years. A very eloquent and dynamic speaker, he became well known not only in Fort Worth, but in the entire state and nation. He was a member of the NAACP's National Board of Directors, National President of Phi Beta Sigma Fraternity, and Grand Vice Chancellor of the Knights of Pythias. Dr. Flemmings was a member of the Mount Gilead Baptist Church and was a dentist associated with the Ransom Hospital, the only black hospital in Fort Worth.

Most students at I. M. Terrell High School who heard Dr. G. D. Flemmings in the school assemblies were deeply impressed by his eloquence and the fervor he exuded for the goals of the NAACP. His stimulating oratory echoed throughout most of their lives. When this writer taught at Dunbar Middle School on Willie Street, he attempted to get black teachers involved or at least contribute to the local branch. Many were afraid to let it be publicly known that they were affiliated and often would anonymously give two or five dollars in support.

When Dr. Flemmings became ill and could not function as the leader of the NAACP, he enthusiastically recommended Ray Bell to be his successor. Flemmings died in 1975. Ray Bell was an underwriter and executive of a local insurance company, but much quieter in his demeanor than Dr. Flemmings. He had been a member of the NAACP for more than thirty years and became its president in 1975. Bell was fortunate to have Attorney Clifford Davis as the legal advisor for the local NAACP. This native of Arkansas was the main legal force that caused segregation to be minimized in Fort Worth. Attorney Davis was successful in getting single-member districts for blacks on the Fort Worth School Board and the Fort Worth City Council. In 1983 he relinquished this role when he was appointed a judge in the criminal court in Tarrant County.

The legal void in the local NAACP was not completely empty. Jessie Gaines, a young attorney and a member of the West Texas Legal Society, carried on the legal work of this organization. Along with this author, he often testified before the state legislature's Redistricting Committee to help insure that more blacks would be elected to positions in Tarrant County.

A constant problem of the NAACP has been the lack of a sustained and wide-range community support. Many critics and members attributed this to the apparent domination of the body by the elderly and ministers in the city, and their goals and aspirations were inconsistent with the younger generation. So, in December 1984, Robert Starr, a young member for twenty years and a member of the National Board of NAACP, attempted to correct this problem seeking the presidency of the local chapter; he was supported by Devoyd Jennings, Jessie Gaines, Reby Cary, and others who felt it was time for a change in the leadership so more community involvement would take place. Several of the older members felt that since Robert Starr was an employee of the federal government, he would be limited to what he could publicly say and do. He was an equal employment specialist with the Federal Aviation Administration and investigator for the Equal Employment Opportunity Commission in Dallas, as well as a director of the Human Relations Commission for the City of Fort Worth. But, on the other side of the coin, he was a successful businessman who had grown up in Fort Worth, graduated from I. M. Terrell High School, attended Southwestern College of Industrial Arts and Texas College, Tyler, and was awarded a Master's degree from Texas Southern University. Robert Starr was the owner of Expert Cleaners and still serves as a member of the National NAACP Board.

However, most of Starr's opposition came from the ministers who dominated the NAACP and felt that other leaders should be subordinated to them because they had always been considered the leaders where the rights of the black community were concerned. Most of the meetings of the NAACP were held at the church of some minister who happened to be a board member, and many potential youth leaders were left out. In 1971, a young black militant group, The United Front, attempted to advance the cause of blacks by calling for a boycott, and the NAACP went against them. The Reverend L. B. George said, "The NAACP does things in a peaceful manner; no demonstrations or riots." Today ministers still dominate the board, and the Reverend Nehemiah Davis is chairman.

However, it should be noted that NAACP board member Robert Starr has always had the support of the ministers on the north side, where he grew up. He has been a member of Shiloh Baptist Church since his youth, and when he became active in community affairs he certainly had the support of Pastor J. W. Washington. Reverend Washington became pastor of Shiloh Baptist Church in 1930 after Reverends Upshaw and C. H. Johnson. Many of us remember how he and members of Shiloh Baptist Church nurtured the development and success of the Community Grocery Store on the Northside in 1948. It was a cooperative endeavor to move the black community to an economic awareness as they developed that store.

Not only did Reverend J. W. Washington become President of the McDonald College of Industrial Arts for World War II Veterans in 1947 in the Masonic Mosque Building in Riverside, he was also a loyal supporter of Mary Allen College in Crockett, Texas. This college was unique in that it was set up as a "Colored Sabbath School" in 1871 by the Presbyterian Church in that city. Later, in 1886, it became a boarding school and teacher-training school for black females; in 1933 it became a two-year junior college that also admitted men. The school was sold in 1944 to the Missionary Baptist General Convention of Texas and became certified as a four-year college. Reverend Washington was an active minister in the convention and continued to push and foster better educational opportunities for black students all over Texas.

Reverend J. W. Washington stands out as a preacher and editor of a black newspaper. *The Fort Worth Defender*, which mirrored the style of the *Chicago Defender*. He had the ability to get messages out from two sources to address many social, economic, and political problems blacks faced in Fort Worth and Texas. His positive religious coverage offset the negative effects produced by the popular *Brotherhood Eye*. This renegade newspaper denigrated black ministers by headlining and exposing their adultery, drunkenness, and other unchristian activities in Fort Worth and Dallas. Reverend Washington's *Fort Worth Defender* defended the integrity of his ministerial cohorts.

The Fort Worth Defender was preceded by the *Fort Worth Mind*, a weekly newspaper owned and published by C. R. Wise and R. L. (Pie) Melton. Professional journalism was ushered into the black community with the development and publication of this paper on December 3, 1932, at the peak of the Great Depression. C. R. Wise, a public school teacher, and R. L. Melton, a Phi Beta Sigma scholar, recognized that white publishers in Tarrant County printed only negative and derogatory accounts of the Afro-American community. They set out to report "the other side of the coin" and appended the title of the paper to the *Fort Worth Mind: A Champion of Race Development*. The paper was a member of Associated Negro Press (ANP).

Other newspapers have imitated the role of the *Fort Worth Mind* and focused on the achievements and problems confronting the black community. In 1957 Audrey Pruitt made a significant journalistic impact on the city of Fort Worth. He commuted weekly from his home in Oklahoma City, Oklahoma, to this urban center in Tarrant County to establish his newspaper, *LaVida News*. For many years he had been the publisher of *The Oracle*, the national publication of his fraternity, Omega Psi Phi. His mother lived in Waxahachie, Texas, and that provided an extra incentive for Pruitt to make Fort Worth the headquarters for his journalistic endeavor.

In 1996 he died and his talented son, Ted Pruitt, continued the publication and is currently the prime articulate voice of the black communities in the Fort Worth-Dallas metroplex and other parts of Texas. It has the largest circulation of any black-owned paper in this state. Ted Pruitt's promotion of the importance of education to our youth and the political consequences of being an uninformed voter-participant gives credence to the secret of his success and his concern about identifying and promoting the achievements of blacks in America. The journalistic model set by Reverend J. W. Washington has come to fruition.

Reverend Washington continued to lead Shiloh to new heights on the north side until his demise; he continued to support his member, Robert Starr, and the NAACP, by setting groundwork for the annual NAACP Day, the second Sunday in January, which started at the Shiloh Baptist Church. Upon Reverend Washington's death, the Reverend Albert E. Chew was chosen as the minister and continues his support to this very day. Reverend

Chew had been the pastor of a church in Abilene, Texas; he is a graduate of Bishop College, a minister plenipotentiary who has an Alphadom educational tenet of "scholarship and love for all mankind," and a veteran of World War II.

Lenora Rolla, Director of the Tarrant Black Historical and Genealogical Society and a nationally known black activist. She was a reporter for the *Dallas Express* and covered the Montgomery, Alabama, bus boycotts that gave her a keener sense of the nature of racial discrimination. Lenora Rolla was a leading exponent of the movement to repeal the poll tax in Tarrant County and the whole state of Texas.

While she served as the director of the Hardee-Adams Funeral Home on Fabons Street, she became interested in the Bicentennial Celebration in 1976 and recognized that there was very little recorded history about blacks anywhere in Texas. In 1977 Lenora Rolla organized the Tarrant Black Historical and Genealogical Society and located it at 1150 East Rosedale. Later it moved to Humbolt Street to the home of Attorney T. S. Boone, one of the pastors of Mount Gilead Baptist Church.

Opal Lee. Another staunch supporter and developer of the Historical Society is Opal Lee, who has been equally involved and continues to preserve historical history and monuments in Fort Worth. She and Lenora Rolla were able to convert the old Hattie Street Fire Station into the East Hattie Haven where poor children who lived in that area would have a place to play. Their work together has resulted in many historical sites in Fort Worth being recognized by the Texas Historical Society, including James E. Guinn Elementary School, I. M. Terrell High School, Mount Zion Baptist Church, and others.

Opal Lee's activism and outreach have left an indelible mark on many citizens in Fort Worth; she seems to be perpetually involved with helping those citizens who are in need. She was born October 7, 1926 in Marshall, Texas, and moved to Fort Worth, where she attended Cooper Street Elementary School (Amanda McCoy) and graduated from I. M. Terrell High School in 1943. In 1948 Opal (Blake) Lee matriculated at Wiley College in Marshall and earned her Bachelor's degree. Later she earned a Master's in Counseling from North Texas State University, Denton, and served as Home/School Counselor for the Fort Worth Independent School District until her retirement in 1977.

Opal Lee is a charter and Life member of the Tarrant County Black Historical and Genealogical Society. In 1970 she formed an organization called Citizens Concerned with Human Dignity to assist the most economically disadvantaged in finding housing in Fort Worth. This social activist has always been involved in leading and encouraging the black community to celebrate Juneteenth, Martin Luther King's birthday, or any other occasion to recognize and preserve the achievements and contributions of blacks to American civilization.

Frank Moss. A long-time advocate of the preservation of black history in Tarrant County is the current president of the Tarrant County Black Historical and Genealogical Society, Frank Moss. He has worked closely with Lenora Rolla and other members of that organization in preserving black heritage and passing it on to young people so they too may be worthwhile contributors to their society. The Society has a permanent exhibit at Fort Worth Town Center Mall, and the Fort Worth Public Library is the custodian of its unique historical collection about black achievement in Tarrant County. Frank Moss is currently working with the city of Fort Worth in placing a marker at the (Ninth and Jones Streets black business center) Intermodal Transportation Center.

Frank Moss is not only a genealogist but also represents District 8 on the Fort Worth City Council. He was elected in 1999 to succeed former councilman Eugene McCray. Moss is a graduate of Dunbar High School and received his degree in business from the University of Texas at Arlington. He was president of that university's Alumni Association. Frank Moss has always been interested in helping his community and that accounts for his activities for many years in the Fort Worth Chapter of the NAACP. His wife, Christene Moss, is a member of the Fort Worth Independent School District Board and has served in that capacity for eight years. The Eastland Elementary School was named in her honor.

Donald Curry, a former Texas and national Golden Gloves Star and a 1980 United States Olympian. This two-time World Boxing Welter-Weight Champion won his first world title at Fort Worth Convention Center, February 13, 1983 and compiled a 9-5 record in world title fights. The son-in-law of Lonnell and Earline Cooper and a member of the New Rising Star Baptist Church, he grew up in Fort Worth and was a graduate of Paschal High School. However, his fame was tarnished by guilt by association when he became a target of the FBI/DEA investigation of drug trafficking in the Bahamas, a charge that was later found to be unsubstantiated. Donald Curry became a successful freelance boxing manager.

Jim Hotel. Fort Worth Press newspaper workers often violated Texas state law by going across the alley from their plant to the black-owned Jim Hotel. They would come from 1:00 A.M. until early morning to hear the black musicians play. Ironically, the jazz center was across the street from one of the leading black churches, Mount Gilead Baptist Church. State laws prohibited blacks from socializing in white hotels and clubs, but racial barriers fell when white patrons wanted to learn and enjoy music as played by black musicians. This fifty-room hotel was originally owned by black millionaire Bill McDonald, who sold it to Levi and Bob Cooper as the Great Depression made an upward turn in the 1930s. In a very story time this hotel became the musical capital of Texas and the nation. Bob Cooper was the owner of Cooper's Taxi Service and Levi Cooper, his brother, was co-owner with Howell J. Atkinson of the historic Greenleaf Café on 9th Street.

Musician Aaron "T-Bone" Walker, who occasionally played for the students at I. M. Terrell High School, developed his musical skills and talents at the hotel and the blues became a main more and folkway of the entire nation. Most of the top entertainers and bands played at the Jim Hotel—Duke Ellington, Count Basie, Cab Calloway, Fats Waller, and others who recognized the outstanding status of this black enterprise. In later years it deteriorated into a drug and prostitute center and was finally demolished in the 1960s as a parking lot for the *Fort Worth Press*.

Elizabeth Branch. Growing up in Jacksonville, Texas, hands scarred from picking cotton, Dr. Branch was motivated to come out of the east Texas cotton fields and improve her servile condition through education; improve and excel she did. In 1958 she matriculated at Jarvis College, Hawkins, Texas, and earned a Bachelor of Science/Elementary Education in 1962. She was employed as an elementary school teacher in Lufkin, Texas in 1962 and 1963, and from 1967 to 1968 she was employed as a remedial reading teacher in Atlanta, Texas. In May 1968 Dr. Branch received a M.S. from Texas Southern University and ten years later in 1979, a Ph.D. degree in education administration from North Texas State University.

From 1973 to the present, this scholar has been an assistant professor and the Director of Special Services for Tarrant County Junior College in Hurst, Texas. Dr. Branch and her husband, James Branch, Sr., targeted teenagers to help them break the cycle of drugs, teenage pregnancy, permanent welfare, and other debilitating hindrances through special training. They established Bee and Bell Daycare and Tutoring Center at 5101 Wichita in Fort Worth as a school qualitatively endowed and consistent with the best educational procedures designed to enable students to live in a dynamic and changing society.

Erma Lewis. The Community Christian Church has always been community-oriented, even before it separated from its parent body, the Annie Street Christian Church. It provided meeting places for the Minority Leaders and Citizens Council and the formation of the Sojourner Truth Players. The Y-Teen Program Director of the Highland Park YWCA and the High School Junior Debs, Erma Lewis used the annex of the church at Riverside Drive and Hattie Street for its first production in 1972. Ms. Lewis was a graduate of I. M. Terrell High School and attended Dillard University in New Orleans and Texas College in Tyler. While at Dillard University, her interest in drama caused her to become familiar with the historical American Negro Academy.

The noted historian Alexander Crummell returned to the United States from Liberia after the Civil War and organized a group of scholarly youngsters who would use their scholastic attainments to lift up the achievements of black Americans. On March 5, 1897, he and some other scholars created the American Negro Academy in Washington, D.C. Erma Lewis used that organization's goals of fostering scholarship and culture in the black community and she involved Fort Worth students in the productions of the dramatic Sojourner Truth Players. She was assisted by many local citizens, but one student attending Texas Christian University was one of her biggest assets.

Curtis L. King, a drama major, was the Artistic Director for the Sojourner Truth Players. He developed exceptional expertise with the community organization and later graduated from Texas Christian University with his Master's in Drama. After a sojourn in New York and Los Angeles, King returned to Dallas to further his career. While a doctoral student in the arts at the University of Texas at Dallas, he interrupted his studying and established the Black Academy of Arts and Letters in 1977. In 1989 he moved into a 250,000-square foot space in the south end of the Dallas Convention Center, where he is estimated to have a $1.7 million budget. King has monumentalized his epochal Black Academy of Arts and Letters as one of Dallas County's top commemorative institution of Art.

Don Mack, writer and publisher of *The Ebony Mart* newspaper and a political activist, came to Fort Worth in 1968 as the director of the Neighborhood Action Incorporated. He remained very pessimistic about the deteriorating relationship between Anglo-Americans and Afro-Americans nationwide. He continually advanced the idea that blacks would barely survive if they didn't have more effective leadership from black and white politicians. Don Mack contended that blacks who have made it need to take another look at their less fortunate brothers and start a real right for their salvation. "With race relations as with pollution, we are approaching the time when our children won't even be able to live here,"[89] he prophesied. Don Mack believed in separation as a way to maintain black identity and self-esteem, but that economic independence should be a mandate for future generations.

Albert Hawkins III. Who would have imagined that a kid growing up on Arizona Street in Morningside would be promoted to an assistant to the President of the United States? Albert Hawkins III had worked in Austin as an economic advisor to Governor George W. Bush, and now he is an assistant to President Bush and a liaison secretary to the President's cabinet. A prince has come out of Fort Worth.

A post-depression education philosophy of his parents, Albert and Myrtle Hawkins, paid off as they admonished their children that you don't have to stay in an educational rut because of your color or where you live. Albert Hawkins III, a 1971 graduate of Paschal High School in Fort Worth, who had an interest in economics and government, matriculated at the University of Texas at Austin. As a student he had an opportunity to work in the post office of the Texas House of Representatives in the state capital, and this nurtured his political career. Albert Hawkins III worked hard and became deputy director of the Legislative Budget Board. His expertise and proficiency in handling the Texas budget placed him high on the list of President George W. Bush's appointment list.

EXTENDED SUPPLEMENT
Fort Worth City Council

Virginia Nell Webber-Huey, 1987-97, Councilwoman, District 8; Mayor Pro-Tem, 1991-95.

Eugene McCray, 1989-93 and 1995-98; Mayor Pro-Tem, 1997. A graduate of Bethune-Cookman College, Florida, and an auditor for Atlanta Life Insurance Company. On November 7, 2001, he was honored for his athletic skills in football by being inducted into Bethune-Cookman's College Athletic Hall of Fame.

The Reverend McKinley Jackson, 1993-95; Councilman District 5; Pastor of Samaria Baptist Church; President of local NAACP.

Bob Terrell, First African-American City Manager, Fort Worth, 1992-2001.

Tarrant County Junior College

Dr. L. L. Haynes. The Reverend Dr. Leonard L. Haynes was born in the rural community of Morales, Texas, in 1898. He was a cum laude graduate from Samuel Houston College in Austin in 1926 and 1936 was given an honorary doctoral degree from that same institution. He did graduate work in Atlanta, Georgia.

Dr. Haynes spent some fifty years as pastor of Methodist churches in New Orleans, St. Louis, Nashville, and Kansas City. In 1932 Dr. Haynes was assigned pastor of St. Paul Methodist Episcopal Church in Dallas. He was one of the founders of the Progressive Voters League, the NAACP, Moorland YMCA, and many other civic groups. He remained in Dallas nine and a half years.

Dr. Haynes served as pastor of St. Andrew's Methodist Church for fourteen years. He organized the first black voters registration as president of the Interdenominational Ministerial Alliance of Tarrant County in collaboration with the NAACP and the Negro Chamber of Commerce. He was recognized as a negotiator, not a marcher, during the civil rights movement. Dr. Haynes worked with local businesses to increase the hiring of minorities and was influential in causing Tarrant County Junior College to be integrated from its inception.

When Dr. Joe B. Rushing became chancellor and opened Tarrant County Junior College in 1965, Dr. Haynes became the first Afro-American trustee on the newly created board. In fact, this author was one of the first black instructors employed as an assistant professor of history when it opened. Recently the college name was changed to Tarrant County Community College.

Dr. Haynes always believed in physical fitness and worked diligently at exercise. Even at seventy years of age, he was still doing forty to fifty push-ups daily to maintain his physical fitness and mental sharpness.

When the Reverend L. L. Haynes did not seek reelection in 1975, the downtown power structure anointed and appointed Harold Odom to succeed the retiring minister. Harold Odom, a native of the Carver Heights Addition in Fort Worth and an employee of the United States Housing and Urban Development Department, was very active in the community. In 1963 he was a member of the Community Relations Committee. Also, he was one of the initial founders of the Fort Worth Negro Chamber of Commerce and had been a key monitor in canvassing the election returns, along with Wilma Alaman, when Reby Cary was elected to the Fort Worth School Board in 1974. Harold Odom had the distinction of being the second Afro-American to serve as a trustee on the Junior College Board from 1975 to 1977.

Gwendolyn Morrison. Tarrant County Community College has a reputation of designating one seat on its board for an Afro-American. They have done so, prior to single-member districts being mandated by the Texas State Legislature. In 1976 Gwen Morrison was the third Afro-American elected to that county board and to this day serves in that position; however, not without controversy. Formerly she was the personnel director of the city of Grand Prairie and later employed as Director of Alternative Certification for the Fort Worth Independent School District. Controversy seemed to follow her and she was charged with theft and tampering with expense money she received from the school district and Tarrant County Junior College for a trip to Detroit.

These charges didn't register well with the black community; generally, they felt that restitution with a reprimand would have been more appropriate as a penalty for filing duplicate expense requests. Many felt that this was a subterfuge for the board's displeasure with Ms. Morrison and a large segment of the black community who challenged the board because they failed to promote Erma Johnson to the vacant position of chancellor of Tarrant County Junior College. The board's reluctance was similar to a prevailing sentiment that caused the city council not to appoint Vernell Sturns to the city manager position in that Fort Worth was not ready for a black to be in that position.

After two years the charges against Gwen Morrison were reduced to a misdemeanor and she agreed to reimburse the school district $1,462 and $2,000 to the county for court-appointed fees. She won reelection in the last Junior College board election in the year 2000 and resumed her voting rights on the board.

Ella Mae Gratts Shamblee. In 1924 she became the first black librarian employed by the Fort Worth Public Library and served for some thirty-eight years. Black children were not allowed in city libraries by state and municipal laws, but Ms. Shamblee received permission and checked books out and made them available to black children and adults who wanted to read. She had special "library days" for them in Lake Como, the Northside, and the Southside of Fort Worth. Branches were later set up in those areas and a Book Mobile became an integral component of the public library. Ms. Shamblee also started the "Children's Hour" at the local YWCA. Today the Shamblee Library in the Southside Multipurpose Center is a tribute to this pioneer librarian; she died in July 1981.

Ella Mae Shamblee had other concomitant librarians. One, Lillian B. Horace, was a librarian at I. M. Terrell High School and an outstanding authoress. She wrote a literary classic, *Sun-Crowned: A Biography of Doctor Lacey Kirk Willliams.* This was a publication supported by the Progressive National Baptist Convention and chronicled the character and career of this outstanding Christian minister.

Sybil Byrd, another native Fort Worthian who was an outstanding librarian, was the daughter of Dr. George M. Munchus and earned a Bachelor of Arts degree from Wiley College in 1938. In 1944 she and her husband, Wilburn Byrd, moved to Galveston, where she worked as an art instructor. In 1955 they returned to Fort Worth when Sybil Byrd received employment with the Fort Worth Independent School District. She earned a Master's of Education degree from Texas Southern University and a Bachelor's in Library Science from North Texas State University, Denton.

Sybil Byrd became the media specialist for seven public school libraries in Fort Worth and organized the services and programs at each school, including African-American historical collections. She served on the Advisory Board of the Fort Worth Public Library.

Another multi-talented librarian is Adelene James, who retired from the Fort Worth Independent School District as a librarian at Meadowbrook Middle School. She is a 1944 graduate of Fisk University, Nashville, majoring in literature and fine arts. Periodically she taught freshman writing workshops at Texas Christian University. She remains active in the community and was one of the members of the Goals of East Fort Worth Committee, which resulted in the building of the East Regional Library. She was also a founding organizer of the Stop Six Community Health Center on Stalcup Street. In 1964 Adelene James became the first African-American to perform at the Greater Fort Worth Community Theater. Her dramatic talent has been ably demonstrated in such productions as *Cat on a Hot Tin Roof, To Kill a Mockingbird*, and many others. She is also an active member of the Fort Worth Chapter of the Links, Inc.

The crowning glory for Fort Worth's pride in its black librarians came in March 1999. A renewed exuberance came to this community when the Library Board elected *Dr. Gleniece A. Robinson* as Director. The appreciation was further enhanced when the *Fort Worth Star-Telegram* and the Downtown Rotary Club awarded the Fort Worth Library the Employer of the Year Award. Robinson's success is no surprise, given her educational background, work ethics, and qualifications as a librarian.

After Governor George Wallace had to compromise on his staunch support of segregation, he introduced a "Freedom of Choice" program for the schools in Alabama. Gleniece Robinson and five other blacks were the first to integrate the schools in Foley, Alabama. Upon graduation, Robinson attended Alabama State University in Montgomery and earned a Bachelor of Science in English/Psychology, June 1973. However, her interest was always in library science and that summer she studied at Emory University. Later the scholar enrolled in the University of Michigan, where she earned her Master's in 1976 and her Doctorate in Library and Information Science.

Dr. Robinson's work experience complemented the quality of her educational training. At the University of Michigan, 1981-82, she selected material and conducted workshops at the University of Michigan Center for Afro-Americans and African Studies Library. In 1980 she worked in the Library of Congress and developed and wrote "A Planning Process for Staff Development and Training." In 1992-94, Dr. Robinson was appointed by Governor Ann Richards to serve on the State of Texas Historical Records Advisory Board. In 1998 Robinson became the first black President of the Texas State Library Association. The library scholar has done extensive research and written many pamphlets and publications.

While working toward all her degrees, Dr. Robinson maintained Dallas as her home base. She was employed by the Dallas Public Library from 1976 to 1999 and received a strong endorsement from Ramiro Salazar, Director of Dallas Public Library System. Fort

Worth has moved to exceptional heights of achievement because of the leadership of Dr. Gleniece Robinson. Her innovative and community coalition-building, outreach services, and program development continues to put Fort Worth on a higher plain of educational and cultural activities.

Bertha Knox Collins. Born in Lorena in the rural Texas prairie land of McLennan County, she was a graduate of Paul Quinn College, Waco. Prior to coming to Fort Worth, Bertha Collins was employed as a testing specialist, teacher, and counselor for the United States Air Force in Clinton, Oklahoma. Bertha Collins migrated to Fort Worth and found employment with the Park and Recreation Department in May 1963. She immediately became involved in the civic affairs of this city. Her foresighted vision focused on the physical and mental development of the youth in Forth Worth. Bertha Collins firmly believed that providing recreational activities for the youth would help reduce the tendency for criminal behavior. In 1969 she was selected as the Mayor's Director of Youth Affairs for the city of Fort Worth. She was so successful in providing these services that Harmon Field Recreation Center was dedicated as a commemorative tribute for her efforts in working with the youth of this city. In 1971 Ms. Collins was one of the winners of the Hercules Award given by the Tarrant County Community Council.

Bertha Collins was also a political activist. When a $1.75 poll tax was required for voting in Texas, she was the first black to be deputized to write the official poll tax receipts. The poll tax was designed to disenfranchise black voters who had gained considerable clout with the Republican Party members who had been successful in the Civil War. She encouraged political involvement as a means of improving the social and economic condition of Afro-Americans in this metropolis.

Better Influence Association. While the United Front was a mixture of Black Muslims and radical Afro-Americans, a more mainstream activist organization remained paramount in Tarrant County. For more than twenty years Robert L. Livingston was the dynamic leader of the Better Influence Association. It focused on the education of youths ages 10 to 19 who were dropouts and involved in drugs. Its goals were to help them develop positive behavior and attitudes, divorce themselves from the militant "hoods," and change their welfare mentality.

The Better Influence Association had several functioning subsidiaries: The Youth Leadership Council, The Nutrition Center, The Accused Rights Commission, Crime Prevention Center, School Counseling Program, and a Career Guidance and Employment Center. Each year the Association gave special recognition to outstanding black leaders in Tarrant County.

Reverend Michael Bell. A tireless and proactive, sometimes provocative man of the cloth with an exemplary love for his community is the Reverend Michael Bell, Pastor of Greater St. Stephen Baptist Church, Fort Worth. He treads where other proclaimers of the Gospel dare not and addresses his concerns through action. His picketing and marching tactics are criticized by many in the black community. Those critics have nothing better to offer but must realize that one can't be a catalyst for change without controversy.

Reverend Bell recognizes the disparity in the quality of education for black students in a semi-segregated school system and led several demonstrations at Morningside Elementary School. He understands the subtleties in the magnet schools and is supported by the Tarrant County Local Organizing Committee, of which he is president. He led daily demonstrations at Tanglewood Elementary School that really got the attention of the school administrators and public. This school is one of the academically and financially elite educational institutions and Reverend Bell agreed to accept former associate superintendent Hardy Murphy as a liaison to monitor the administration's progress in addressing the concerns of the minority community. It was finally resolved to the satisfaction of all.

James Cash. Anyone who has the ability to excel and major in mathematics and physics has the major mental components for success. Math was not this author's long suit when I attended I. M. Terrell High School. Since I couldn't find the "known," I certainly couldn't find the "unknown." James Cash, a resident of the Morningside area, played basketball at James E. Guinn Elementary School and later attended I. M. Terrell High School in 1960. Cash helped to integrate athletics at Texas Christian University in 1965-69 and break the racial barriers in the Southwestern Conference. In his junior and senior years he was honored by being named to the Academic All-American Basketball Team.

After graduating from T.C.U., Cash matriculated at Purdue University and earned his Master's in Computer Science and his Ph.D. from Purdue's Krannert School of Management. In 1976 he was appointed Professor of Business Administration and Associate Dean of Harvard Business School. He is the first Afro-American scholar to become a tenured full professor at that institution. James Cash has been selected to serve on the Microsoft Corporation, General Electric, and Knight-Ridder boards of directors.

Adair Optical. A basic economic and political hypothesis blacks have advocated since 1980 is that they can't continue to run for political office or establish a profitable business solely on the color of their skin. They must broaden their appeals to all groups and that's what one ideal young female entrepreneur has done. Alyce Jones was born when overt and flagrant racial prohibitions had been reduced in Tarrant County. Her father was the Reverend C. A. Holliday, pastor of the Greater St. James Baptist Church in 1952, and was honored to be the first black minister to be elected President of the General Ministers Association of Fort Worth in 1967-68. He was also Vice-Moderator of the Saint John Landmark District Association. His daughter, Alyce, graduated from O. D. Wyatt High School in Fort Worth in 1980 and has been in the optical eyewear business for more than twenty-one years.

Alyce Jones opened her first store at Camp Bowie and University; later she established a store at Sundance Square and now has plans for her third store in the Chapel Hill Center, Hulen, at I-30. This store will also include an optical training classroom because Ms. Jones knows the need for more students to become professionals in this field and reduce the shortage of experts in the optical field. To keep abreast of revolutionary changes in the optical market, Alyce Jones travels regularly to Milan, Italy. Her ambition is to create an optical boutique that focuses on gaining the trust and respect of her clientele by offering sincere, professional consultations and providing the best optical solution for an individual's appearance and lifestyle.

Reverend Paul A. Sims. The pastor of the Community Christian Church for many years was Paul A. Sims. This church had a reputation as a seven-day-a week church which served the community continuously. This dynamic leader was a civil rights activist who previously marched with Dr. Martin Luther King, Jr. in other states and constantly challenged the Fort Worth City Council for not addressing the concerns of minorities in that city. At the same time he challenged young blacks to quit making excuses and set worthwhile goals for their own development and success in life. Reverend Sims was closely associated with the Paul Quinn College in Hawkins, Texas.

Robert L. Hughes. No history of Fort Worth would be complete without the inclusion of a living educator-coach-legend in the person of Robert L. Hughes. His power to inspire and motivate students to achieve and overachieve is an exceptional quality. He was born and reared in Sapulpa, Oklahoma, a small town that is an industrial suburb of Tulsa. Sapulpa was settled by Jim Sapulpa, a Creek Indian from Alabama who established a farm along Rock Creek in 1850. With the coming of the Frisco Railway in 1886, more settlers arrived and the town developed into an agricultural shipping center. It is in this environ that Robert Hughes grew up and in 1946 graduated from high school.

From 1951 to 54, Coach Hughes attended Texas Southern University and received his Bachelor of Arts degree from Tulsa University in 1958. Upon graduation he became the head basketball coach at I. M. Terrell High School and established many records until the school closed in 1973. His teams won nine district championships from 1962 to 73; three state championships in the years 1963, 1965, and 1967; and one state runner-up in 1966.

In 1973 Coach Hughes was employed as the head basketball coach at Dunbar High School, where he presently serves. In 1983 Coach Hughes received his Master of Arts degree from Texas Wesleyan College in Fort Worth. At Dunbar he had twenty district championships from 1976 to 1997; nineteen bi-district championships from 1976 to 1994; ten regional championships from 1977 to 1991 and 1993; three state runner-ups in 1977, 1979, and 1988; and state championship in 1993. Coach Hughes was elected to the Texas Sports Hall of Fame in 1993 and to the Southwestern Athletic Conference Hall of Fame in 1995.

Ruth Charity Club, a historical first in "helping the one that is lowest down," the motto of this community helper. Fannie Mae Williams organized this charitable group in 1932 and each year hundreds of persons in need were helped. They assisted the sick and shut-ins and gave food, clothing, and blood donations. The Ruth Charity Club had a membership of more than two hundred Christian members; it included young children in ages from four years and up. All workers were volunteers; there were no paid workers.

The Club received a charter in 1948 and was awarded its tax-exempt status in 1954. Fannie Mae Williams was the founder and served as president of the Ruth Charity Club for forty-four consecutive years.

Velma T. McEwen. In 1951, when the NAACP was losing support because of its aggressive agenda in promoting black goals of equality, the National Urban League grew into prominence as it focused on an emerging concept that blacks didn't need welfare, they needed job training and work opportunities. This was certainly an acceptable agenda in Tarrant County, and the Fort Worth Urban League was organized. Velma T. McEwen, a native of Mississippi, came from Washington, D.C. to assume the position of Executive Secretary of the local chapter.

Ms. McEwen was a graduate of St. Augustine College and received her Master's degree from American University in Washington, D.C. Her work began in Fort Worth and she used her past connections to influence mortgage companies and developers to fund housing in the black community. Subsequently, Carver Heights was developed and a street in this area carries the name of McEwen Court in her honor. However, supported by the aggressive Dr. Marion Brooks, who served as one of the presidents of the Fort Worth Urban League. Velma McEwen became perceived as too militant for the downtown business community. She pushed hard for fair employment at General Dynamics and other aeronautical centers; she challenged the labor unions to accept blacks in some of their skilled craft unions. Her actions prompted many city leaders to classify her as "anti-white," and they demanded that the United Fund stop all funding for the Fort Worth Urban League. This action accelerated the demise of the league and to this day there has not been a movement to reestablish an Urban League in this city.

This theological and metaphorical prediction that analyzes the history of black Americans in the United States is a challenge to the youth and young adults in this country today. In this new millennium, it's time for more princes to come out of Egypt! Where do we start? It starts with you! The new leadership is you! Don't look for a leader, you be one; cast aside the mass of trivia, set your own goals, and go after them. Don't let your friends deter your important quest. Individual and collective discipline is essential.

Set worthwhile goals of economic independence and take aggressive steps in education to make progress, because technological illiteracy won't help us. Get politically sophisticated to understand and work effectively in the system. Discipline yourself with good manners, decent appearance, and dependability, and work for the greatest needs for the largest number of people. Then you too will be able to join in the chorus: "Stony the road we trod, bitter the chastening rod, felt in the days when hope unborn had died; yet with a steady beat, have not our weary feet come to the place for which our fathers sighed."

NOTES, PART III

1. H. P. N. (Camp) Gammel, *The Laws of Texas, 1822-1897*, III, Volume 10 (Austin 1898), p. 206.

2. Joe B. Frantz, "The Significance of Frontier Forts to Texas," *Southwestern Historical Quarterly* (The Texas State Historical Association: Vol. LXXIV, No. 2, October 1970), p. 204.

3. Gammel, *The Laws of Texas*, II, p. 326.

4. Kenneth Wiggins Porter, "Negroes and Indians on the Texas Frontier, 1831-1876, A Study in Race Culture," *Journal of Negro History* (Volume XLI, No. 4, October 1956), p. 309.

5. Seymour V. Conner, *The Peter's Colony of Texas* (Austin: The Texas State Historical Association, 1959), p. 105.

6. Julian Kathryn Garrett, *Fort Worth: A Frontier Triumph* (Austin: The Encino Press, 1972), p. 127.

7. Ibid., p. 129.

8. James Farber, *Fort Worth in the Civil War* (Belton, Texas: Peter Hansbrough Press, 1960), p. 15.

9. Ibid., p. 15.

10. Duane Gage, *Scenes from the Past: A Mid-Cities Album* (Tarrant County Jr. College (NE), Local History Museum, 1975), Photo #22.

11. The *Denton Record-Chronicle* (Sunday, May 15, 1977), p. 2B.

12. "In Old Ft. Worth: The First Time I Saw Ft. Worth," *The News Tribune* (July 2, 3, 4, 1976), p. 6.

13. Ibid., p. 15.

14. Ray Billington, quoted in Bracy Meier, *Rudwick Blacks in the Abolitionist Movement* (Belmont, California: Wadsworth Publishing Co., Inc., 1970), p. 5.

15. P. Garrett, Op. Cit., *Fort Worth: A Frontier Triumph* (Austin: The Encino Press, 1972), p. 177.

16. Oliver Knight, *Ft. Worth: Outpost on the Trinity* (Tulsa: University of Oklahoma Press, 1953), p. 48.

17. Garrett, p. 177.

18. *Ft. Worth Chief* (July 25, 1860).

19. Madeline William, "How Reporter's Questions Opened Parks to Negroes," *The News Tribune* (July 2, 3, 4, 1976), p. 14.

20. Sheridan, *Memoirs II, Texas Negroes* (New York: Charles L. Webster & Co., 1888), p. 261.

21. Williams Mack, "In Old Ft. Worth: The Trials of J. Frank Norris," *The News Tribune* (_____), p. 33.

22. William Hamilton, "In Old Ft. Worth: Memories of Tarrant County Slaves," *The News Tribune* (July 23, 1976), p. 15.

23. Ibid., p. 15.

24. Farber, p. 54.

25. *Fort Worth Democrat* (Saturday, May 2, 1874).

26. *Fort Worth Democrat* (Saturday, April 11, 1874).

27. *Fort Worth Democrat* (Saturday, May 2, 1874).

28. Edgar P. Sneed, "A Historiography of Reconstruction in Texas: Some Myths & Problems," *Southwestern Historical Quarterly* (Vol. LXXII, No. 4, April 1969), p. 443.

29. Farber, p. 58.

30. *Fort Worth Democrat* (Sunday, March 20, 1881).

31. "In Old Ft. Worth," *The News Tribune* (February 11, 1977), p. 15.

32. Gage, photo #17.

33. _____

34. "Civil Rights: Disgraceful Conduct," *Fort Worth Democrat* (April 17, 1875).

35. Rayford Logan, *The Betrayal of the Negro: From Rutherford B. Hayes to Woodrow Wilson* (New York: Collier Books, 1968), p. 23.

36. "More Rope Wanted: A Negro Outrages a Lady at Bremond," *Fort Worth Daily Democrat* (December 27, 1877).

37. *Fort Worth Daily Democrat* (April 14, 1848).

38. *Fort Worth Daily Democrat* (December 27, 1877).

39. *Fort Worth Daily Democrat* (January 13, 1878).

40. *Fort Worth Daily Democrat* (March 2, 1878).

41. *Fort Worth Daily Democrat* (December 6, 1878).

42. *Fort Worth Daily Democrat* (March 26, 1878).

43. *Fort Worth Daily Democrat* (August 25, 1878).

44. *Fort Worth Daily Democrat* (April 18, 1878).

45. Ibid.

46. *Fort Worth Daily Democrat* (January 22, 1884).

47. *Fort Worth Daily Democrat* (August 3, 1881).

48. Julian K. Garrett, *Fort Worth: A Frontier Triumph* (Austin: The Encino Press, 1872), p. 130.

49. See Claire Eyrich, "Inn Set Standard of Elegance," *Fort Worth Star-Telegram* (February 13, 1963), and Reby Jones, "Story of the Como Community," *Fort Worth Como Weekly* (1964), pp. 3, 8.

50. *Ninth Annual Report of the Superintendent of the Fort Worth Public Schools for the Scholastic Year Ending June 30, 1881*, p. 21.

51. Superintendent of Education, *Sixth Biennial Report* (1888), p. 288.

52. *Fort Worth Public Schools* (June 1899).

53. Jackie Grey, "Mama Hazel Was a Legend at Terrell," *Fort Worth Star-Telegram* (May 24, 1977).

54. "Negro Baptizing," *The Democrat* (Tuesday, July 27, 1880).

55. Lauraine Sharp, *100 Years of the Black Man* (Fort Worth: L. Sharp and Co. Publishers, 1973), no numbered pages.

56. "Laying the Cornerstone," *The Democrat* (Saturday, May 1, 1881).

57. Program, "Centennial Festival: Mount Gilead Celebrates Its Centennial Festival," (November 19-23, 1975).

58. "Pioneering AME Bishop to Speak," *Dallas Morning News* (January 17, 2001).

59. *The News Tribune* (June 25, 1976), p. 17.

60. Ibid., p. 17.

61. Joyce E. Williams, *Black Community Control: A Study of Transition in a Texas Ghetto* (New York: Praeger Publishers, 1973), p. 204.

62. *Fort Worth Star-Telegram* (April 3, 1949).

63. Ibid.

64. *Fort Worth Star-Telegram* (April 4, 1949).

65. *Fort Worth Star-Telegram* (April 4, 1949), p. 3.

66. *Fort Worth Star-Telegram* (April 7, 1955), p. 3.

67. *Fort Worth Star-Telegram* (April 2, 1967), p. 6D (m).

68. Ibid., p. 6D.

69. Ibid., Editorial (April 2, 1967).

70. *Fort Worth Star-Telegram* (December 21, 1999).

71. *Fort Worth Star-Telegram* (June 7, 1970).

72. Bill Eden, personal communication.

73. *Fort Worth Star-Telegram* (March 16, 1971).

74. "Gardner With a Black Thumb - Clifton Tinsley Speaks," *Melodies of Blackness* (Fort Worth: National Consortium for Humanizing Education, 1976), p. 65.

75. *The Phoenix* (April 7, 1979, Vol. I), p. 1.

76. *Fort Worth Star-Telegram* (October 29, 1980).

77. *Fort Worth Star-Telegram* (April 30, 1985), p. 9A.

78. *Fort Worth Star-Telegram* (August 13, 1986), p. A13.

79. *Fort Worth Star-Telegram* (February 17, 1988).

80. *LaVida News* (October 16, 1982), p. 4.

81. *Fort Worth Star-Telegram* (September 24, 1982), p. 12S.

82. Doug Harlan, San Antonio columnist, Oliphant University Press Syndicate (January 15, 1983).

83. Carl Freund, *Dallas Morning News* (January 30, 1983).

84. *Fort Worth Star-Telegram* (October 2, 1991), Section B, p. 3.

85. *Fort Worth Star-Telegram* (October 30, 1999), Section A, p. 20.

86. Debra Dennis, "Bagsby Retains Commissioner's Seat in Tarrant County," *The Dallas Morning News* (November 8, 2000).

87. *Fort Worth Star-Telegram*, "Obituaries" (Thursday, July 27, 1978).

88. Don Mack, "We Have a Few Years While We Still Can Talk," *Fort Worth Star-Telegram* (February 13, 1970), p. 12A.